WINNING THE VOTE FOR WOMEN

Winning the Vote for Women

The Irish Citizen *Newspaper and the Suffrage Movement in Ireland*

LOUISE RYAN

FOUR COURTS PRESS

Typeset in 10.5 pt on 13.5 pt CaslonPro by
Carrigboy Typesetting Services for
FOUR COURTS PRESS LTD
7 Malpas Street, Dublin 8, Ireland
www.fourcourtspress.ie
and in North America for
FOUR COURTS PRESS
c/o ISBS, 920 NE 58th Avenue, Suite 300, Portland, OR 97213.

A catalogue record for this title is available
from the British Library.

ISBN 978-1-84682-701-3

Printed in England
by TJ International, Padstow, Cornwall.

Contents

Acknowledgments

The first edition of this book was published in 1996 by Folens as *Irish feminism and the vote: an anthology of the* Irish Citizen *newspaper, 1912–20*, and I am very grateful to them, especially Conor Walker, for agreeing to release the book so it could be republished in this updated and revised edition by Four Courts Press. I am delighted that the book could be republished in time for the 100th anniversary of female enfranchisement.

This was my first book, and it still means a great deal to me. It grew out of my PhD research at University College Cork in the 1990s, which now feels like a lifetime ago. I will always be grateful to my supervisor, Piet Strydom, for all his encouragement and support.

There are a number of people who encouraged me in my efforts to have the book republished: Margaret Ward, Linda Connolly, Sinéad McCoole, Grainne Blair, Donna Gilligan and Cait Beaumont. I am particularly grateful to Isobel Ní Riain and Pádraig Ó Snodaigh for their advice and practical help.

A special word of thanks to Donna Gilligan for helping to find the lovely image of Margaret (Meg) Connery accosting politicians that is used on the front of this book. Additional thanks to Berni Metcalfe at the National Library of Ireland and Nikki Braunton at the Museum of London for permissions to use images.

Republishing this book would not have been possible without the enormous enthusiasm and support of Sam Tranum, the team at Four Courts Press and two anonymous readers for their helpful comments and suggestions. I am also very grateful to Eileen O'Neill for the indexing.

I would like to thank the University of Sheffield, faculty of Social Sciences, for the practical assistance I received in support of this book.

Finally, a special word of thanks to my family: Donatus, Finnian, Isobel, Jean and John.

Foreword

MARGARET WARD

It is extraordinary to realise that Louise Ryan first published *Irish feminism and the vote: an anthology of the* Irish Citizen *newspaper, 1912–1920* in 1996. Its reappearance is very welcome at this historic time when we celebrate the centenary of the Representation of the People Act of 1918, which enabled women over 30 to vote and to stand for election. The *Irish Citizen*, the voice of the Irish suffrage movement during some of the most turbulent years of campaigning for the franchise, is utterly indispensable as a source for understanding those times. Even its title is subversive, throwing out a challenge at a time when no one in Ireland was a citizen, being subjects of the British monarchy. The *Irish Citizen* was proud to be a paper that reflected the concerns of all those committed to the fight for a society based upon principles of justice and equality.

Those who enter its pages encounter an exciting world of debaters and hecklers, of feminist crusades into the countryside, prison experiences, hunger strikes, debates on militancy and exposés of white slavery and other abuses against women and girls – coupled with a celebration of womanhood in pageants, fancy dress, theatre and literature. We find opinions of all shapes and sizes, as well as news and reviews. We can read about key events, including the home rule crisis, Ulster Unionist response to the home rule bill, the Dublin Lock-Out, the First World War, the Easter Rising and the first elections of women to the Dáil and to local government, helping us to gain a gendered understanding of those turbulent times. Documents from that early feminist movement throw new light on topics as varied as the relationship between religious affiliation and political identity; the role of Irish political movements within the international community; sexual morality in turn-of-the-century Ireland; and the culture of the times, reflected in feminist critiques of plays and books. The selections contained in this book provide us with some of the most essential articles produced by the *Citizen*, while also whetting our appetite for more.

The Irish suffrage movement continues to suffer from neglect however, despite the richness of documentation that exists. Its membership was comprised of some of the most literate and best-educated women of the period, and their writings provide us with polemical articles, vivid journalism and sober analysis. Although there has been some increase in publishing on Irish suffrage since the first edition of this book appeared, we still have no organisational account of the Irish Women's Franchise League, and neither do we have any full-length biographies of key figures in the group, other than Hanna Sheehy Skeffington. Women like Margaret Cousins, Meg Connery and Margaret McCoubrey – fine militants all – are some of the women deserving of far greater attention. As Louise Ryan acknowledges in her introduction, 'history has not been kind to feminists. The under-representation of feminists in our history books has denied us a thorough knowledge and understanding of the legacy of feminism.' The pages of the *Irish Citizen* and the Sheehy Skeffington collection in the National Library of Ireland hold rich treasures for researchers. My hope is that a new generation of historians will be inspired by the publication of this essential collection so that in the coming years we will enjoy learning much more about those 'smashing times'.

Introduction

> Our little paper stands for a great deal to us women. It is the visible demonstration of our continuity and purpose and of our capability in action, our self reliance even when our men supporters are withdrawn from our field: it is the voice of the woman crying in the wilderness that destruction of life will never make for construction of the fundamentals of peace, which are indeed equality, liberty and humanity … [its] files will be as valuable to future women as are the published records to us of the steps in history by which our predecessors won the education which now makes our political enfranchisement inevitable. (Margaret Cousins, *Irish Citizen*, Jan. 1917)

The *Irish Citizen* newspaper, published in Dublin from 1912 to 1920, provides a very valuable insight into the philosophy of Irish suffragism. As Margaret Cousins prophesied in the above quote, the paper stands today as a record of the women and men who campaigned, not only for the vote, but for the feminist movement in Ireland.

Today, in the early decades of the twenty-first century, this little newspaper provides us with a vivid picture of the issues that concerned suffragists more than one hundred years ago. It clearly illustrates that the suffrage movement was interested not only in the franchise but in a much wider array of issues affecting women generally.

Women in Ireland have made great strides since that time, and many rights and entitlements have been achieved. According to Máire Geoghegan-Quinn, Ireland's first female European commissioner, the advancement of equal rights and opportunities for women and men in Ireland in recent decades has been 'transformational' (cited in EC, 2017). Indeed, it has been noted that Irish women in the early twenty-first century 'have more rights than their mothers, grandmothers and great grandmothers' (EC, 2017). Nonetheless, there is plenty of evidence to show that women in Ireland still have a long way to go to achieve the full equality sought by the suffrage movement.

For example, women's paid employment has increased steadily since the 1970s, despite a slight dip during the recession years, but women still make up the majority of part-time workers in Ireland. Women are seriously under-represented on boards of management in Ireland's leading companies (EC, 2017). Women continue to be under-represented in politics. After the general election in 2016, only 22 per cent of TDs in Dáil Éireann were female (although 55 per cent of Irish members of the European Parliament were female). When it comes to violence against women, data on domestic and sexual assaults tend to 'shock those who are not familiar with them' (EC, 2017). The results from an EU survey on violence against women found that 14 per cent of Irish women had experienced physical violence by a partner. In 2015, Women's Aid recorded over 16,000 incidents of domestic violence against women in Ireland. Thus, as will be seen throughout the chapters in this book, many of the issues addressed by suffragists remain pertinent today.

The history of the Irish suffrage movement must be understood against the background of Ireland's particular economic and political situation (Ryan & Ward, 2007). In some ways the suffrage movement developed in Ireland as part of a specific cultural and nationalist renaissance. However, the movement was not isolated from international events. In fact, Irish suffragists maintained regular contact with suffragists in Britain and America, and on the European continent (Murphy, 1989).

Among the pioneering suffrage campaigners in Ireland was Isabella Tod, who established the first suffrage association in Belfast in 1872 (Watkins, 2014). Another early suffrage group was set up in Dublin in 1876 and, after a number of name changes, became known as the Irish Women's Suffrage and Local Government Association (IWSLGA). Because women in Ireland, unlike British women, did not achieve complete local government franchise until the 1890s, early Irish suffragists had to campaign for both the local government and parliamentary franchise simultaneously. The IWSLGA was founded by Anna Haslam and her husband Thomas (see Quinlan, 2007). They were later described by the *Irish Citizen* as the 'pioneers of feminism in Ireland'. The IWSLGA remained small throughout the 1800s, with a dedicated core of about fifty members. Its main tactics included writing letters and petitions to Parliament, and holding small meetings, usually in the drawing rooms of members' houses (Cullen & Luddy, 1995). Nonetheless, the campaign for women's local representation was broadly successful. The women's poor law guardian bill of 1897 and the Local Government Act of 1898 allowed women to run for district councils and poor law boards. As Virginia Crossman has shown, the elections in 1899 saw the return of thirty-one women district councillors and eighty-five women poor law guardians, which demonstrates the appetite for public office among Irish women at that time (Crossman, 2006).

From these early seeds, the 1900s saw the suffrage movement grow and develop a higher profile. There are a number of reasons for this: the emergence of a group of highly educated women who had obtained university degrees but found most professions closed to them; the example of the large British suffrage movement; and the cultural revival that was then taking place in Dublin (Cullen Owens, 1984; Cullen, 2007). In 1908 a new suffrage group was set up by two young university graduates, Hanna Sheehy Skeffington and Margaret Cousins (Ward, 1997). Named the Irish Women's Franchise League (IWFL), it was impatient for change and not afraid to challenge contemporary social values. In contrast to the 'lady-like' behaviour of the earlier suffrage groups, the new IWFL adopted so-called 'militant' tactics by flouting social conventions about the acceptable behaviour of women. From addressing crowds on the backs of lorries to picketing public meetings and heckling politicians, the militant movement broke new ground in the Irish campaign for the vote.

The period 1912–14 can be described as the heyday of Irish suffragism, and the movement grew to an estimated membership of over 3,000 (Cullen Owens, 1984). Several new societies sprang up around the country. In Galway the Connacht Women's Franchise League arranged public lectures and published suffrage papers (see Clancy, 2007). The Munster Women's Franchise League (MWFL) was set up and soon had more than 300 members in Cork alone. It also had branches in Limerick and Waterford. The president and vice president of the MWFL were the well-known novelists Somerville and Ross, famous for their books on the 'Irish R.M.'. These women were from Ireland's landowning Protestant unionist community, who dreaded the prospect of Irish independence from Britain. The fact that these two women were among the leaders of the suffrage movement in Ireland indicates some of the conflicts and tensions that existed within it (Ryan, 2006). Another leading member of the MWFL was Susanne R. Day, also a writer. She was elected as one of Cork's first female poor law guardians and was among many suffragists who gained valuable political experience through local government (Watkins, 2014).

In Dublin the Irish Women's Reform League (IWRL) was set up by Louie Bennett to promote the rights of working women and their need for the vote. Bennett was later to become the general secretary of the Irish Women Workers' Union and, as such, maintained an important link between the women's suffrage and trade union movements (Jones, 1988; Cullen & Luddy, 2001).

Meanwhile, in the North, the Irish Women's Suffrage Society had branches in Belfast, Derry, Whitehead and Bangor. The Lisburn Suffrage Society was formed in 1909 by Lilian Metge (Hill, 2007). In addition, as Hill notes, the formation of the Church League for Women's Suffrage in Belfast in 1912 provided a 'forum for those suffragists of a religious nature to demonstrate their support' for the cause of female enfranchisement (Hill, 2007: 215).

By 1911 there were so many small suffrage groups scattered around the country that an umbrella group, the Irish Women's Suffrage Federation

(IWSF), was established and soon had around twenty member societies. These various societies represented the different political, religious and geographical divisions in Ireland at the time (Ryan, 2006).

Throughout this period, various attempts were made to introduce suffrage bills at Westminster. In 1912 the Irish Parliamentary Party (IPP) was instrumental in bringing about the defeat of the conciliation bill. Why was the party so hostile to the enfranchisement of women? The IPP, led by John Redmond, was dedicated to the cause of home rule for Ireland and had managed to win the support of the Liberal Prime Minister H.H. Asquith. Since Asquith was well known as an opponent of women's suffrage, it was feared that if women were enfranchised, Asquith would resign. If a general election was held, it was widely suspected that the Conservatives would sweep into power. The IPP feared that home rule would never get through Westminster if a Conservative/Unionist alliance was in government. This is one reason why the IPP consistently voted against the enfranchisement of women. This earned it the resentment of not only the British suffrage movement, but also the suffragists in Ireland (Ward, 1982; Cullen Owens, 1984).

The IWFL decided that the only way to get the attention of the government and the Irish Party was through militant activities. The IWFL had always described itself as militant, but it was not until 1912 that this policy was put into practice. On 13 June, eight women were arrested for throwing stones at government buildings in Dublin. This will be further explored in chapter 1.

Before proceeding, it may be useful to distinguish between the terms 'suffragist' and 'suffragette'. The term 'suffragette' has become synonymous with the militant activities of the British Women's Social and Political Union (WSPU), led by Emmeline and her daughters Christabel and Sylvia Pankhurst. The term 'suffragist' is a more general term used to describe all those who supported votes for women, and is usually applied in particular to constitutional (as opposed to militant) campaign groups. The British movement can be broadly divided into two large camps: suffragettes (WSPU); and constitutional suffragists (the National Union of Women's Suffrage Societies, led by Millicent Fawcett). However, it would be inaccurate to analyse Irish suffragists through the lens of the British movement. As will be discussed in more detail in chapter 1, although the IWFL described itself as militant, it never achieved the levels of militancy associated with the WSPU. For that reason, I will use the more general term 'suffragist' throughout this book.

In the case of Irish suffrage militancy, it is questionable whether such tactics really did attract the kind of nationwide publicity for which the militant suffragists had hoped (Ryan, 2006). Much of the press was hostile to suffrage militancy, as the *Irish Citizen* indicated on 5 April 1913: 'The Irish Press continues as usual its campaign of misrepresentation and suppression against the suffrage movement.' Faced with such hostility, the IWFL decided to take action and set up their own newspaper, which would not only help to differentiate them from the British suffragettes, but would also provide a forum for positive publicity for the suffrage movement in Ireland.

The origins of the paper

Francis, husband of Hanna Sheehy Skeffington, had some journalistic experience and had already tried and failed twice to start a paper of his own (Ward, 1997). He firmly believed that the Irish suffragists needed a paper of their own in which to express their views and spread propaganda. The more militant the Irish suffragists became, the more their activities were boycotted by the press. In the autobiography James Cousins wrote with his wife, he described how he and Francis decided to begin a suffrage paper.

He remembered seeing Francis in Dublin one day and the latter simply announced: 'We must have a paper of our own to keep the British and Irish suffrage movements distinct and carry on propaganda along our own lines.' Cousins was enthusiastic but wondered about the financing of such an undertaking. They decided to approach Mr and Mrs Pethick-Lawrence who ran the British suffrage newspaper *Votes for Women*. Cousins describes how, a few days later, a strange woman arrived at his house with an anonymous donation of £260. She handed over the money and left as mysteriously as she had arrived. The Cousinses always believed that the donation was from the Pethick-Lawrences (Cousins, 1950: 203–4).

Thus with Cousins and Sheehy Skeffington as editors, the first issue of the paper appeared on 25 May 1912. The motto of the paper, which Cousins claimed he thought up, was as follows: 'For Men and Women Equally the Rights of Citizenship. From Men and Women Equally the Duties of Citizenship.' In explaining these words, he said:

> The new paper was to be the organ of human relationships, of adjustment between the needs of the community; in short, of citizenship ... of the social construction in which the feminist and masculine sides of humanity should share equally the work of life, and enjoy equally the products of their work. (Cousins, 1950)

Not surprisingly, then, the paper was called the *Irish Citizen*, a name chosen by the two men. Cliona Murphy says the word 'citizen' was popular among suffragists internationally at that time, and used in the titles of other publications (Murphy, 1989: 35). As Margaret Ward notes in her preface to this book, the word 'citizen' took on an added significance in the Irish context, because Irish people were not then 'citizens' but were instead 'subjects' of the British crown.

Being a professional journalist, Francis Sheehy Skeffington did most of the work on the paper. He wrote unsigned editorials and articles on the political aspects of Irish suffrage agitation. Cousins wrote on the more general principles of suffrage. An eight-page weekly publication, the *Irish Citizen* consisted of the aforementioned editorials plus an 'Activities Page', with notices about forthcoming suffrage events, advertisements and, most importantly, articles submitted by suffragists from all the various suffrage groups in Ireland, and on occasion from those abroad as well. Within one month the paper was claiming weekly sales of 3,000 and an estimated readership of 10,000 people (*Irish Citizen*, June 1912). The paper sold for a penny, and an annual subscription was 6 shillings and 6 pence with free postage, though this was reduced later on when the paper became a monthly. The paper was sold at suffrage events and by the enthusiastic efforts of volunteer street sellers. The front cover of this book shows a detail of a photograph of one such enthusiastic seller, Margaret (Meg) Connery, wearing an *Irish Citizen* poster, while accosting political leaders (see p. 20 for the full photo).

Though the two editors were men, they were associate members of the IWFL. Both men and their militant wives were also active in the literary and Gaelic revival going on in Ireland at that time. The *Irish Citizen* reflected this interest in all things Irish. There is little doubt that those behind the paper were sympathetic to the cause of Irish self-determination. This point will be further explored in chapter 5.

That the *Irish Citizen* was edited by members of the IWFL gave that group an unfair advantage over the other suffrage societies in the country, one could argue. For example, the militancy of the IWFL was given much positive publicity. However, the *Irish Citizen* was still very much the paper of the movement (Ryan, 2006). It was a forum for debate among the various scattered suffrage societies in Ireland. Letters condemning militant activities, representing the viewpoints of the constitutional suffrage groups, were frequently printed in the paper. In addition, opinions were invited on such topical issues as home rule (see chapter 5).

In March 1913 the Cousinses, who had been experiencing serious financial difficulties, left Ireland to work in England and later India (Candy, 1994). Francis Sheehy Skeffington was left as sole editor, though his wife Hanna was very active in contributing and helping to produce the paper (Ward, 1997). The *Irish Citizen* was anti-militarist and vehemently condemned the First

World War. This complex issue will be the subject of chapter 3. Francis spoke out publicly against the war and was arrested and imprisoned. Though given a one-year sentence, he was released before his time was served owing to weakened health while on hunger strike. On his release from prison, he managed to escape to the USA, where he remained for almost one year (Levenson & Natterstad, 1986). Thus, from July 1915 to early 1916, Hanna was the editor of the paper. Unlike many other suffrage groups in Ireland, the IWFL (and therefore the *Irish Citizen*) remained loyal to the 'suffrage first' policy, and refused to engage in any relief work – arguing that it might prolong the war. Hanna worked tirelessly for the cause. In 1915, the IWFL organised sixty suffrage meetings, including those that were part of speaking tours to remote rural areas (Ward, 1997). However, the divisions caused by the war had a deep effect on the suffrage movement. As we will discuss in chapter 3, some suffragists so disagreed with the *Irish Citizen*'s anti-war policy that they withdrew their subscriptions (Murphy, 1989: 41; Levenson & Natterstad, 1986: 55).

During the Easter Rising in 1916, tragedy struck the paper. Francis Sheehy Skeffington, recently returned from the USA, was shot dead by a British firing squad. Though he had played no part in the Easter Rising, he was arrested while trying to prevent looting in the devastated Dublin shops. His widow attempted to find out why her husband had been shot. With the help of John Dillon MP and Tim Healy MP, she eventually succeeded in bringing Bowen-Colthurst to trial. He was found guilty of 'murder while insane', sent to Broadmoor, and then released eighteen months later (Ward, 1997). There were those, like Eva Gore-Booth, who believed that Skeffington's murder had not been the work of a mad soldier – that he had been deliberately shot for his pacifist ideals. Gore-Booth described his 'unarmed yet insurgent idealism' as the worst enemy of militarism (Roper, 1987: 51). In fact, Bowen-Colthurst had initially been promoted after Skeffington was shot and before the public outcry (Ward, 1997). It is worth noting here that the pacifist cartoonist Ernest Kavanagh, who contributed many humorous cartoons to the *Irish Citizen*, was also killed during Easter Week 1916.

Late in 1916, Hanna relinquished her role as editor of the *Irish Citizen* and went to the USA on a lecture tour to attempt to win American support for Ireland's cause. Louie Bennett, founder of the Irish Women's Suffrage Federation and Irish Women's Reform League and general secretary of the Irish Women Workers Union (IWWU), became joint editor of the paper, along with IWFL member Mary Bourke-Dowling. Louie seems an odd choice for editor, as she had been so outspoken against *Irish Citizen* policy in the past. She had actually withdrawn her subscription to the paper one year previously. A well-known pacifist and internationalist, she was not a nationalist per se (Hazelkorn, 1988; Cullen Owens, 2001). While the paper had always been pacifist and supportive of workers' rights, she brought to it an increased concentration on international pacifism and trade unionism.

However, all was not well at the paper. For some time, it had been in debt. By early 1916 it had shrunk from its original eight pages to just four, one of which consisted entirely of advertisements, and was published only on a monthly basis. The editor described the cuts as due to 'the debt incurred in the paper's three and a half years struggle as a weekly, with the forces of reaction' (*Irish Citizen*, mid-Feb. 1916). The single issue that appeared in July carried the following statement: 'The *Irish Citizen* will be carried on if an adequate response is made to the appeal for funds. It behoves every good suffragist to promote the success of the fund.' As a mark of the perceived importance of the paper, money poured in and the paper was saved. Well-known people such as Maud Gonne, George Bernard Shaw and Mr and Mrs Pethick-Lawrence were among those who contributed.

On her return from the USA, Hanna was arrested under the Defence of the Realm Act. She was imprisoned in Holloway Gaol in England with her old friends Countess Markievicz and Maud Gonne. Unlike her nationalist cellmates, Hanna had experience of using the 'hunger strike' strategy as a way of assuring her speedy release from prison (McDiarmid, 2015). She returned to Dublin in 1918, resumed her role as editor of the paper and immediately began working hard to bring it back to its original eight pages, and to increase circulation. She succeeded on both counts, but financial constraints kept the paper as a monthly publication only. Louie Bennett continued to play an active part in the paper. By 1919, two pages of the *Irish Citizen* were devoted to women's trade union news. The paper all but became the organ of the IWWU. The relationship between suffragism and labour will form the basis of chapter 4.

Women won partial enfranchisement in 1918 under the terms of that year's Representation of the People Act. However, this act granted voting rights to all men over 21 years of age, while women were only granted the vote if they were over 30 years old and if they were either a member or married to a member of the local government register, a property owner or a graduate voting in a university constituency. In this way, the act significantly increased the number of male voters, and therefore prevented a female majority in the electorate.

The *Irish Citizen* was unmoved by the winning of the vote on such limited terms. Both it and the IWFL insisted that women must have the right to vote equally with men, and that they would continue to fight until that equality had been won. But historians suggest that many women now began to lose interest in suffragism (Cullen Owens, 1984). As discussed in chapter 5, Ireland was by now on the brink of war, and nationalism was threatening to swamp feminism. Hanna Sheehy Skeffington saw this as one of the major reasons for the demise of the *Irish Citizen*:

> There can be no woman's paper without a woman's movement, without earnest and serious minded women readers and thinkers, and these have dwindled perceptibly of late partly owing to the cause above mentioned [national crisis] and because since a measure, however limited, of suffrage has been granted women are forging their own destiny in practical fields of endeavour. (Hanna cited in McKillen, 1982: 84)

Other reasons for the demise of Ireland's only feminist paper included a severe lack of funding, which itself was indicative of dwindling support, and a dispute between Hanna and Louie Bennett about it becoming a trade union paper. Also, Hanna, as a local councillor and member of Sinn Féin, found her own interests shifting away from the paper in 1920. The printing presses themselves fell victim to the War of Independence in Ireland – they were smashed by the Black and Tans. There was simply no recovery, and so the paper appeared for the final time in September 1920.

The eight-year history of the *Irish Citizen* covered a significant period in Irish history. During these years the labour movement underwent expansion in Ireland, the infamous 'lock-out' of striking workers took place in Dublin, the home rule issue came to a head, the First World War occurred, the Rising of 1916 erupted, Sinn Féin won a landslide victory in the general election of 1918, Dáil Eireann was set up in 1919, and the War of Independence broke out. In the midst of all of this – and perhaps lost in all of this – was the feminist movement. Ignored by history for so long, this movement is vividly recorded in the pages of its very own paper. But the *Irish Citizen* does more than simply record suffrage history; it also provides us with a deeper analysis of Irish suffragist and feminist ideas and policies (Ryan, 2006). Few of these women ever published their ideas in books, but the paper provides us with fascinating insights into their thoughts. More than that, the paper takes us through an extremely interesting and important period of history from a feminist point of view.

By analyzing the way such topics as the legal system, the war, nationalism, women's work and votes were dealt with by the paper, and by those who contributed to it, we can come to a better understanding of the philosophy of the Irish suffrage movement. This book, however, does not offer an exhaustive account of the *Irish Citizen*. It would be impossible to include every issue. So this book has, of necessity, been selective. The paper tackled such issues as divorce, prostitution, housework and temperance. However, only five particular topics will be explored. In making my choice of topics and writers I have attempted to represent the range of the movement, including less well-known groups like the Irish Women's Reform League and active, but less well-known women like Marion Duggan and Margaret Connery.

Each chapter of extracts from the Irish Citizen begins with a brief introductory discussion. My aims are first, to locate the extracts within their historical contexts, and second, to explore some of the feminist analyses used by the suffragists. In my writings on the Irish suffrage movement over the last twenty years or so, I have sought to demonstrate that early feminism in Ireland was highly sophisticated, encompassing an impressive array of theoretical positions, ranging from socialism to liberalism (Ryan, 1995, 1997, 2006; Ryan & Ward, 2007). While some of the suffrage writings may seem old-fashioned and conservative, some still appear quite radical and challenging.

The *Irish Citizen* stands today as a testimony to the courage and determination of Irish women and men. However, it also indicates how generations of feminists have reinvented the wheel. History has not been kind to feminists. The under-representation of feminists in our history books has denied us a thorough knowledge and understanding of the legacy of feminism. Unaware of our forgotten foremothers, we approach taboo subjects like incest and marital rape as if for the first time. The extracts included in this book illustrate the depth of analysis and theorising in which the suffragists were engaged. They also demonstrate that the Irish suffrage movement was far more than merely a 'votes for women' movement. For many of those women writing in the *Irish Citizen*, the vote was but a means to an end. In the words of Meg Connery, in the August 1918 edition of the paper, it was merely a step on the 'road to freedom'.

Abbreviations

IPP	Irish Parliamentary Party
ISF	Irishwomen's Suffrage Federation (same as IWSF)
IWFL	Irish Women's Franchise League
IWRL	Irish Women's Reform League or Irishwomen's Reform League
IWSF	Irish Women's Suffrage Federation (same as ISF)
IWSLGA	Irish Women's Suffrage and Local Government Association
IWSS	Irish Women's Suffrage Society
IWWU	Irish Women Workers' Union
MWFL	Munster Women's Franchise League
NUWSS	National Union of Women's Suffrage Societies
WSPU	Women's Social and Political Union

Margaret 'Meg' Connery wearing an *Irish Citizen* advertising board and accosting politicians including unionist leader Edward Carson. Reproduced courtesy of the National Library of Ireland.

Irish suffragists, including Hanna Sheehy Skeffington (back, centre, dark dress, to right of woman wearing 'Banner Captain' sash), attending a rally at Hyde Park, London.
Reproduced courtesy of the Museum of London.

CHAPTER I

Feminism and the vote

Citizenship and the vote

As will be discussed at length in later chapters on work, war and justice, the suffragists, in general, believed that giving women the vote would give them access to political power, and that once they achieved this power everything in society would be different. Women would bring different qualities into the political sphere. Thus the struggle for the vote was linked to a wide range of campaigns for equality in the workplace, in the legal system and in society generally.

As noted earlier, the motto of the *Irish Citizen* summarised the demands of the movement: 'For Men and Women Equally the Rights of Citizenship. From Men and Women Equally the Duties of Citizenship.' The very name of the paper itself, the *Irish Citizen*, is important; it indicates that equal rights and equal citizenship were the centre point of the movement. The editorial of 10 August 1912 makes this point clearly:

> The full citizenship which British women have found essential alike for their protection and for the realisation of their responsible humanity, is claimed today for the same reasons by Irishwomen as their inalienable part and lot in the guidance in their country's destinies.

In this piece the editor makes it clear that:

> It is just possible that an actual majority of the women of the country may never have given utterance to a definite opinion (on the question of votes for women) ... the mere question of numbers is immaterial ... great questions are never decided by a counting of heads ... but by the force of the spirit of right and justice which makes a handful of determined souls carry along with them a host of the merely ignorant and undecided, of the selfish and the cynical.

Suffragists, especially those most closely associated with the paper, believed that they had justice and right on their side in demanding votes, even if they did not have the majority of the people behind them. The article also explains why women needed access to political decision-making, not just of right but also of necessity. Women, according to the editor, simply could not trust men to make decisions for them. However, this article implies a certain level of elitism. A small number of campaigners had the right to go ahead and fight for the vote on behalf of the ignorant and the apathetic. As will be discussed at length in chapter 4, class divisions were a contentious issue within the suffrage movement. Let us now begin to explore this point.

The Suffrage Catechism

In its first anniversary issue of 17 May 1913, the *Irish Citizen* printed the Suffrage Catechism. This takes the form of questions and answers and comes up with some surprising statements. In answer to the question, 'Do you want all women to get the vote?', the catechism replies: 'No!', and then goes on to explain, 'Because every man has not got a vote. Men have to qualify for the vote in certain ways ... what we ask is that women who qualify in the same way should have the same right to vote.'

However, in reply to the charge that some suffragists agree with restricting the vote to people of property, the catechism says that some suffragists do and some do not. In response to the question of what use votes would be to women anyway, the catechism explains that the possession of a vote makes somebody a citizen and gives him or her some power over the way laws are made and administered. In anticipation of the old question, 'Why don't women stay at home and keep out of politics?', the catechism says:

> There are vast numbers of women in every country who have no 'homes' in the sense in which you use the word. There are large numbers of women at work in the world in factories, in shops and in offices earning their bread as independent beings. For them politics are vital because they affect wages.

It may seem surprising that this catechism only demands votes for women on the same basis as men. One would perhaps have expected this from the more conservative suffrage groups but surely not from the likes of the IWFL. Indeed, as the Catechism went on to explain, suffragists were not all in agreement about such restrictions.

One woman who certainly opposed restrictions on who could and could not vote was Marion Duggan. A qualified lawyer and a graduate of Trinity College Dublin, she was originally from Co. Westmeath (Watkins, 2014). Writing on 8 August 1914 under the pen name 'M.E.', Duggan pointed to three basic divisions among suffragists. First, there were those who wanted suffrage immediately, while others felt that votes should be postponed until after home rule had been established – I will discuss this division further in chapter 5. Second, she argued, there were those suffragists who wanted to employ only peaceful constitutional campaigning in an effort to win the vote, while groups like the IWFL, the IWSS and the British WSPU had grown impatient and so adopted militant tactics, which frequently resulted in arrests and imprisonment. Third, and perhaps most serious, Duggan argued, was the division between those suffragists who wanted votes for all and those who only wanted votes for 'ladies'.

Duggan states that the real division within the suffrage movement was between those who wanted a 'high franchise', in other words those who wanted votes on the basis of a property qualification, and those who wanted 'universal suffrage', i.e. votes for everyone. She indicated that there were a number of 'ladies' who wanted the vote simply for the 'aggrandisement of all persons of their own class' (*Irish Citizen*, 8 Aug. 1914). Duggan revealed her own socialist beliefs (Watkins, 2014) when she agreed with James Connolly that the organisation of working-class women must be a fundamental aspect of the suffrage campaign. She expressed her disapproval of the English militants for the way they distanced themselves from the labour movement. This, she argued, was due to pressure from the wealthy and aristocratic members of the WSPU, who refused to be associated with labour politics. Duggan stated her politics very clearly when she wrote: 'I should like to see the forward suffrage policy of tomorrow decided by labour suffragists, militant and non-militant, meeting together and taking the opinion of all as to what their common course should be.'

This problem of class bias applied right across the suffrage movement and cut across militant and constitutional groups. For example, the non-militant Conservative and Unionist Women's Franchise Association (which established a branch in Dublin in 1909) was far more concerned with winning votes for their mainly upper-middle-class members than with listening to the needs of working women (see Murphy, 1989: 27). We return to this discussion in chapter 4.

Militants versus non-militants

On 1 June 1912 a mass meeting of suffragists was held in Dublin. The newly founded *Irish Citizen* gave detailed coverage of this important event in Irish feminist history. The meeting was chaired by Professor Mary Hayden (the first woman professor of Irish history) of the IWSLGA and was an attempted show of unity on the part of a range of women's groups. Hanna Sheehy Skeffington wrote of this meeting: 'Constitutional joined militant – for the day at least; Unionist was allied to Nationalist, Party claims (so dear to our loyal women) were for once subordinated to sex principle' (*Irish Citizen*, 8 June 1912).

Hence, as I have argued elsewhere (Ryan, 2006), despite this show of unity, the divisions within the movement were clear. Even Hanna Sheehy Skeffington's article revealed some of the obvious tensions – unionist/ nationalist, militant/constitutional. In addition, her article highlighted the presence of women from a range of socio-economic backgrounds: a doctor, teachers and factory workers. Nevertheless, one must question the ability of the movement to maintain a unity of purpose across such a range of diverse class backgrounds and interests. We will return to this point later.

At this mass meeting a resolution was passed calling on the government to amend the home rule bill by including a provision for the enfranchisement of women on the basis of the local government register. Copies of this resolution were circulated to cabinet ministers and to all the Irish MPs. When no reply was received, the Irish Women's Franchise League decided to embark on a campaign of militancy (Levenson & Natterstad, 1986). On 13 June 1912 eight members of the IWFL were arrested for breaking the windows of government buildings in Dublin (Cullen Owens, 1984). These Irish women were, in a number of cases, seasoned campaigners who had previously been arrested for militancy in Britain (*Irish Citizen*, 25 May 1912). They were: Kathleen Houston, Marjorie Hasler, Maud Lloyd, Jane Murphy, Margaret Murphy, Marguerite Palmer, Hanna Sheehy Skeffington and Hilda Webb.

Two hundred women packed the courtroom for the trial (Levenson & Natterstad, 1986). Cliona Murphy argues that the trial took on a 'carnival atmosphere' as the suffragists in the dock used the opportunity to gain full publicity for the cause (Murphy, 1989: 93). The women were each sentenced to a fine of 40 shillings or a month's imprisonment. All eight refused to pay the fine, opting instead to go to prison (Cullen Owens, 1984). According to Levenson and Natterstad (1986), they were well treated in prison and received all the privileges of political prisoners including having meals sent into Mountjoy prison from Jennie Wyse Power's restaurant.

The reaction to the outbreak of militancy in Ireland was mixed. Even among the suffragists themselves it proved contentious. The veteran campaigner Anna Haslam said that she could not condone the actions of the militants, but she still visited Hanna Sheehy Skeffington in prison, bringing food and gifts (Ward, 2017). As the following extracts from the *Irish Citizen* indicate, militancy remained a site of disagreement for a number of years.

In July 1912 an event occurred that was to harden public attitudes against the militants. During the visit of Prime Minister Asquith to Dublin he was attacked by three women from the English Women's Social and Political Union who had travelled to Ireland with the intention of disrupting this official visit. The women – Lizzie Baker, Gladys Evans and Mary Leigh – also attempted to set fire to a theatre where Asquith was due to speak. Leigh and Evans were arrested and sentenced to five years imprisonment. In protest at the length of their sentences, four of the Irish suffragists in Mountjoy, including Hanna Sheehy Skeffington, went on hunger strike. After one week of this, the Irish women were released due to their deteriorating health. Interestingly, while the English militant prisoners in Irish jails were forcibly fed, the Irish prisoners were not (W. Murphy, 2007).

While the militant Irish suffragists attempted to show some solidarity with the British militants, this does not mean that there was no ill feeling. Hanna later wrote that she 'deplored the fact that they [the English women] had not left the "heckling" to the Irishwomen' (Levenson & Natterstad, 1986: 38). She added that 'even the best meaning English have blind spots where the Sister Isle is concerned' (quoted in Ward, 1997: 93). The non-militant Munster Women's Franchise League immediately condemned the actions of the English militants as 'wicked' (Cullen Owens, 1984: 59).

This was not the first or last time that English women from the WSPU came to Ireland. Members of the WSPU were particularly active in Belfast. Such was the defection of its members to the WSPU that the IWSS collapsed in 1914 (Urquhart, 2000; Hill, 2007). In September 1913, Christabel Pankhurst wrote to Hanna Sheehy Skeffington to say that the WSPU intended to target Dublin. The *Irish Citizen* described this as a 'regrettable' move (Levenson & Natterstad, 1986: 54). In any case the First World War intervened and the WSPU abandoned militancy.

As noted in the introduction, it would be misleading to associate Irish militancy with that of the English WSPU. The Irish women rarely embarked on anything more militant than smashing windows, while the English women engaged in far more violent and dangerous tactics, including blowing up buildings (Edwards, 2014). However, in the north of Ireland, militant activism was more marked than in the south, and it lasted for more years, with attacks on Belfast Bowling and Lawn Tennis Pavilion, Newtownards Race Course and the greens at Knock Golf Club, as well as the infamous fire at Lisburn Cathedral (Hill, 2007).

The government decided that firm measures were needed against suffrage militancy, especially in the light of the frequent use of the hunger strike, which meant speedy release from prison on health grounds. In the spring of 1913 the famous Temporary Discharge Act became law. Under the terms of the act a hunger-striker could be temporarily released to recover her strength and then rearrested to continue her sentence thus prolonging her sentences indefinitely. It quickly became known as the 'Cat and Mouse Act', as the prisoners were being released and re-arrested like mice being taunted by a cat.

The first test of this act in Ireland occurred in the case of the so-called 'Tullamore Mice'. A number of women from the IWFL, including Marguerite Palmer, had been arrested for smashing windows in Dublin. They were sent to Tullamore prison. As the extract from the *Irish Citizen* graphically reveals, the women were treated badly and denied political prisoner status, illustrating the hardening of attitudes of the legal authorities towards militant suffrage tactics. When the women went on hunger strike they were punished with the withdrawal of all privileges, including books, pillows and a fire. Marguerite Palmer's article is a powerful piece of writing, which illustrates very clearly the suffering of those women who chose to go on hunger strike.

The women were released under the Temporary Discharge Act, but ordered to return within weeks to complete their sentences. A massive protest meeting was quickly arranged in Dublin's Mansion House. It drew an 'overflowing audience representing all shades of suffrage opinion' (Levenson & Natterstad, 1986: 51). No attempt was made by the authorities to re-arrest the Tullamore Mice.

The division between militants and non-militants seems to have been largely about tactics. Although there were some ideological differences, it would be an error to see the militants as politically more radical than the constitutional suffragists (Ryan, 1994, 2006). In fact, some of the more radical, universalistic suffragists, like Duggan, vehemently opposed militancy. Writing on 5 April 1913, Duggan asked 'Are Militants Suffragists?' She picked up and took issue with many of the arguments used by militants in earlier editions of the *Irish Citizen*. She was particularly angered by the assumptions made by militants that it was they, not the constitutional suffragists, who were furthering the suffrage cause. Militants dismissed constitutional suffragists like Duggan as naive and ineffectual. However, according to Duggan, the militants were underestimating the achievements of constitutional methods. She saw militancy as merely damaging the suffrage cause. For example, she blamed militancy for the defeat of the conciliation bill (1912) in parliament. She argued that the quiet, educational methods of the IWRL had done more to help Irish women and expose inequalities than the militant tactics of smashing panes of glass. Despite what Duggan said, it is not easy to say whether militancy lost the suffragists public support or, as the IWFL claimed, won them valuable publicity.

On 4 January 1913 Hanna Sheehy Skeffington had written in the *Irish Citizen* to justify militancy. Her main argument was that militancy kept suffrage demands in the public eye. In legitimating such riotous behaviour she said that it was a social revolution. 'Society as at present constituted must go.' She expressed surprise that Irish people in general did not condone militancy, since they had used it on numerous occasions to attain nationalistic ends (such as in 1798) and in the Land War (1879–82). She added that in almost fifty years of the suffrage movement in Ireland nothing had been achieved, so obviously a change in approach was required. 'Desperate diseases need desperate remedies,' she concluded.

On 25 July 1914 Margaret Cousins wrote on the 'defensibility of militancy'. Women, she claimed, were effectively held in slavery. Therefore militants' motives were pure, which in itself absolved them from guilt. Militancy was, in her view, a form of self-defence. She compared the militants to mothers who use desperate measures to protect their children. Women who were prepared to do nothing even when their children went hungry or lacked proper shelter were not worthy mothers, she declared:

> What individual mothers dare not do, the suffragettes with mother love for the race burning in their hearts are doing ... There can be no peace without honour and justice, for while the injustices remain unredressed coercion must be met with spirited resistance.

This argument is very similar to the one cited earlier (*Irish Citizen*, 10 Aug. 1912) in which it was argued that 'great questions are never decided by a counting of heads', and which spoke about the 'handful of determined souls' who carry along the ignorant and apathetic. This is how members of the IWFL justified their militancy. By so doing, did they perhaps inadvertently take the initiative away from working-class women instead of trying to help such women organise? The militant women meant well; and they endured prison, hunger strikes and, in the case of the Cousinses, bankruptcy, for the cause of suffrage. However, their attitude does appear patronising. They saw themselves as the saviours of women, 'suffragettes with mother love burning in their hearts', who would get the vote for the poor, uneducated and oppressed women.

On 5 June 1915 Lucy Kingston, originally from Co. Wicklow, a pacifist and member of the Women's International League for Peace and Freedom and of the Irish Women's Suffrage Federation (see also Swanton, 1994), wrote that snobbery was creeping into the suffrage movement. There was a danger, she warned, that highly educated and intellectual feminists would be greatly disappointed by their 'sisters', who found it harder to reason. The movement could not afford, she said, to have some women looking down on other women, as it was bad enough to have one sex looking down on the other.

It is all too easy to condemn the suffragists, especially the militants. Undoubtedly, they were dedicated to their cause and caught up in an extremely exciting and dangerous campaign. In their enthusiasm it was perhaps easy to feel frustrated with those women who showed no interest in the cause of women's rights. However, such a problem was not unique to the Irish suffrage movement. How should feminists react to women who are either apathetic or even hostile towards the women's rights movement?

In the extracts from the *Irish Citizen* these issues are discussed from different perspectives. Among these extracts I have included two interesting and very different accounts of the reactions that suffragists encountered in their efforts to spread the feminist message, especially outside of Dublin.

Regional tours

The accounts of regional campaigning are relevant for a number of reasons. First, they give a fascinating insight into the harsh realities of organising a feminist propaganda tour into rural Ireland in the early years of the twentieth century. Although there had been active suffrage campaigning for many decades in urban centres like Belfast, Dublin and Cork, the lack of transport and communication meant that certain counties had been virtually untouched by the suffrage movement. The accounts of these tours indicate the sharp divide between urban and rural Ireland, and also suggest another possible division within the suffrage movement. As the suffrage movement was largely, though not exclusively, urban did that mean that the majority of rural women felt alienated and excluded from the campaign for enfranchisement? While the *Irish Citizen* made strong efforts to include features on factory women, there was virtually nothing on rural and agricultural women. Susanne R. Day's article on touring in Kerry suggests that the country women she met were broadly sympathetic to the cause. Day, a Protestant Cork woman, as noted earlier was a well-known writer and active campaigner for poor law reform (see Day, 1916; Watkins, 2014).

Second, I have included these two articles because they are so different. While Day's tour of Kerry went relatively smoothly (although she does hint at some difficulty booking the local hall), the tour of the West described by Hanna Sheehy Skeffington was plagued by boycotts. Her article highlights three of the main power brokers who had the ability to impose a boycott; the church (both Protestant and Catholic), the politicians (in particular those who were members of the Ancient Order of Hibernians) and the press. She describes very vividly how the church, in collusion with the local press, had managed to create such a sense of fear in a small town that nobody was prepared to display a poster advertising the suffrage meeting or even to sell the women the necessary equipment to build a makeshift platform. In addition to these barriers to public speaking imposed by the power brokers, there was the sheer challenge to convention of women getting up on a public stage and addressing an audience in early twentieth-century Ireland. Dealing with the constant heckling was an ordeal. However, Day illustrates very nicely how an experienced speaker could deal effectively with a heckler, including a noisy 'anti-suffragist' and even turn the situation to her advantage. Clearly, as Cliona Murphy has argued (2007), humour was an important aspect of suffrage campaigning. It is also likely that Day's years of experience as a poor law guardian in a male-dominated environment equipped her to deal with heckling and antagonism (see Day, 1916).

There is perhaps a temptation to divide suffragists into two stereotypical categories; the constitutional lady hosting a genteel drawing-room meeting over a cup of tea, and the militant 'suffragette' virago smashing windows in Dublin. While in reality both types of activity went on, both of these stereotypes are exaggerations that simplify the diversity and complexity of suffrage strategies (Ryan, 2006). The two accounts of the speaking tours go some way towards challenging these stereotypes. Day was a constitutional suffragist and a member of the MWFL, which condemned militant violence. Yet her account of touring Kerry indicates the courage, determination and energy of the non-militants. Hanna Sheehy Skeffington's account of the tour of Longford and Roscommon equally illustrates the courage and determination of the IWFL, who had to overcome significant obstacles, including the threat of personal assault. The militant and constitutional suffragists in Ireland had far more in common than may be supposed (Ryan, 1994, 2006).

Suffragism and feminism

Throughout this book I will argue that the suffragists were involved in a complex and multifaceted campaign that cannot be simply dismissed as a single-issue effort to win the vote. This was a feminist movement going well beyond enfranchisement (Ryan, 2006). As the *Irish Citizen*'s October 1919 editorial stated, the paper's aim had always been to promote both suffragism and feminism in Ireland.

Clearly, many suffragists did not see the struggle ending when women got the vote. The *Irish Citizen* proved that it was not satisfied with token gestures when it refused to acknowledge as a victory the 1918 Representation of the People Act, which granted votes to women over 30 years of age (subject to property qualifications). The policy statement of October 1919 promised that the *Irish Citizen* would continue the fight:

until women have secured the other rights that enfranchisement involves of which the vote is but a small part and but a symbol ... the complete abolition of various taboos and barriers – social economic and political – that still impede women's progress and consequently that of the race.

While some women were satisfied to accept the 'victory' in 1918, others were less convinced.

The *Irish Citizen* and the IWFL were not at all happy with the partial vote. Margaret Connery, writing in April 1917, called the then proposed restriction on women according to age an 'illogical and lopsided suffrage proposal'. The IWFL would, she wrote, continue to demand: 'votes on the same terms as it is, or may be, granted to men'. She accused Millicent Fawcett, of the National Union of Women's Suffrage Societies in England, of favouring expediency over principle. The Irish suffragists would, Connery said, accept this 'shabby and make-shift measure' under protest and continue the campaign.

The same writer in August 1918 writing on the subject of the forthcoming general election discussed the 'new force in Irish politics' – women voters. Connery remarked how newspapers and politicians who had condemned 'sexless viragoes' for wanting the vote were now flattering these women and trying to attract their votes. She wondered if the voting Irish women would be any different from generations of voting Irish men: 'For years the Irish electorate has been fed on flapdoodle and flagwagging. Will the women show their judgment by demanding a more sustaining mental diet?'

She was well aware that 'many women' would not challenge social inequality or tackle such controversial topics as excessive drinking, double moral standards or the hypocritical attitudes towards unmarried mothers in a so-called Christian country. Instead, many women would demonstrate a 'slave-like' obedience to male standards. The effects of centuries of submission would not disappear so quickly. She concluded 'there are still many milestones on the road to freedom'.

Connery's article is extremely important because it shows that suffragists were not totally naive about the immediate effects of women winning the vote. There was an acknowledgment that the socialising influences of centuries would not disappear as soon as the first vote was cast. This article also shows that many suffragists, particularly those who regularly contributed to the *Irish Citizen*, saw the vote merely as a first step to freedom, not as the end in itself. Only after they had won the vote could women even begin to address the numerous challenges, problems and inequalities within Irish society. This theme is clearly articulated in the extracts from the newspaper that follow.

THE IRISH
CITIZEN

Printed in
Ireland
on
Irish Paper.

For Men and Women Equally
The Rights of Citizenship;
From Men and Women Equally
The Duties of Citizenship.

Weekly
One Penny.
Annual
Subscription
6s. 6d. post free.

Vol. 1.   JUNE 22nd, 1912.   No. 5.

PRISONERS FOR LIBERTY.

Members of Irish Women's Franchise League on trial for breaking Government windows.

"No better allies than women can be found. They are in certain emergencies more dangerous to despotism than men. They have more courage, through having less scruples, when their better instincts are appealed to by a militant and just cause in a fight against a mean foe."

(Michael Davitt.)

"For where a man's will hangs above men's heads, sheer as a sword or scourge might, and not one save by his grace hath grace to call himself man—there, if haply one be born a man, needs must he break the dogleash of the law to do himself, being wronged, where no right is, Right."

(Marino Faliero)

MISS MARGARET MURPHY.

(Miss Margaret Murphy took part in the deputation of Black Friday, Nov. 21, 1910, and was brutally ill-treated. She has just completed a sentence of two months' hard labour for her share in the militant protest of last March. She went through the Hunger Strike, and was forcibly fed).

(Miss Jane Murphy has just completed the period of two months' hard labour to which she was sentenced as a result of her last protest. She went through the hunger strike as a protest against not receiving the treatment of political prisoners in Holloway, and was forcibly fed).

MRS. PALMER.

(Mrs. Marguerite Blanche Palmer joined the I.W.F.L. at its formation, and was a member, as Miss Bannister, of its first Committee. Heckled Mr. Birrell at Law Students' Debating Society, Oct. 21, 1910, owing to his refusal to receive deputation from any Irish Suffrage Society. Heckled Sir Edward Carson at Rathmines Town Hall, Dec., 1910, as a result of his refusal to receive deputation. Hon. Sec., I.W.F.L., Nov., 1910; resigned June, 1911. Organised Census Resistance, March, 1911. May, 1911, lobbied Irish members on behalf of I.W.F.L. prior to Second Reading of Conciliation Bill. Participated in militant protest in London, Nov., 1911; sentenced to one week's imprisonment for breaking two windows in new War Office).

MRS. SHEEHY SKEFFINGTON.

(Mrs. Sheehy Skeffington is the eldest daughter of Mr. David Sheehy, M.P., who was six times imprisoned for political offences in connection with the agrarian and Home Rule agitations. Her uncle, Father Eugene Sheehy, was the first priest imprisoned as a "suspect" by Forster. She graduated with distinction in the Royal University, winning Scholarship, 1897; Honours B.A., 1899; M.A. with First Class Honours and Special Prize, 1902. Member of Committee, Irish Association of Women Graduates. One of the founders of the I.W.F.L., 1908; Chairman of Committee, 1911. With Miss Hilda Webb, heckled Mr. Birrell at Greystones, Oct., 1910. Heckled Sir Edward Carson, Dec., 1910. Went on deputations to Mr. Redmond, Dec., 1909; July, 1910; Jan., 1911, and April, 1912. Took part in Poster Parade, Home Rule Sunday, and in deputation to National Convention).

MISS JANE MURPHY.

"What rights are hers that dare not strike for them?"

(Tennyson).

Four of the militant suffragists who were arrested in Dublin, June 1912.

Extracts from the *Irish Citizen*

Irish Suffrage Prisoners

25 MAY 1912

The following is a list of the members of the Irish Women's Franchise League, the Irish militant organisation, who have undergone imprisonment for their share in militant protests in London:

1. Miss Allan – one month, November–December 1910.
2. Mrs Cousins, Mus. Bac. – one month, November–December 1910.
3. Mrs Garvey Kelly – one month, November–December 1910.
4. Miss Houston – two months, November 1910–January 1911.
5. Miss Eva Stephenson – two months, November 1910–January 1911.
6. Miss Hilda Webb – two months, November 1910–January 1911.
7. Mrs Baker – one week November 1911.
8. Miss Bourke-Dowling – one week, November 1911.
9. Mrs Connery – one week, November 1911.
10. Miss Maud Lloyd- one week, November 1911.
11. Mrs Palmer – one week, November 1911.
12. Mrs Emerson – two months with hard labour, March–May 1912.
13. Miss O. Jeffcott – two months with hard labour, March–May 1912.

Miss Jeffcott went through the hunger-strike and was forcibly fed.

In addition to those who went as delegates from the IWFL, a number of other Irishwomen – of whom it is not possible to compile a full list – joined in these protests on their individual responsibility, and were imprisoned. Among these should be mentioned:

From Dublin – Mrs Earl and the two Misses Murphy; from Belfast – Miss Robinson and Mrs Bennett. Of these Mrs Bennett and the Misses Murphy had hard labour sentences of two months; they went through the hunger strike, and were forcibly fed.

A large number of Irish women resident in Great Britain also took part in these protests and were imprisoned.

Mass Meeting of Irish Women: an Impression from the Platform

by Hanna Sheehy Skeffington

8 JUNE 1912

Some weeks ago – when, in fact, we first learned that we were excluded from the home rule bill – the Irish Women's Franchise League conceived the thought of rallying all Irish suffragists under a common standard to voice our common demand. Suffrage societies and other women's organisations throughout the length and breadth of Ireland instantly responded. Constitutional joined militant – for the day at least; Unionist was allied to Nationalist, Party claims (so dear to our loyal women) were for once subordinated to sex principle, and the result was Saturday's delegate meeting, the first women's congress held in Ireland. Its memory and its inspiration will survive long after its definite purpose – the pressing of a Government amendment to the home rule bill – has been achieved or blocked; long after it has been resolved once more into its individual elements and scattered, the thought of it will abide: Dublin will be inspired by the demonstration of the keenness of the provinces, and the provinces will gain new energy by contact with the centre.

Women possess the genius for organisation, for skilled manipulation of effect. Their unfailing attention to details give their meetings an element of the picturesque lacking in male-run assemblies. Those twenty shields of plain black and white lettering, bearing the names of the various provincial centres represented at the meeting, those banners and pennants of orange and green, azure and silver, dark-blue and gold that lined the hall, added a further emphasis to the exclusively feminine platform, representative of so many varying feminine activities, from medicine and the law to artistic needlework and craftsmanship. One woman doctor had snatched some moments from her crowded professional day to come, a woman labour-organiser joyously told of a strike, happily settled, where her girls had won, another came from a teachers' congress brimful of economic sex-grievances.

The spirit of the audience, as judged from the platform, was throughout deeply earnest and, to my mind at least, stirringly militant. It was a woman's audience; one felt, moreover, that every woman present represented many others, as their chosen delegate. It was an audience of experts: every subtle point, every political allusion was at once appreciated; those women were unanimous as to what they wanted and how what they wanted was best achieved. Moreover (and this to me was the most cheering sign of all) they were so strong in their sense of absolute right, of unswerving sex-faith and constancy, that they did not take over seriously the prospect of political wiles and delay. Home Rule or no Home Rule, Westminster or College Green, there is a new spirit abroad among women: whether the vote is reluctantly granted by a Liberal Government or wrested from an Irish Parliament, to women in the end it matters but little.

Politicians and parties (Irish and English alike) if they do push on their Home Rule ship, regardless of warnings, 'full steam ahead', will be iceberged and their male monster will founder – that is all. But the women who are behind this world movement will most surely achieve their purpose. I am almost sorry for the politicians at their party play, those little legislators blindly making little laws for those who make the legislators.

Editorial: What Is a Political Prisoner?

10 AUGUST 1912

Considerable confusion of thought appears to exist, even in Ireland, where people ought to know better, as to what constitutes a political prisoner. The lack of any discrimination, in English law, between political offences and ordinary crime doubtless accounts for this lack of clear standards on the matter. In some quarters the idea seems to be entertained that, whereas a small offence like window-breaking may be properly placed in the political category, law-breaking of a more serious character, such as attempts to fire public buildings, or personal violence likely to result in bodily injury, must be treated as ordinary crime. Such a classification ignores the only real basis of distinction between political offences and ordinary law-breaking – namely, the political motive. Any offence, small or great, which is committed with a political motive, ranks as a political offence; and the offender, during whatever period of detention may be deemed necessary by the courts, must be treated with the respect and regard due to a political prisoner. People who do not think clearly may be horrified at this deduction; but no other is logically possible. And English Governments, so savage against political offences committed within their own jurisdiction, have fully recognised this principle in dealing with refugees from other nations. These refugees, even when charged with assassination by their own governments, have always been sheltered by England, so long as their political motive was unmistakable.

'Crime is crime', said Mr Justice Madden, in his address to the Grand Jury with reference to the English Suffragettes charged with law-breaking in Ireland, 'and we have nothing to do with the motive'. That is the view of the legal pedant, not that of the historian – not, therefore, that of the Statesman, whose task it is to anticipate history's verdict and to shape his acts in accordance with it. The offences for which Mrs Leigh and her colleagues were arraigned this week cannot be confused with ordinary crime. They are symptoms of a deep-seated political grievance, of political unrest not to be assuaged otherwise than by the removal of that grievance. They are warnings – serious warnings, one may admit, yet mild in comparison with similar manifestations in the past on the part of men suffering injustice – that, in the words of Mr Birrell, 'the time for shuffling and delay is past'. For every woman who is goaded to the point of action such as taken by Mrs Leigh and Miss Evans, there are hundreds suffering under a profound sense of indignation at tyrannical government; there are thousands, less profoundly moved, yet deeply in earnest in the struggle for their rights. These hundreds, these thousands, will not be appeased or cowed by the spectacle of prison torture being inflicted on these few who have offered themselves up as sacrifices in voicing the sentiments of all. Rather they will be provoked to emulation, to open defiance of the Government, the law, the state of society which makes it possible for women of the hero-type, such as Mrs Leigh, to be ranked with criminals. Tyranny is here, as always, not only a crime, but a blunder.

English law being mainly an assemblage of heterogeneous judicial decisions, not a rationally ordered code, there is, naturally, no consistency in its workings with regard to political prisoners. The Irish suffragettes now in Mountjoy are treated as political prisoners, because their protest did not sufficiently alarm the authorities; the English suffragettes consigned to the same prison last Wednesday, whose political motive is equally manifest, and was commented on and recognised as honest both by judge and prosecuting counsel, are treated as convicts; – because they succeeded in striking terror into the Government, and the first thoughts of terrified tyranny, gauging by its own cowardice the effect of brutality on others, is to resort to savage repression. Another reason, doubtless, was the expectation that the inflaming of popular passion against the English Suffragettes would enable the latter to be degraded and tortured with impunity – an expectation doomed to disappointment in the revulsion of feeling caused by Judge Madden's ferocious sentences, quite as much as by Mrs Leigh's eloquence, amongst the Irish Suffragists who are most sincerely opposed to militancy.

Editorial: Do Women Want the Vote?

10 AUGUST 1912

One of the most frequent assertions which take the place of arguments on the part of those who oppose the political enfranchisement of women is that women do not want the vote. The statement bears a suspicious resemblance to the language used by the supporters of privilege and oppression in all ages. Persons who are comfortably placed, and therefore, in most cases, satisfied with existing social arrangements, are always so anxious to believe that revolutionary movements are not the spontaneous issue of a feeling of widespread discontent among the unprivileged, but the wicked work of a few unnaturally restless 'agitators'! It is true that, as we have previously maintained, to mistake the effect for the cause, to confound the outward manifestation with the inward soul, of great social and national movements has invariably been the error of those who denied justice the world over. But they have gone further than that; not satisfied with denying justice, they attempt to deny that any demand exists for the removal of injustice. The ostrich is, in fact, as notable and characteristic an ingredient of the undesirable side of human nature as ever was the ape and the tiger. Those who do not want to be convinced of the justice and expediency of a certain course are never at a loss for excuses and subterfuges and evasions of the plainest facts in order to maintain an indefensible position; and in no country has this been more universally noted of persons in power than in Ireland.

If the disaffected are in active rebellion, they are unfit for liberty. If they are peaceable, they do not ask for liberty. This is the two-edged dilemma with which the obstinacy of reaction essays to cut the Gordian knot of Revolution.

Women do not want the vote. The phrase brings comfort especially to the placid souls of persons, mostly easy-going, unprogressive, and moderately well-to-do, whose ideas on the duties of active citizenship are, to use no term of stronger quality, sufficiently cloudy and unsubstantial to keep them in the darkness of ignorance as to the real conditions under which the vast majority of women's lives are passed. A limited view from the standpoint of upper or middle-class social prosperity leads at once to the rather obvious conclusion that the women of these classes are adequately housed, clothed, and nourished. Whereupon the want of imagination, which consists in seeing nothing but the superficial fact, infers that what is true of some known women must also be true of all women, known and unknown; and at the same time, commonplace Philistinism suggests that the satisfaction of the most immediate animal necessities can leave no possible or conceivable ground for discontent in the hearts of women. We have, on previous occasions, adverted to the fallacy, so prevalent among writers in the fashionable Press organs, of ignoring the existence, not to say the hardships, of women of the proletariat and working classes in their estimates of the importance of the Suffrage for women. A similar fallacy in regard to a true valuation of the volume and intensity of the demand of women themselves for enfranchisement is no less common.

We are informed on excellent authority that, in a recent canvass of the women municipal voters in certain wards of the city of Dublin for a petition to the Corporation on Woman Suffrage, nine out of every ten women who were canvassed declared themselves in favour of the enfranchisement of their sex. It is a fact of common observation that audiences of working people, whose hard lives induce in them a keen sense of the realities involved in political questions, listen attentively to Suffrage speakers, and invariably, when not previously inflamed by party bias, give an almost unanimous assent to the principle of sex equality. We have, in fact, been often struck with the superior quickness of the working woman to grasp the essentials of the Suffrage question, and with her vivid, if resigned, consciousness of the subjection of her sex to men.

In England the strength of the demand has received more extensive and complete expression than has been possible in Ireland, where the immense preponderance of agriculture over industrial conditions of life and the peculiar political position have combined to retard the growth of women's organisations for the defence and furtherance of their economic interests. In England working and professional women are largely organised; and we believe that, with the single exception of the Anti-Suffrage League – which has recently, in fact, surrendered its exclusively feminine character – no single organisation of women in England, whether existing for the defence of economic interests or for social reform and temperance work, has failed to declare in favour of the principle of Woman Suffrage. The women of Great Britain have repeatedly held demonstrations and processions on a vastly greater scale than would be possible for any other political party at present. What is true of women in England, Wales, and Scotland, is true also of the women of Ireland. The full citizenship, which British women have found essential alike for their protection and for the realisation of their responsible humanity, is claimed today for the same reasons by Irishwomen as their inalienable part and lot in the guidance of their country's destinies. We say Irishwomen advisedly, though it is just possible that an actual majority of the women of the country may never have given active utterance to a definite opinion. What of that? The mere question of numbers is immaterial. Great questions are never decided by a counting of heads in the manner of the market-place, but by the force of the spirit of right and justice, which makes a handful of determined souls carry along with them a host of the merely ignorant and undecided, of the selfish and the cynical. Women truly representative in the highest sense of the term, overwhelmingly representative of the finest feminine intellect and prestige in Ireland, women distinguished in many walks of life, mothers of families and leaders of opinion, have united to ask for the measure of justice. Are they not worthy to be accounted a part, at least, of the Voice of Ireland which our Liberal and Nationalist legislators delight to honour?

Are Militants Suffragists?
by M.E.
5 APRIL 1913

Readers of the last two numbers of the *Irish Citizen* will readily understand that I was keenly interested in the article, entitled 'A Holy War', which appeared in last week's issue. It told me so many things about my own views I never knew before! There was, however, just one trifle which the author no doubt inadvertently omitted to make clear. It is a small point, but without some explanation I find great difficulty in answering her. It is this: Do militants believe that women should have votes; or, in other words, do they hold that the women who suffragists propose to entrust with the Parliamentary Franchise, are capable today of making an intelligent use thereof? The 'militant movement' started to secure votes for women, and loudly its teachers declared women were fit to vote; but on reading 'A Christian Militant's' personal opinion (by the way militants say they never abuse constitutionalists!) I cannot really believe that she thinks 'one who discloses an inexcusable and appalling ignorance', 'a dishonest distortion of facts', 'a blind leader of the blind', etc., is fit to vote on questions of national importance. My views are those of the National Union of Women Suffrage Societies, and the Labour Party, who must, therefore be equally guilty and equally unreliable. It is a pity, because the man in the street reading such an article, and the similar one by Miss Pankhurst in the 'Suffragette' of 21st. March 1913, will have no doubt come to the conclusion that as the militants believe constitutionalists morally dead, they do not intend to cease from militancy upon the enfranchisement of the morally dead. I was recently told that 'many people' believe that had it not been for militancy, the Liberal women would never have insisted upon the passing into law of the White Slave Traffic Bill, i.e., that without militancy an educated body of women, knowing all the facts of this diabolical trade, would have done nothing to put an effective end to it!

Therefore, you must worry them into it! It is an intelligent theory, but you can't call it suffrage. It brings home the necessity of declaring non-militant societies anti-militant. It supposes that had we been enfranchised in 1910, militancy would have still been required to rouse women voters in 1912. It is necessary to keep non-militants up to the mark. Mr Maurice Wilkins makes a really fine defence of 'militancy', but both critics make the mistake of substituting the particular for the general. 'All humanity got a trumpet call to militancy.' Pillarbox outrages are militancy. Therefore, humanity got a trumpet-call to destroy letters. Every form of spirited protest must be tried. This is exactly where 'A Christian Militant' and I part company. She holds that the need to wage 'a holy war' justifies any weapon, except possibly murder. I do not.

Let me illustrate from actual warfare. I believe an international agreement exists by which the powers bind themselves not to use 'explosive bullets' (I think they call the things). Would 'A Christian Militant' excuse their use in 'A Holy War' by men? Does Christianity authorise 'forcible conversions'? Each form of protest must be judged on its own merits, both as regards its moral aspect and its effect on public opinion. Does violence tend to make opponents sympathetic? I object to modern militant methods, and to the hunger strike, because as a matter of fact, I do not believe their effect on the public has been such as to lead to the speedy enfranchisement of women. No stronger evidence of this could be quoted than that supplied last week by Miss Montgomery.[1] 'A Christian Militant' has discovered that I prefer that 'the lives of women should be wasted in prison rather than that inanimate property should be destroyed', etc., etc. This is simply begging the question. She assumes that I, like herself, believe that destruction of inanimate property actually prevents this waste. Taking it for granted that militancy would cease for a time if the vote was won, I do not think 'outrages' bring the day of victory any nearer.

More, I am afraid that public opinion is being so stirred up that the militants will bring upon themselves greater suffering. A sacrifice I regard as perfectly useless, since we will certainly get the vote without it, since the heaven-born current of Social Reform cannot be delayed.

May I point out that there is a mean between 'every quiet constitutional means of obtaining the vote' and modern militancy – i.e. spiritual militancy. As

---

[1] This possibly refers to a Miss Montgomery who was a Belfast militant.

I said in my last article, protests could have been directed against specific social wrongs, against which women ought to struggle. Take indecent assault on girls and children.

I do not see how the destruction of a pillar-box calls direct attention to this wrong! Whereas the destruction of the windows of the magistrates who impose a nominal penalty would probably do so.

I carelessly gave a wrong impression in one respect. I spoke of the endurance of the militants being the cause of the success which has attended the 'movement'. This was, quite naturally, read to mean 'the Suffrage movement'; but I should have made it clear that I was referring only to sympathy with the militants in their fight for political treatment. I really do not believe that had there been no Christabel Pankhurst there would be no suffrage. I think quiet constitutional methods produced feelings of rebellion in all thoughtful women, Christabel among them! She lit a flame, but there is no proof that the fire would never have started without her; while it is clear that it could never have spread without inflammable material to work on.

The previous failure was due to the strong Conservative element in the British Constitution. The House of Lords had to go before there was any chance of Women's Suffrage. We might have been voting to-day had militancy not defeated the Conciliation Bill! Militancy does not educate those against whom it is directed. 'A Christian Militant' doubtless would say that Mrs Leigh, or some other militant, had done more for women than anybody else in Dublin. Now I would be inclined to say that the most useful persons in the Dublin Suffrage are the Hon. Lit. Sec. and Literature Committee of the I.W.R.L.

One goes into 29 South Anne Street, one selects a well-chosen volume in that admirable library, with the pleasing conviction that it will make every reader better fit to vote; that fine thoughts will enfranchise the spirit; and that those alienated by militancy will be restored to the Suffrage. One criticism is necessary; it is this: I think few or no books relating to the special conditions of Irishwomen are to be found in it.

There are no books on the subject! Now I think our native militants would be waging a more effective war if they devoted themselves to investigating the actual conditions under which their countrywomen live. We need a democratic Women's Council to inquire into questions of Women's Unemployment, 'Half-Time' Employment of Children, Girls' Schools, Trade Education, etc. All of which would throw illumination on the reasons why women need votes. My position is this: I hold that a woman sitting quietly in an office, making out statistical returns, may be a more effectual fighter in the 'Holy War' than a much-advertised 'hunger-striker'. Again, personal bravery is no criterion of political acumen. I suppose it is my moral blindness that prevents my seeing quite how 'militancy' made non-militants see the need of demanding a Government Bill policy. I should have thought they, like the militants, learnt it from experience of M.P. human nature. Militancy does not convert; its defenders assume that certain actions must have certain results without, as a matter of fact, finding out whether their theories are in fact true. They don't study psychology.

The Suffragists' Catechism

17 MAY 1913

What do suffragists want?

Votes for Women.

What does that mean?

That women should be allowed to vote at the elections of members of Parliament, just the same as the men are.

Does that mean that you want every woman to have a vote?

No.

Why not?

Because every man has not got a vote. Men have to qualify for the vote in certain ways – they have to be owners or occupiers of certain property, or lodgers in rooms of a certain value. What we ask is that women who qualify in the same way should have the same right to vote as the men who qualify.

Then you approve of restricting the vote to people of property?

Not necessarily. Some suffragists do and some don't. What they are all agreed on is that whatever entitles a man to vote should entitle a woman to vote also – that she should not be forbidden to vote simply because she is a woman.

Then if all men had votes, you would be in favour of all women having votes?

Certainly. Equal voting rights for the sexes is our demand.

What good would it do a woman to have a vote?

The same good as it does a man.

What is that?

Ask any man voter if he would like to have his vote taken away from him, and what good it is to him. He may not be able to tell you in detail what good it has done him personally – many men who have votes are not intelligent enough to know how to use them – but he will make it clear to you that he would resent any attempt to take it away from him. He feels, whether he can explain it or not, that the possession of a vote makes him a citizen – gives him some power over the way laws are made and the way they are administered.

But women don't understand politics; would they know how to vote right?

Plenty of women understand politics, just as well as the men, and very often better. But even those women who don't understand politics now would learn all about them quickly enough if they got the vote.

How would having the vote help them to learn about politics?

Because the voter is a person of importance to the people who want to get into Parliament. As soon as women get votes, the political parties, on all sides will make it their business to educate the women in politics, so that they may hope to get their votes.

But isn't it better for women to know nothing about politics, and to mind their homes instead?

There are vast numbers of women, in every country, who have no 'homes' in the sense in which you use the word. There are large numbers of women at work in the world, in factories, shops and offices, earning their own bread as independent beings. For them, politics are vital, because they affect wages.

The Tales of the Tullamore 'Mice'

by Marguerite B. Palmer

26 JULY 1913

Sentenced to six weeks' imprisonment for non-payment of fines and compensation imposed for the breaking of the United Irish League fan-light on May 11th, we were taken to Mountjoy Prison, and immediately on arrival applied to the Lord Lieutenant and the Prison Board for 1st Division Treatment. It will be remembered that Mr Macinerney, the magistrate who tried us, was prepared to recommend 1st class treatment on condition that we paid the amount of compensation; this, of course, we refused to do, and were accordingly committed as ordinary prisoners. This initial mistake and want of foresight on the part of the magistrate has since been the cause of not only the ruined health of three women, but the ruined prestige of the Irish Prison Authorities.

Our petition traversed the usual ground of the political offender, pointing out the absence of moral guilt in our offence and requesting the same treatment as had been granted to all previous Irish Suffragist prisoners committed under the same circumstances, namely 1st Division with the right of association and conversation at exercise. On being transferred to Tullamore the morning after our committal, we were allowed on application certain minor ameliorations pending the reply to our petition, but our needlework, books, bags and all extra clothing were removed – a petty and unnecessary piece of tyranny. Even a harmless needle and thread for urgent repairs had to be literally fought for; the point was only won by our calling attention to Clause 6 of the Prison Rules which requires the prisoner to keep herself decent in her person, and declaring that to comply with this Rule we would either have to be given the wherewithal to sew on certain hooks and buttons, or retire to our beds for the rest of our 'time'. And these details had to be confided to two men officials!

When will the prison authorities develop a sense of the fitness of things and appoint women officials for women's work?

Such was the treatment which was being meted out to us at the time when an official statement appeared in the Press that 'Suffragist prisoners were receiving 1st class treatment from the date of their committal'. A full week of this 'neither fish, flesh, nor fowl' system went by before the reply to our petition arrived. The reply proved to be one quite worthy of officialdom – it gave with one hand what it took away with the other; it spelt weakness, indecision – bluff. It consisted of three paragraphs, the first nobly granting 1st class treatment, the second pointing out the absence of the 'legal status' of the 1st class Misdemeanant (that old, worn-out legal quibble), and the third arbitrarily placing us outside the jurisdiction of the Visiting Committee, a body which holds almost supreme power over the prisoner of the 1st Division, possessing the right to allow the prisoner to wear her own clothing, supply her own food, books, work, etc., to have newspapers, writing material, friends, etc., in fact, all that goes to make up what has hitherto in this country been known as 'political treatment'. The Prison Board were to deal direct with us in all matters, the rights of the 1st class Misdemeanant (as set forth on the Card of Rules and Regulations supplied to us) were to be applied for to the Prisons Board, and would be doled out by them according to their favour and their caprice. 'Killed with Kindness' would be the effect of this pet treatment if it were put into operation; we would receive all the physical comforts of 1st class treatment, but the stigma of the criminal, and the pampered criminal, would remain on our souls. As is now well known, we do not fight for political treatment to soften the rigour of prison life, but to force the prison laws to recognise the difference between the honourable prisoner and the criminal prisoner – a difference which has already been established by force of precedent in Ireland, but which still remains to be fixed by statute. Every other

country in Europe acknowledges that the political prisoner is on the same
footing as a prisoner of war and gives him like consideration.

After fully digesting this, to us, insulting proposal we again petitioned the
Lord Lieutenant, pointing out that as full 1st class treatment had been granted
to other Suffragist prisoners without restriction or reservation, we resented this
unfair discrimination and requested that full 1st Division treatment be granted
in the spirit as well as in the letter. To this no satisfactory reply was received,
necessitating the dread prospect of the Hunger Strike, resulting in our release
in five days under the 'Cat and Mouse' Act – that 'last ditch' of the 20th
century coercionist.

Before passing to the details of the Hunger Strike, a word must be said on
the functions of the Visiting Committee, for the enlightenment of those who
have never invaded the sorry precincts of a prison. The Tullamore Visiting
Committee is elected by the Grand Jury, and approved by the Lord
Lieutenant, for the purpose of acting as an outside and unbiased check on
behalf of the public upon the prison authorities and system – to ensure that
the prison Rules and Regulations as fixed by Statute are fairly administered;
in short to guard against the possible victimisation of any prisoner. As will
readily be seen, the political prisoner is above all others the most liable to
suffer from victimisation through political bias. Did the Visiting Committee
of Tullamore realise that in submitting to the usurpation of their Statutory
powers by the Prisons' Board, they were leaving us at the mercy of the
undoubted political animus of the authorities? If they did, they are guilty of a
gross betrayal of public trust.

On the declaration of the Hunger-Strike a series of petty and vindictive
methods of punishment began; little refinements of cruelty, hitherto untried
in Ireland, were inflicted upon us by the direction of the Prisons' Board,
evidently in the hope that each additional turn of the screw would weaken our
resolve, and in the end break our spirit – that old, old error which every
Oppressor, since the world began, has made. The policy of the authorities,
particularly during the period of the Hunger Strike, was unstatesmanlike in
the extreme. One would have thought the pain of slow starvation would have
satiated the thirst for punishment which the present day prison system
inevitably creates in the heart of the official. Not so – we were immediately
removed from the association cell which we had occupied, and thrust into cold
cells which had been unoccupied for many months, in complete solitary
confinement – that worst of all punishments known in prison. For the first
time in the experience of Irish Hunger-Strikers, all our belongings were
removed from our cells, neither reading, writing, nor work of any kind was
permitted; complete solitude, silence and idleness was the order. Suffering

from cold was a special feature of the punishment, and one which in the case of one of us, has had more lasting results than the Hunger-Strike itself. Despite the warm weather at the time, the cells were so cold that, before the Hunger-Strike, a fire had been supplied by the doctor's orders; this was withdrawn as a punishment on the declaration of the Strike, at a time when it was most required. The suffering from the cold, resulting from the sudden change in temperature, coupled with the lowered vitality and the inability to take any measure of vigorous exercise, owing to the increasing weakness, equalled any of the choice methods of torture of the Middle Ages.

Further, even that merciful provision of Nature, sleep, was rendered impossible by our own pillows being taken away, and that instrument of torture, the prison pillow, substituted. It is filled with horse hair, so tightly stuffed that even the most vigorous treatment will produce no impression upon it – the effect upon its unfortunate victim is to leave every bone in the head, neck and back bruised and aching. A further hardship was the withdrawal of the privilege of association and conversation at exercise, which necessitated our refusing out-door exercise altogether, on principle.

To the Hunger-Striker, one day is the same as another, and each hour as it comes is exactly the same as the last. The day is spent sitting upright on one's chair, looking at nothing, doing nothing, but thinking, thinking always. The blood stagnates at the knees, one creeps over to the bed to seek a change of position and get relief, but none comes. At last, too weak to sit upright, one is forced to lie down – still no relief; every pulse in the body throbs, throbs incessantly, the heart thumps heavily through the body to the back, no sleep will come, and the hours creep slowly, slowly on.

It is this sickening monotony, the awful silence, the ever present evidence of punishment, the barred windows, and above all, the relentless enemy, waiting, watching, to take any possible advantage as one's bodily strength gives out inch by inch – these are the things which play such mental havoc with the Hunger-Striker.

This, then, is the real meaning of the Hunger-Strike, and to their everlasting honour and glory be it said, that of all the hundreds and hundreds of women who have engaged in it, weak and strong, old and young, rich and poor, there has never yet been found one to throw up the fight, even in the face of the horror of forcible feeding. Evidence enough this, surely, that a strong principle exists behind the agitation – a principle that no prison cell persecution can stifle, not even in its latest form, the brutal and futile 'Cat and Mouse' Act. This will be fought as dauntlessly and successfully as was forcible feeding, at the cost, no doubt, of many women's lives, but crushed it shall be, and perhaps by then the authorities will have learned the folly of playing with the deeply rooted convictions of earnest reformers, and recognise the wisdom of falling in line with the spirit of the age, by granting the reform we fight for – political treatment for political prisoners.

Touring Kerry
by S.R. Day
20 SEPTEMBER 1913

The campaign opened in Cahirciveen on Tuesday night, when the Carnegie Hall was filled with an audience which listened intently to the speeches. No need to drive home the principles of liberty and emancipation in the town which gave birth to Daniel O'Connell! The speakers were on sure ground, and as point after point was raised and emphasised, it was encouraging to see men and women, who had lounged carelessly back in their seats at first, lean forward now eager to catch every word of this newest phase on the emancipation of Irish people.

From Cahirciveen we went to Waterville where, owing to difficulties connected with the halls, we had to speak in the open air to a crowd composed of fishermen, shopkeepers, farmers and farm labourers, telegraphists from the cable station, and English visitors. It was not an easy matter to pitch a speech in a key to ring harmoniously over such a mixed assemblage, but the meeting was held principally for the inhabitants, so we spoke directly to them. Here again, we were received with the utmost courtesy and interest, and the constant 'that's true' and 'you're right' showed how the points went home.

Valencia was, in speaker's parlance, a 'soft job'. The island has been splendidly worked by the Hon. Mrs Spring Rice, who enrolled numbers of 'Friends of Suffrage' there last year, and is still doing invaluable work, sustaining old interest and enthusing new. As an example of what can be done by individual effort, Valencia, in our experience, stands supreme. Here the proceedings were enlivened by the presence of a real live 'Anti' (English of course), whom the Lord delivered into our hands, with the humility characteristic of his tribe. He took refuge behind the petticoats of a woman, Miss Violet Markham, to whose opinion he attached so much importance, we shrewdly suspect he would like to see her in the Cabinet! (If only she might keep all the other women out.) His total, abysmal ignorance of Ireland and Irish conditions, made him an easy prey, especially when addressing the speakers he said: 'You say you need social reform but you send John Redmond to Parliament.' 'But we don't,' we protested. So he tried again, but the 'You elect

John Redmond,' was soon making the room laugh. For the 'Anti' was the only person present who failed to realise the delicious irony of crediting voteless women with the election of John Redmond, or any other politician.

Driven to the last ditch (behind a woman!) 'Well Miss Markham thinks otherwise,' he declared. 'Wouldn't you find life very monotonous if all women were cut to one pattern?' the platform retorted, and then he told us we were flying too high, going too fast. We should cut our wings and move more slowly. 'There is a woman in the room tonight who signed a suffrage petition in '66', was the quick response. When he spoke of the law 'favouring' woman, he was sharply reminded of the Queenie Gerald case;[2] when he praised the laws against the White Slave Traffic, of Australia, where enfranchised women have abolished the Traffic. Several converts were made – and we thank our heckler for his assistance in making them!

In Killorglin there was the largest crowd. A thick mass of men and women standing at the back, and the chairs filled, with the exception of the front row. They inclined to be facetious at first, and 'out for a lark' many of them. A few trenchant remarks on the labour question, the importance of the vote for working women, and its benefits through them to working men, soon caught their attention, and in spite of an element in the audience which might easily have spoiled it, the meeting was one of the best we held. One or two attempted interruptions were put down with a firm hand by those who had come to listen. The inevitable 'local celebrity' sat prominently in the front row, shouting his approbation, but a quiet 'please don't interrupt' from the platform was taken in good part, and he too, composed himself to listen. One determined reactionary, also in the front row, informed us several times that we should be at home. We appreciated the compliment, but finally driven to suggest that he had Turkish ancestry, he became so flustered that he informed us that Germany was the finest country, and the Germans the finest nation in the world. Being ourselves convinced that the Irish are, we said so, and after that the Turk took refuge in discreet silence.[3] Good collections were taken at all these meetings, over 130 pamphlets sold, and between 70 and 80 'Friends of Suffrage' cards signed. These total would, we are convinced, be much higher, but we were short-handed in Waterville, Miss Cummins combining the duties of chairman, literature seller and collector. A number of *Irish Citizens* were also sold.

Travelling over to Tralee on Saturday, we heard three countrywomen talking. They discussed their own affairs, and presently the inevitable happened. 'Weren't the young ladies saying in Killorglin last night that the

---

2 This was a notorious case involving procuring teenage girls into prostitution.
3 The reference to 'Turkish ancestry' is probably an attempt to suggest traditional, patriarchal attitudes towards women.

poor man's child hasn't such a good chance in the world as the rich man's child, when it goes hungry to school.'

'Sure enough, and the want of a hunk of bread making all the difference.' And so on, till we told them who we were, and after that a suffrage meeting of informal kind was held for the benefit of these three women, four others, and one man, who serenely told us 'he would not give women too much liberty!' 'Ara don't mind him', whispered one of our friends. 'Sure his wife is that hot, she do what she likes, and faith, he daren't say a word to her!' 'Aren't two heads better than one?' asked another, summing up the suffrage question in a nutshell.

It was exhilarating to talk to such women; shrewd, capable, honest, they knew they wanted the vote, and knew why. Yet they had not been at the meeting. They could not leave their homes and their children. One of them disposed of government by sex succinctly. 'The men?' she said with fine scorn. 'What do they know of women or of children? They fill their bellies and they walks out!'

They took our pamphlets and leaflets eagerly, they shook us warmly by the hand, and they wished us 'Good Luck' and we clambered into a train for Ventry, to enjoy a well-earned holiday, convinced that three stalwart missionaries will further the cause of Woman Suffrage in Killorglin!

Message from Mrs Sheehy Skeffington

13 DECEMBER 1913

Mrs Sheehy Skeffington is making favourable progress towards recovery after her five days' Hunger Strike. She is under the care of Dr Kathleen Lynn, whose report (read at the I.W.F.L. meeting on Tuesday) states that Mrs Skeffington's heart shows signs of improvement, and that the sleeplessness which at first caused anxiety is disappearing. Mrs Sheehy Skeffington, who is ordered absolute quiet for some time, has sent the following message to her friends through the *Irish Citizen*:

> I desire through the medium of the *Irish Citizen* to thank most heartily all my friends in the Franchise League who worked so strenuously during my imprisonment, and who organised the fine series of protest meetings outside Mountjoy Prison on my behalf. Their splendid enthusiasm and matchless energy were the battering ram that forced open the jail gates! It is gratifying to realise that Sergeant Thomas, by

his assault on me, and the police who illegally attempted to break up the protest meetings, have unwittingly rendered us a great service, and given a fine impetus to our movement by rousing public indignation against police methods and the ways of police magistrates. I congratulate the I.W.F.L. on its victory over the police, those arch-disturbers of the peace, who were afraid to face even a Police court judgment of their disgraceful conduct. During this period of enforced inactivity I am happy to know that our work goes forward unimpeded, and that the Franchise League keeps its flag flying, no matter how many of us fall by the way. Later I hope to be able to acknowledge more adequately, and in person, the many messages of sympathy and the many acts of kindness of my friends during my illness – just now I must ask them to take the will for the deed!

I wish also to express my thanks to the sister suffrage societies, the I.W.S.S. and the I.R.L., and to the I.L.P.I., for their resolutions and help on my behalf, and to all those who have rallied to us at this juncture with generous financial support.

Votes for Women in the West

by Hanna Sheehy Skeffington

14 MARCH 1914

Longford, Leitrim and Roscommon lay long a dark disfiguring blot on our suffrage map, for there no suffrage speaker had ever penetrated, while, with the exception of Clare, every other county in Ireland has now been opened up by some pioneer. Accordingly, Mrs Connery planned to wipe out the stain by holding three meetings, one in the chief town of each county, namely in Longford, Carrick-on-Shannon and Boyle. She organised the tour in advance, visiting the towns one after one, interviewing the local magnates and engaging halls. In Longford alone did there seem difficulties, the Bishop being hostile, refusing 'to argue with a woman', and using his influence against the granting of the Catholic Hall. As we had heckled the local M.P.s a few weeks previously, and as one of them, a pronounced 'anti', owns the chief newspaper in the town, we looked for some trouble in Longford. But, as usual, a suffragette's life is full of surprises and in Longford alone did we find everything smooth in our path – a crowded hall, an enthusiastic meeting. Many converts who had come to jeer remained to join. One interrupter, who essayed dubious jests, was sternly quelled, and we were apologetically informed that he was 'no Longford man', an excuse which seems all sufficient to the native.

Next day we passed on to our next halting-place, Carrick, not many miles away – but what a difference! It is a small town of 1,100 inhabitants, containing thirty-two public-houses. It lies in marshy swamps, then half engulfed owing to persistent rains, miles of sodden bog-land stretching to the horizon. Here we experienced the nature and horrors of a sympathetic lockout, a steady boycott. The explanation of the mystery we learned later, bit by bit. The Canon had denounced us at first Mass on the Sunday previous, with other Lenten abominations, including a Patrick's Night dance that the young people were arranging. He advised the women of the town to remain at home, look after their families, and to have nothing to do with Votes; and, to make assurance doubly sure, the local publicans, trustees of the promised hall, were advised by their spiritual director 'to withdraw their permission and break their agreement', the sacredness of contracts apparently not being recognised in Carrick. Everywhere we met with stony silence, any occasional gleam of hope or approval being instantly suppressed with a kind of tremulous fear.

The publicans particularly (whose activity is not impaired by the Lenten season) seemed most afraid of contamination. Some of the younger spirits, railing at the 'rages of old men' seemed interested, but paralysed with a nameless fear: doubtless any help given or sympathy shown would be visited on the offenders hereafter.

Failing to get the Town Hall, which had been duly billed and advertised, we tried to secure one of those under Protestant management, only to find the non-Catholic section equally fear-ridden and evasive. The fiat having gone forth that suffrage was taboo, vestrymen, churchwardens, rectors, freemasons vied in putting us off with futile equivocation and shallow subterfuges, each shifting the responsibility on to the shoulders of someone else. At last, abandoning all hope of securing even a barn, we managed to enlist a journeyman carpenter to hammer a few planks on a couple of soapboxes, so that we might address Carrick from the Market Square. By this time night had descended upon wet and badly lighted streets: still an open air meeting had possibilities. But true to the tacit boycott, no Carrick shopkeeper would sell a board, or even a nail, for a free platform; no crier would cry the meeting through the town. When the carpenter, at half-past eight, after a weary search for materials, came to tell us, he was followed by a howling, raging mob, led by a drunken virago. In spite of Lent, in spite of the proximity of the church, they paraded the space before the hotel, creating a pandemonium for over two hours with motor-bombs, savage yells and obscene jeers, mock 'suffrage' orations and wild charges across the street. After two hours' vigil they were dispersed at the sight of two policemen. So much for Carrick. A friend told us later that the only way to hold a suffrage meeting there would be to insinuate it into the middle of a picture show, by collusion with the management and without previous announcement. As a matter of 'free speech' it is not to be thought of.

In Boyle a similar fate threatened. Here the local priests were sympathetic. We had secured St. Patrick's Hall without difficulty, till a local faction (Boyle is a town of factions and faction-fights) brought pressure to bear to prevent free-speech, threatened to wreck the hall, to cut off the lights, and make the speakers forever silent. A local paper, which had accepted an advertisement, calmly announced, on its own, that the meeting would not take place. The distributor of handbills was suborned to suppress the bulk of them, shopkeepers who had placed them in their windows were bullied into withdrawing them. The local politicians (partly Hibernians, of which there are two opposing camps) had determined that by fair means or foul we should not be heard. But for the kindness of the Rev. J. Watson, in giving us Clew's Memorial Hall, and but for a chance encounter of a brave and public-spirited knight-errant, no meeting would have been possible. As it was, we had to collect our audience by house to house canvass in the midst of a pig fair; no crier would give his services, none would hire or lend a chair to eke out the school-benches. Many feared the wrath of politicians, and remained away. Yet we had a goodly meeting in the little schoolhouse, a small charge keeping out the hooligans. We won many converts, and uttered some home truths to the foul-mouthed 'horse-blocker' from Belfast who attempted heckling, only to cover his discomfiture with obscenities and to be repudiated by the decent-minded people of Boyle for his pains. Towards the close of the meeting we had red pepper scattered by some boys, and a broken pane from outside, and when the meeting was over the rival factions made use of the occasion for a fight, during which they rolled over the police in the mud of Boyle's chief thoroughfare, and got their heads broken in consequence. Plate glass was shattered as a further diversion: five baton charges took place, stones rained. As one of the combatants said next day, 'Shure, we hadn't such a grand time since the Parnell split!'

Who Said Hysteria?

On our side we had compensations in the shape of a few trusty stalwarts (among the progressive spirits who recognise the bane of faction-mongering), several new recruits, a good collection, brisk sale of literature, unbroken heads, in spite of flints and in spite of police 'protection' (sixty police had been hastily drafted into the town to 'keep order', yet no arrests were made), and, lastly, the luxury of column-long reports, not only in the local, but in Dublin and English papers. Reporters may overlook with impunity enthusiastic meetings, as in Longford, but five baton charges, yards of shattered glass – what journalist could resist these appeals to 'copy'?

Next day the great Horse Fair took place, and we wandered freely among the wild colts from Connemara, and their haggling sellers and buyers, too bent on bargaining to give a thought to the doings of yesternight. In the intervals of sales one could catch snatches of suffrage debate going on all around. Decidedly ground has been broken in Boyle – and glass incidentally.

Votes for All Women
by Marion E. Duggan, LLB ('M.E.')
8 AUGUST 1914

Mr F. Sheehy Skeffington's recent article on 'The Function of Militancy' was so fair and so true that one feels a little reluctant to call attention to a serious inaccuracy. He says that Parnell never repudiated 'his extreme wing'. This does not at first sight convey the fact that Parnell did repudiate an extreme party who were not 'his'! I allude to the Phoenix Park murderers, to whose 'will' we owe modern Unionism. I quite decline to believe there is no moral difference between a good republican and the anarchist who uses bombs to abolish royalty! Mr Skeffington believes that without militancy suffrage would sink back to the despair of 1884; if women will not work for Votes unless inspired by militancy, how can we be sure they will, when enfranchised, work for any other reform? Shall we not always have militant spirits, whose impatience of delay will make them prefer direct action to persuasive methods? It is very interesting to note how militant apologists are more and more attributing militancy to provocation and strong feeling, rather to any intellectual conviction of the superior effectiveness of their actions. This is not surprising when the great majority of the intellectual educated women are opposed to militancy, while the leaders of the various working-women's organisations are equally non-militant (and, of course, equally intellectual). I agree with Mr Skeffington that an extreme wing is a necessity in any movement. It is the extremists who make immediate compromise possible. I do not agree that the dividing line is best drawn between the women who feel (or will) and the women who think.

We have so far shelved the question of adult suffrage.

I think the real point at issue is between those who want a 'high franchise', votes for all who pay a large amount of taxes, and those who desire one person one vote. The time is at hand when there must be war between those who want votes to protect the rich, and those who want votes to help the poor. Government rests upon the consent of the governed, and the advocates of votes for gentry are faced with the difficulty of making their 'social inferiors' obey laws as to which they have not been consulted. Shoot down resisters? The syndicalist asks, who is going to provide food, etc., for the soldiers? Money is useless if the workers refuse to work. No government can compel obedience; they can merely, if superior in strength, kill the disobedient.

Women cannot fight? Men cannot force women to bear children, since physical force will kill the unborn. Hitherto our suffrage societies have fallen into two divisions, militant and constitutional. Both parties demand 'votes for women on the same terms as given to men': Socialists and Conservatives are found in the same ranks – though I have been assured, on competent authority, that all the militant leaders are in sympathy with labour, and it is a matter of common knowledge that the largest suffrage society in England is definitely in alliance with the Parliamentary Labour Party. What are we Irishwomen going to do in the interval which must elapse before we can get the vote from our own Parliament? At present we are divided into those who believe that our fellow countrymen will give it to us for the asking, and those who fear we may have to fight for it. Non-militants deprecate recourse to violence on principle, and to any impatient immediate action from expediency. Militants ask what do they gain by waiting three years if the non-militants still refuse to join them in any line of action which may be necessary.

It is obvious, therefore, that we want some scheme that will satisfy the intellects, consciences, and 'divine impatience' of both parties. Mr Connolly declares himself in sympathy with the militants, but has outlined a Syndicalist scheme for securing the votes from an Irish anti-suffrage Government. In other words, he is not intellectually convinced that the present English policy of outrages is the most effective method imaginable. The labour leader wants us to organise working women, and so make sure of the vote.

To me the great merit of his suggestion lies in the fact that even if the vote is pressed upon us by our Irish M.P.s, workingwomen will still need to be organised. Votes and Trade Unions go hand-in-hand. Is it to be said that suffragettes had to take to violence because they knew it would be absolutely impossible to organise them? Those who have heard Miss Larkin tell the tale of the three hundred little girls who walked out of Jacob's when one of their number was ordered to remove her badge will think better of Irishwomen. If we cannot organise women before we get the vote, how can we organise them afterwards?

Of course, it is very easy to say (I have said it myself), that all women are not fit to vote, and that one would prefer it to come by degrees! Let us be honest with ourselves. Will we be content with votes for some women, or do we mean to go on and work for votes for all women and men? Do we honestly believe that wealthy women or educated women, can be trusted to make laws for poor workingwomen? It is said that during the time the W.S.P.U. was working in semi-alliance with Mr Lansbury's party, large subscriptions ceased to come in. The 'peeresses and American millionairesses' who support the Pankhursts are alleged to prevent their leaders openly declaring their labour sympathies. Really, however, we do not need hearsay evidence from England to convince us that militants are not necessarily democrats. How many Irish W.S.P.U. members took part in the recent fight for a Police Enquiry? I know at least one excellent militant who advocated ending the recent troubles in Dublin by hanging Mr Larkin. I need not waste time by proving that many non-militants are quite hopelessly opposed to the claims of organised labour.

We stand at the parting of the ways. Do we want to see workingwomen free and independent, or humbly receiving the legislative bounty of their better-off sisters? Women can do invaluable work for the various men's parties. Let us see to it that the labour women are not slaves, but free women, giving their services in consideration for support in getting the vote and other reforms. I should like to see the forward suffrage policy of to-morrow decided by Labour Suffragists, militant and non-militant, meeting together and taking the opinion of all as to what their common course should be. If honest and fair-minded women come together and deliberate in a straight, honest fashion, taking into account all the circumstances of the case, I think we need not fear the result. What we have to fear now is seeing our plans spoiled by rude, unsympathetic 'ladies', who merely desire the aggrandisement of all persons of their own class. 'Suffrage first' has no meaning if we allow any suffragists to interpret 'non-party' as 'never Labour'.

The New Force in Irish Politics

by M.K. Connery

AUGUST 1918

The political wiseacres are busy prophesying a General Election before Xmas. It will mean an anxious time for the party politicians of every school, for it will introduce a new and hitherto unknown force into the political arena – namely, the woman voter. What a perplexing problem for the seasoned manipulator of votes, for how can one be certain that the old wiles, the old cajolery, the well-worn platitudes of yesteryear, will beguile the woman voter? To the militant suffragette, with a sense of humour, the coming electoral battle should provide many amusing situations, and much food for philosophic reflection. It will be pleasing to observe the sudden transformation, in the press and on the platform, of erstwhile virtual enemies into suave and flattering friends, and we ourselves shall 'suffer a sea change' almost as bewildering.

The 'wild women' and the 'sexless viragoes' of the militant era shall blossom into 'ladies' endowed with the wisdom of Solomon and a monopoly of all the civic virtues. The anxious concern for the fate of the 'home', the condition of the family darning and the daily ablutions of the baby – problems which used to keep some of our public men awake of nights not so long ago, will vanish like a dream in the arduous work of capturing the woman's vote. It will then be the woman's turn to play the role of critic. To what extent the women outside the suffrage movement have developed the critical faculty there is no certain means of judging until the testing time comes.

This much, however, is certain, that amongst the men voters of the older generation the critical faculty had become practically atrophied through lack of use, producing an inevitable crop of shifty, compromising, time-serving, place-hunting, backboneless humbugs in the public life of the country. It is the fashion to rail against these moral jellyfish nowadays, and pour derision on them, but it is only the bare truth to point out that these men were a very faithful reflex of the mentality and conception of public probity of the electors who placed them in power and authority. It therefore behoves women to take warning from the mistakes of others, and try to develop the faculty of clear and critical thinking in the time before us. When the stage thunder of the General Election is let off and all the vendors are shouting their wares at the top of their lungs, clear thinking and cool judgment will be taxed to the utmost. In times of emotional crisis the unwary are betrayed into mistaking noise for work and mere talking for constructive thinking. For years the Irish electorate has been fed on flapdoodle and flagwagging. Will the women show their judgment by demanding a more sustaining mental diet? Let it be remembered that flapdoodle is a malady which any and every party is liable to develop if the faculty of critical judgment is lacking amongst its supporters. 'Where the populace rise at once against the never-ending audacity of elected persons', says Walt Whitman, 'there the great City stands'.

Some suffragists are greatly concerned lest a few dozen or a few hundred women may have failed to get on the Register. There doesn't seem much ground for this apprehension in view of the fierce struggle for votes we have been witnessing at Irish by-elections for the past year, and which has done more to wake up the potential voter on the importance of getting registered than would hundreds of verbal appeals and tons of instructive literature.

Anyway, the number of voters is the politician's look-out. It is also unfortunately, his out-look, for he is all for quantity; but it is a superficial view. For suffragists and progressives of all sorts it is the quality of the woman's vote that matters. Quality alone can make any essential difference in the tone and in the aims of our public life.

If the new woman voter in Ireland has the courage and independence to set a new standard I believe the men of the new generation would try hard to live up to it. There are some questions of burning interest to women which men, even the best of them, will obstinately refuse to face or to think out, unless and until women compel them to face them. Are women satisfied that the double moral standard should continue to regulate the relations of men and women in this country, with its accompanying spectacle of a section of every large town and city given over to the unrestrained practice of bestiality? Are they content with a legal code which pursues the erring woman with merciless vengeance while it winks at and encourages the practice of male vice? Are they content that a Christian community shall continue to treat the unmarried mother as if she were a mad dog while it relieves the father of her child from all direct moral responsibility to the child or to the community? Is the married mother satisfied that the law should deny her all legal right to her own children? Are decent Irishwomen proud of the fact that outside of Ulster the manufacture and sale of intoxicating drink is Ireland's best known and most flourishing industry?

These are the kind of nuts which our women might well offer would-be politicians to crack. This is the kind of test to apply to fine sentiments, if they are genuine they will stand it.

Will Irishwomen set a new standard for their country? Will they pierce through the froth of politics to the eternal verities beneath? Irishwomen have a long-inherited passion for national liberty. They will ring through on that issue. May they be equally true and uncompromising on the deep human issues here indicated.

While there are hopeful signs of awakening, it cannot be denied that many women still exhibit a spirit of slavish deference to existing masculine standards. Lacking self-confidence and intellectual courage they prefer, like sheep, to follow a beaten track. How clearly Connolly visualised this weakness in their moral fibre is shown in 'The Reconquest of Ireland', when he says:

In Ireland the soul of womanhood has been trained for centuries to surrender its rights, and as a consequence, the race has lost its chief capacity to withstand assaults from without and demoralisation from within.

In Tennyson's 'Princess' there is a picture of woman's abject condition in the Victorian era which first stung me into a fury of revolt against woman's degradation. This is how the poem describes them:

> Live chattels, mincers of each other's fame,
> Full of weak poison, turnspits for the clown,
> The drunkard's football, laughing-stocks of time,
> Whose brains are in their hands and in their heels,
> But fit to flaunt, to dress, to dance, to thrum,
> To tramp, to scream, to burnish, and to scour;
> Forever slaves at home, and fools abroad

Out of this Pit Feminism has sought, not unsuccessfully, to lift our sex. There are still many milestones on the road to freedom.

Editorial: Our Policy and Our Critics

OCTOBER 1919

From time to time it seems to be necessary to restate one's position and reformulate one's policy, for public memory is short and liable to confusion. The *Irish Citizen* was founded in May 1912 to further the cause of Woman Suffrage and of Feminism in Ireland; as its name implies, its ideal was to urge 'For men and women equally the Rights of Citizenship, from men and women equally the Duties of Citizenship.' In addition it has stood for the rights of Labour, especially of the women workers (often overlooked) and for the rights of small peoples, beginning not with the far away Balkans but at home in Ireland. During the war, in the almost universal stampede of British (and even some Irish) suffragists and feminists who prostituted their movement to militarist uses, the *Irish Citizen* under the guidance of Francis Sheehy Skeffington stood firm for Peace, believing that the cause of Woman and the cause of Peace were inextricably bound together. When partial franchise to women of thirty was granted during the war some British suffragist papers ceased activities and left the struggle for complete emancipation, 'for the suffrage on the same terms as it is or may be granted to men', to valiant papers like *The Vote* and to the more conservative *Common Cause*. Other papers like the *Woman's Dreadnought*, edited by Sylvia Pankhurst, became Socialist, changing the title to the *Workers' Dreadnought*. The *Irish Citizen*, like *The Vote* still continued its feminist and suffragist propaganda, and hopes to do so until all women have the vote equally with men and until women have secured the other rights that enfranchisement involves, of which the vote is but a small part and but a symbol. We want equal pay for equal work, equal marriage laws, the abolition of legal disabilities, the right of women to enter the hitherto barred learned professions, women jurors and justices, in short, the complete abolition of various taboos and barriers – social, economic and political – that still impede women's progress and consequently that of the race.

There is much need in Ireland, as well as in most other countries (for women can hardly be said to be fully emancipated in any country to-day), for a distinct feminist organ devoted primarily to the advancement of women and holding a watching brief for their interests.

It is obvious that such a paper must not belong to any party; one set of critics would deflect us entirely to Republicanism or to Labour, while another would have us 'non-political' in the Unionist sense of the word, which means non-Irish. With both sections of these friendly critics we differ. We stand for the rights of all Irish women as women, independent of party or sect. But, at the same time, we recognise the right of the majority of the Irish people to mould its own destinies and accordingly, like Irish Labour, we stand for self-determination of Ireland – accordingly, we are anathema to some Belfast women 'loyalists' to whom the mere word 'Irish' in our title is an offence. The cause of Woman in Ireland has suffered too much from party rancour: it is time that women tested these party shibboleths for themselves. No party, unhappily, is yet quite free from sin where women are concerned. It is to hold the mirror up to the failings and shortcomings of each in turn that the *Irish Citizen* exists, and we reckon it a sign of grace that we are blamed in turn by each party for not becoming mere camp-followers of this or the other side. While we shall always be glad to publish divergent views, our editorial policy must remain feminist and non-party on the lines that we have stated. We hope that we have made this clear. We shall be glad of our readers' views on the question. It is good for women from time to time to do a little mental stock-taking and spring cleaning, to tot up gains, estimate improvement or deterioration, to clear out rubbish and to sweep away the cobwebs. If we have assisted the process, even at the risk of raising a dust, we shall be satisfied.

CHAPTER 2

Women, morality and the law

S uffrage movements in the USA and Britain have long been associated with
what have been called 'social purity' movements (Kent, 2014; Hall, 2004;
Bolt, 2014). Many suffragists clearly believed that women would bring new,
better qualities into public life that would raise moral standards and tackle
various 'social evils'. Such arguments usually highlighted the caring, mothering
role of women. In Ireland, from its very early history, suffragism had strong
links with campaigns for social purity. Anna Haslam, founder of one of the
first suffrage groups, worked closely with Josephine Butler and her campaigns
to tackle double moral standards and the sexual exploitation of women (Cullen
& Luddy, 1995).

In campaigning to improve social morality, suffragists argued that
women were well suited to tackling many of the 'evils' prevalent throughout
society. One way in which early activists sought to increase women's public
role was by becoming poor law guardians. In their campaign at the end of
the nineteenth century for women poor law guardians, activists emphasised
the particular qualities that women would bring to managing workhouses.
Haslam argued that women would bring a 'practical humanity' which would
improve the diet and clothing of inmates in Irish workhouses (Quinlan,
2007). Carmel Quinlan notes that: 'Twenty-first century feminists might
well deplore Haslam's perception of women poor law guardians' strengths
as essentially the application of their domestic skills to the workhouse'
(2007: 36). However, as Quinlan notes, Haslam used these traits to
overcome male opposition and to argue that women were uniquely qualified
for this public office.

It may be tempting to criticise Irish suffragists for using arguments
about 'womanly' qualities of caring and motherhood or women's moral
superiority over men. Through the pages of the *Irish Citizen* we come to
learn more about the suffragists' notions of morality and purity. However,
rather than seeing them in terms of a narrow, reformist, moral conservatism,
it is important to locate suffragists' attitudes within a social and historical
context. In the late nineteenth and early twentieth centuries, suffragists had
to engage with the prevailing negative stereotypes of women. Women were
commonly dismissed as weak, cunning, deceitful and lacking moral

integrity. In the face of these criticisms the suffragists had to construct a counter-narrative to justify a public role for women as full citizens.

In the pages of the *Irish Citizen* suffragists made various arguments for women's place in public life. As will be apparent in the extracts later in this chapter, some suffragists argued that women were actually morally superior to men. Others made their argument based not on moral superiority, but on grounds of equality between the sexes.

Violence against women and children

Irish suffragists addressed a huge range of issues, including prostitution, temperance, divorce, etc. However, here there will be a focus on two issues that were recurrent themes throughout the history of the *Irish Citizen* – child abuse and violence against women. The extracts included in this chapter are fairly representative of the wide range of articles appearing in the *Irish Citizen* over its eight-year history.

These include editorials as well as contributions from individual suffragists and the regular reports from the Court Watch Committee set up by the IWRL to monitor court cases involving women and girls. Child abuse and violence against women continue to be relevant in Irish society and, indeed, many societies worldwide (see Steiner-Scott, 1997; and Maguire & Ó Cinnéide, 2005). In addition, these two topics are important because they illustrate quite well the suffragists' critique of the legal system. As discussed below, these discussions also call into question the relationship between the public and private spheres.

As Sandra Holton (1992) has argued, the suffrage movement generally was more aware of the dichotomy between the public and private than has previously been recognised. As part of the growing appreciation of the suffrage movement in Britain, Holton acknowledges the sophistication of suffragists' analysis of the complex inter-relationships between the public sphere and the private sphere. I will argue that the Irish movement was equally prepared to tackle such complex concepts. In particular, the article on wife-beating, cited below, illustrates the complex and blurry line between the sanctity of domestic privacy and the necessity for public protection against domestic abuses.

As seen in the previous chapter, in October 1919, Hanna Sheehy Skeffington, as editor, outlined the policy of the *Irish Citizen* throughout its history. Among the main issues that the paper had always supported were equal marriage laws, the abolition of all legal disabilities affecting women, the right of women to enter all hitherto barred learned professions, and the right of women to be jurors and justices. The *Irish Citizen* stood 'in short [for] the complete abolition of various taboos and barriers – social, economic and political – that still impede women's progress and consequently that of the race'. Indeed, equal marriage laws had always been a concern of the editorial board of the paper. For example, on 16 November 1912, the editorial argued that a prerequisite for true citizenship was equal divorce laws. However, a heated debate on divorce in 1919 suggested that at least some suffragists did not support *Irish Citizen* editorial policy on this contentious issue.

It is interesting to look at the attitude of the *Irish Citizen*, and those who contributed to it, towards the law and their suggestions for its improvement. As suffragists, and especially militants, these women often experienced the wrath of the legal system, and many of the regular writers in the paper had been imprisoned, including Hanna and her husband Francis Sheehy Skeffington, Margaret Cousins, and Meg Connery. Suffragists seem to have been in agreement in explaining why the legal institutions took such a harsh view of women who broke the law. The legal system was made up entirely of men: male judges, male barristers and male jurors.

On 19 July 1913 a case was reported concerning a 16-year-old woman who was sexually assaulted by her employer and subsequently became pregnant. In court the jury was unable to reach a verdict. The writer of this article surmises that one reason why the all-male jury was not able to convict the man was due to the way in which the all-male council 'played upon their masculine prejudices, pointing out to them that any one of them might one day find himself in a similar position to the man in the dock'. A woman on the jury might, says the writer, have reflected that any other girl might one day find herself in a similar position to the unfortunate 'ruined' girl in the case.

The paper's editorials, as well as individual suffragists who wrote on the subject of the law, espoused the view that women could expect no justice from the legal system so long as it remained a male preserve. 'Is it not time we had women on the bench and on the jury when such crimes as murderous and indecent assault receive nominal or no punishment?' (Feb. 1919). This refers to the case of a soldier who got six months in prison for beating his wife almost to death with a poker. She was still in hospital, many months later, when the case went to court (see also Steiner-Scott, 1997).

The IWRL's Court Watch Committee sent reports of cases to the *Irish Citizen* on a regular basis, often under the heading 'Watching the Courts', and frequently were penned by Marion Duggan, LLB. Although her name may not be familiar today, she was one of the most prolific contributors to the *Irish Citizen*. As noted in the previous chapter, she opposed militancy and often engaged in heated debates with militant suffragists. Duggan was a socialist, a member of the Irish Women Workers' Union and the IWRL. Her involvement in the labour movement and her strong commitment to social justice underpinned many of her articles in the *Irish Citizen*. Although she wrote on issues as diverse as Irish theatre and the rights of women workers, it was in the 'Watching the Courts' column that she most regularly contributed to the paper, initially using the pen name 'M.E.' and then reverting to her own name.

The articles on child sexual abuse (including incest) are still upsetting to the modern reader. One can only imagine what readers in early twentieth-century Ireland would have made of them. These articles reveal a side of Irish society that has been carefully hidden and denied until very recently. These accounts in the *Irish Citizen* are so important not only because they illustrate the fact that child abuse, especially sexual abuse, has a long history in Ireland but also how attempts were made to conceal its prevalence (Ryan, 2007). The suffragists reveal the processes through which such abuses were silenced and rendered invisible. For example, suffragists argued that the press played a key role in perpetuating the myth that sexual viciousness did not exist in Ireland. The *Irish Citizen* gives many examples of cases that were either not reported at all in the Irish press or, if reported, were made light of by journalists. Beyond simply reporting these crimes, the *Irish Citizen* goes further and offers a feminist analysis of the underlying causes of this form of abuse against women and children. According to suffragists, the courts, by refusing to take such matters seriously and handing down light sentences, also contributed to this silencing process. The suffragists, in particular the IWRL, demanded access to court hearings with the expressed intention of publicising what went on. However, they frequently complained of not receiving the cooperation of the courts (11 July 1914).

Suffragists made it their business to publicise the 'private' abuses against women and children that were occurring within domestic settings. In so doing they sought to broaden the public role of women and to politicise what had hitherto been labelled 'private', family matters. In this way, as I have argued elsewhere (Ryan, 2007), they challenged the public/private dichotomy in two ways. First, they wanted the right, as women, to actively contribute to the public sphere and leave the narrow constraints of domestic life. Second, they challenged what was considered 'private' by attempting to call public attention to what went on in the home, 'behind closed doors'.

In September 1919, Elizabeth Priestley McCracken, a unionist, a member of the IWSS and a well-known novelist, wrote an article on the subject of wife-beating. In this article, she was very critical of the tradition of the privacy of the family. 'An age-long tradition prevails that in matrimonial affairs what transpires in the home must be carefully concealed from the world without.' Such secrecy could mask physical abuse and so lend security to the more dominant partner, she argued. McCracken then examined the reasons why women were forced to keep such abuse secret: 'Wife beating is of common occurrence, and is suffered, for the most part, in silence by the victim for the sake of her social or financial position, or for the sake of her children.'

Even when a woman did take an abusive husband to court, she could expect little satisfaction. The crucial factor in wife-beating was the woman's economic dependence on the male breadwinner. Even the courts, according to McCracken, took this into account and rarely sentenced the man. In fact, the legal system actually went so far as to excuse male violence against women 'in effect creating in the minds of cruel and tyrannical men an idea that it is the male prerogative to beat wives'. She saw wife-beating as not only a cruel crime but also as the negation of trust, love and morality. And, true to her suffrage principles, she ended the piece by arguing that women voters should bring about social change and ensure the personal safety of all women. She advocated setting up a society for the protection of women similar to societies already in existence to protect children.

This article is extremely important as it illustrates feminist analysis of the complex power relationship between the privacy of the home and the public institutions of law and order. McCracken began by asserting how the privacy of the home masks male violence. In addition, she also indicated how male financial power keeps women in a position of dependency. She further illustrated how the male-dominated public institutions were unable or unwilling to represent women and instead reinforced male authority both inside and outside of the home.

The underlying attitude of many suffragists was that women within the legal system would be different from men. This is in line with their attitude towards women in parliament. As mentioned earlier, many suffragists seemed to presuppose that there was a fundamental difference between men and women. They appeared to assume that women within the legal system, or indeed women in government, would bring different and better morality to public life. As Mary Cullen notes:

> The demand was never simply for equality of rights with men within existing structures and value systems. Nor did feminists promote men's patterns of behaviour as the norm to which they should aspire. Their aim was more ambitious, a transformation of society through the promotion of 'female values'. (2007: 15)

While this raises many questions about their faith in women and their notions of morality and immorality, it does not mean that they had absolute trust in all women. For example, in January 1919, the *Irish Citizen*'s 'Current Comment' column addressed the issue from a more pessimistic perspective. The nomination of women as magistrates in England had not included suffragists and those women who had struggled for so long to win rights. Instead the 'parasites', those women who were indifferent to the cause of women, were being called to serve as magistrates. These women, who included members of the nobility, were chosen because of their social class. The writer hoped that in Ireland such women would not be chosen as magistrates. This article, at least, indicates that suffragists were not naive and realised that not all women could be trusted to act in the best interests of their sex.

Nonetheless, implicit in many of the articles in the *Irish Citizen* is the assumption that women are more trustworthy than men and so are better suited than their male peers to be the moral guardians of society.

Women as moral guardians

On many occasions suffragists appear to be embracing the conservative ideology prevalent in Victorian society that women were the moral guardians of the home. The only apparent difference between Victorian moralists and the suffragists was that the latter wanted to extend the moral guardianship of women from the home into public life. It would be easy to condemn this attitude in suffragists. However, as Karen Offen (1992) has argued, such attitudes were common among suffragists across Europe. But these attitudes were often mixed with notions of rights, citizenship, equality and democracy. It would be simplistic to claim that Irish suffragists employed only arguments of moral superiority. Nevertheless, morality was a recurrent theme in the suffrage newspaper.

The November 1917 article 'Morality: Conventional or Otherwise' reveals a major suffragist dilemma. In it, Margaret Connery explored what she called the 'modesty cult'. This cult was particularly prevalent in Ireland and was perpetuated by the clergy, she said. Men in all ages have been sticklers for the observation of a strict moral code on the part of women. Women, for example, were not supposed to have legs or necks, these should be concealed at all times. While priests could publicly criticise women from the altar for their supposed nakedness ('glad necks'), the women were powerless to defend themselves. She cited the example of Cardinal Logue addressing an all-male audience on the topic of the decadence among women. He referred especially to women wearing short skirts and thin stockings. Yet, Connery is outraged that the cardinal made absolutely no mention of the immorality of low wages and bad housing experienced by many of these women. This was, according to Connery, ample evidence of the double standards and 'modesty cult' in action. She pointed to the hypocrisy of a church that did not condemn war, saving its sharpest criticisms for women. Connery viewed such attacks on women by the church as: 'a despairing attempt on the part of the old Adam in man to assert its ancient domination over women's lives before it is finally swept away' (Nov. 1917). As I have written elsewhere, the Catholic church regularly attacked women's fashions, lifestyles and leisure pursuits as evidence of moral decline in Ireland, especially after the establishment of the Free State in the 1920s and 1930s (Ryan, 1998, 2002). That suffragists like Meg Connery had the confidence to take on such criticisms and challenge them, in print, is a testament to their courage and commitment to women's rights. Nonetheless, it is interesting to note that Connery did not sign her full name to this controversial article, instead using her initials, M.K.C.

In some ways, Connery's piece has much in common with the article by Elizabeth Priestley McCracken, discussed above. Here Connery examined the power of all-male institutions to reinforce male privilege and so disadvantage women. Like McCracken, Connery was challenging the public/private dichotomy by exposing how private morality was publicly constructed by all-male bodies. The message of this article is that women must break free of male definitions of morality. But what did Connery see as the alternative morality? If women were to define their own morality what would it be like? Connery's other writings for the *Irish Citizen* give us some clues.

In an earlier article of September 1917, for example, Connery wrote that at the age of 16 years a girl may consent to her own 'moral ruin', in other words, may have sex. Connery, like many of her suffrage colleagues, identified women's subjection with sex. Therefore, she advocated freedom from sex rather than a freedom to enjoy sex. This is similar to an argument put forward by Marion E. Duggan when she referred to the unwed mother as 'ruined'. On the subject of 'free love' and sexuality, Duggan wrote an article in response to criticism from the English anarchist press. The anarchists had criticised the suffragists for opposing 'free love'. While Duggan acknowledged that suffragists may oppose 'free love', she asked if that is necessarily a reason for reproach. Dangerous diseases, she warned, were the inevitable results of sexual laxity. She went on to say that motherhood without marriage was bad for women: 'It is a thing we want to stop, we deplore its prevalence' (4 Sept. 1915). The question is when she said 'we', did she mean the majority of the suffragists or just the Watch Committee, of which she was a member?

In the interests of balance, Duggan then went on to look at the sexual activities of men. Was sexual laxity in men immorality, a sin, or simple necessity? She suggested that if it was a result of immorality on the part of men then they should reform and live more moral, Christian lives. To return to the subject of unwed mothers, she said that in Ireland such women were left to battle alone in a hostile world. They had two choices: living at home with their parents and suing the man for financial support, or else going to the workhouse. She suggested that in order to discourage unmarried women from having children, suffragists should make the child their chief concern. All children born to unwed women should be made wards of court, she argued, which would ensure that the father paid for the maintenance of the child. She then linked certain forms of sexual immorality with madness, especially in the case of men who assault children. She advocated that such men should receive medical attention, not prison.

This article points to three immediate problems for the suffragists in relation to sex: disease, unwanted pregnancy and exploitation by men. While these fears persisted, the suffragists recoiled back into the safety of high moral standards, which they then sought to impose on men. Are there any other possible reasons for the suffragists' negative attitudes to sex? In her book on Irish suffragists, Cliona Murphy says that the anti-suffragists used to accuse the suffragists of being obsessed with sex and sexuality (1989: 131–3). This could be another reason why the Irish suffragists were so anxious to play down the issue of sex. As was common at that time (Candy, 2007), most of the suffragists did not credit women with any sexual needs of their own. And it would appear that at least some of the suffragists were very ignorant on the matter (see Cousins, 1950: 108; Levenson & Natterstad, 1986: 16; Candy, 2007). Of course, these attitudes were not unique to Irish suffragists and need to be understood within the socio-historical context of the early twentieth century (Bland, 1995). Nonetheless, the following extracts illustrate that behind this moral conservatism was a sharp, insightful analysis of society that included some elements of radical feminist critique. As we will see, suffragists took on controversial and contentious topics and were not afraid to suggest some rather radical solutions.

Suffragists cleverly reinterpreted the story of St Patrick banishing snakes from Ireland.

Extracts from the *Irish Citizen*

Editorial: Is the Law an Ass – or Worse?

10 AUGUST 1912

Suffragists – and especially those who have good reason to take special interest in the law-courts – can well appreciate the saying that 'the law is an ass'; but in common justice to that much-harassed quadruped, let it be said that the comparison in this case is odious, as the ass, unlike the law, does not reserve its most vicious kicks for women – either at the bidding of its master or to gratify the wish of vulgar onlookers.

The law, as administered in the Irish Courts during the past week, furnishes interesting material for reflection; the following cases were picked at random from an evening paper, and compare most strikingly with the heavy sentences passed recently on suffragists in Ireland:

1. (a) On August 2nd, at the City Commission, Judge Madden sentenced Mary Anne West to 6 months' imprisonment for breaking the window on a public house, value £7 8s. No less than 62 previous convictions were against her, of assault, larceny, ill-treatment of her child, drunkenness, and glass breaking. The woman had a thoroughly bad character, but the Judge actually apologised for the heavy sentence of 6 months, saying he had to give it as 'the offence was so rife'.
(b) Be it noted – Miss Webb and Miss Lloyd, charged with breaking £5 17s. 6d. worth, are undergoing a similar sentence of 6 months; not only were there no previous convictions against them, but the Recorder said he was quite convinced their motive was a perfectly pure one.

2. (c) At Rathcoole Petty Sessions, on August 2nd. Jas. Mulally was charged with an aggravated assault on his wife by 'striking her on the neck with a knife, thereby inflicting a serious wound and placing her life in danger, the doctor certifying that she was in a serious condition and had to be detained in hospital for three weeks'. The Bench decided 'with some reluctance not to send the prisoner to jail this time: he must instead find securities, himself in £10 and two sureties of £5 each to keep the peace for 12 months, or in default go to jail for 2 months'.
(d) Be it noted –The first four Irish militants convicted of window breaking were sentenced to 2 months' imprisonment (one month, and

one month in lieu of an undertaking to keep the peace for 12 months) for damage ranging from 10s. to 30s.

If, pro rata, the gash in Mrs Mulally's throat is valued by the Bench at from 10s. to 30s., and is only deserving of the alternative penalty of 2 months' imprisonment, why should a few pounds' damage in a theatre be rated so much higher, and the penalty inflicted be five years. By what vagary of the law can Mr Mulally get off, relatively speaking, scot free, while Mrs Leigh is imprisoned for such a term?

In connection with the Mulally case, it is also interesting to note, that for such an aggravated assault the maximum penalty the law can impose is 6 months' imprisonment; an attempt upon life, therefore, according to the judicial mind, is evidently only a serious matter calling for unlimited punishment when the perpetrator of the crime is a Suffragist and the victim a Cabinet Minister, or a Cabinet Minister's pet.

Such is the law as framed by men and administered by men; it stands by the strong and deserts the weak, not because it is the natural enemy of the weak, but because it only hearkens to the voice which cries the loudest – and the dominant note in public affairs is the masculine.

Lest it may be thought that the 1st Division treatment granted to Irish Suffrage prisoners excuses the long sentences imposed, let it be clearly understood that no such thing is the case. The better treatment was conceded solely in recognition of the political and non-criminal motive which prompted the so-called misdeeds, and was not in any instance given in mitigation of punishment.

Current Comment: Irish Girls in Peril

3 MAY 1913

Last week in Limerick three young girls were attacked on their evening walk by a satyr, who gagged and bound one of them, a child of 15, rendering her almost unconscious. But for the timely assistance of some young men who heard the girls' screams, the brute would have escaped. This is the gist of the matter.

The Press reports, however, with their usual finesse, entirely obscure the main issue in their plaudits for 'a young solicitor's plucky act'. Without belittling the rescuer of the maidens, would not he himself be the first to deprecate undue praise for what must be a natural act to any decent man – the prevention of criminal assault upon an unprotected child? We have too high an opinion of Irish manhood to suggest, as does our Press, that such a deed shows more than ordinary heroism.

What strikes the mere woman about the tale is the fact that such a foul outrage could be committed in the neighbourhood of a quiet Southern city and that no attempt to lynch the would-be assassin of maidenhood is recorded. Meanwhile the Press reserves its leaded type for 'Dastardly Outrages' of Suffragettes on unprotected golf-greens and empty mansions of the rich. It can find only the callous appellation of 'exciting incident' for attempted rape.

Editorial: The Ruin of Young Girls in Ireland

19 JULY 1913

Last week we commented upon the danger of Irish girls under the present state of the law. This week we have a much worse example at our own doors. A case came before the Recorder of Dublin last Friday, in which a man was charged with criminal assault on a girl under sixteen. The girl gave birth to a child last January, when she was fifteen years and eight months old. This was the second time the case was tried, and for the second time the jury disagreed.

No one, therefore, has been made responsible for ruining this girl's life. The jury's disagreement was, no doubt, in some measure due to the very able manner in which the defending counsel played upon their masculine prejudices, pointing out to them that any one of them might any day find himself in a similar position to the man in the dock. A woman on the jury might have reflected that any young girl might any day find herself in the pitiful plight of the ruined girl. The suggestion of the defence was that the Crown had prosecuted the wrong one of two brothers, in whose house the girl lived, employed as a servant by their sister; and that the girl herself was charging an innocent man in order to shield the real culprit. The Recorder commented strongly and very properly on the undoubted fact that the girl had been ruined while in this employment. Proceedings were not instituted till after the birth of the child; and consequently only the assaults which took place within the preceding six months could be made the subject of a prosecution. This brings out a serious defect in the law: the six months limitation rendering it quite possible that a guilty man may escape all punishment for offences of this character which have been clearly proved against him, but the proof of which was not attainable until too late a date for him to be made legally responsible. All the parties concerned belonged to County Dublin. Not a word of this case was allowed to appear in any Dublin newspaper. This is how the press created the legend that there is no sexual viciousness, and no danger to young girls in Ireland.

In the Courts

by M.E. Duggan, LLB

11 JULY 1914

Two cases involving sexual offences against little girls were before Mr Hunt in the Northern Police Court on Monday, June 29th, and have been returned for trial at the City Sessions on 9th July.

John Madden, a 'free labourer', now an ice-cream vendor, is alleged to have attempted to assault a child aged six years and eleven months in Lower Gardiner Street. Dr Boyd Barrett deposed that the victim is suffering from venereal disease (gonorrhoea). Bail refused. A Protestant clergyman is said to have gone bail in £20 for a man named Jones, resident in Drumcondra, who is accused of indecent conduct towards an eight-year-old girl.

It will be remembered that the Irishwomen's Reform League, some months ago, resolved to take action with view to bringing before the notice of the Court their desire that such cases should be punished with the utmost severity.

Accordingly, Messrs. Cochrane and Co., 18 Harcourt Street, have been instructed to hold a Watching Brief on our behalf, and in Madden's case we trust the Court will not deny that we have a right to be interested in the proceedings. We have in hand a number of subscriptions towards the expense, but more are needed. We trust that those who feel that children ought to be protected from human beasts will try to spare us a trifle.

It must be clearly understood that: (1) A refusal to allow our representative to speak will not necessarily mean that our trouble has been for nothing. (2) We are not out to try and force the conviction of innocent men; but merely to assist in getting at the truth and to voice the 'women's point of view', in order that sympathy with the prisoner will not lead to a short sentence. (3) We do not propose to be represented in every case, but will, if allowed, intervene from time to time, in order to create strong public opinion and to prevent secrecy. (4) There is a need for our urging stern measures. See last week's *Irish Citizen* 'A Distorted Sense of Humour'. The notorious Edelstein, when guilty of assaulting a girl of ten, was allowed by the Recorder to go free, 'on account of his services to his co-religionists'. (The said co-religionists have since got the individual in question sent out of the country.)

It is said that a father was found guilty at last sessions of continued offences against his ten-year-old daughter, and received nine months imprisonment. We are not content to hear rumours about these things afterwards; we want our representatives there at the time with a view to getting accurate information. Mr Justice Dodd, in a seduction case recently expressed a desire to take into account 'the natural and irresistible impulses animating the man'.

We spent a profitable hour in court on Wednesday 1st July.

Two women, named Brogan and Tore, were accused of fighting.

The question of previous convictions being raised, it was suggested that Brogan had served a sentence on another occasion for assaulting the police. She denied indignantly, 'it was for soliciting'. It appeared she had done a month on more than one occasion for this offence, of which she did not seem in the least ashamed. Doubtless, thinking herself indispensable to the 'natural and irresistible impulses of men'. Is it safe to shut our eyes and trust that the courts will maintain a high moral standard?

We would be glad if some responsible person would come down to court for the trial (even though it may take place in camera). Full information as to when it may come on will be available at 29 South Anne Street.

The Woman Lawyer – Her Work for Peace
by M.E. Duggan, LLB
24 APRIL 1915

Two reasons may be given to justify the entrance of women into any new sphere of human activity. First, that women, being in some ways superior to men, may be able to effect reforms and to breathe a new spirit into the dry bones of Conservative stagnation. In the second place, women have failed to cultivate certain admirable qualities which men have learned (and also forgotten) by experience, and the discipline of a hitherto untried kind of work may materially assist her moral development.

With the woman doctor, a change has come over medicine. Drink and vice are no longer believed to be necessary preservatives of male health and strength. The importance of preventive medicine is more and more being realised since the days of Florence Nightingale. What about preventive law? Why is it that the nations are not content to abide by the decisions of international tribunals? That is the question which the women delegates at the Hague Conference have got to answer. Can we separate the ordinary law administered in the various countries of the world from the proposed International Courts? I do not think we can. If any nation really respects and believes in the law as administered in its midst, that nation will probably put its trust in international justice too. If, on the other hand, the people have been brought up on the axiom, 'the law is an *hass* [*sic*]'; if they know that rich and poor fare very differently, and that petty red tape has bound the hands of justice, are they likely to favour the establishment of International Tribunals? In England and Ireland, law is very expensive, and many reforms are needed. How then, can the peoples of these two countries learn to trust International lawyers? Here is work for women. We are beginning to ask to be admitted to the administration of justice as lawyers, jurors, magistrates and Judges. We base our claim on the principle that those who are affected by the administration of our laws should be consulted as to that administration on equal terms with men. A man who beats his wife, or outrages a child answers to men alone for his crimes! Is this educating him as to the rights of women and his duty to them? It encourages men to believe themselves capable of deciding upon the destinies of other folk, and from thence it is but a short step to believing themselves entitled to settle the destinies of small nationalities. Law needs to be made something real, vital and respected by all classes. The woman lawyer is the pioneer of women jurors and judges. All the reasons that are advanced on behalf of Votes for Women can be applied to their being allowed their parts in the Courts. Women desire to be represented on Courts of Arbitration, and that carries with it the obligation to make themselves fit to sit there. Now the mere book-learning of International Law is easy enough; women seem to do particularly well on that subject in the Law School of Trinity College Dublin. Doubtless, the same state of things prevail elsewhere; but unless allowed to become lawyers, how can we qualify properly? I come now to my second reason for admitting women as a sex to the administration of justice. We urge this, because we believe it would be good for justice and good for women. We believe that this reform would tend to evolve a calm, impartial, fair-minded type of woman, while women's good qualities would educate male lawyers and politicians. At present it is not thought necessary for a woman to learn the judicial virtues. Were every schoolgirl a potential juror, countless instructors would take her education in hand. How can women, educated in total ignorance of these virtues, educate their sons to believe in law rather than in force?

Has not this unhappy war come upon us because men and women are so unfair to one another? They will not stop to enquire into motives or to weigh actions. Men have come to take for granted their own fitness to 'judge the earth'. Did women's claim to share this duty do nothing else save turn attention of humanity to the need for and the beauty of that calm consideration of both sides of the case which is the essential feature of justice, our work would not have been in vain. How educative it is to hear a judge sum up!

Space will not permit me to dwell upon the needs of India's daughters and of women doomed to Mahommedan harems. They need women lawyers to help and advise them.

International Peace presupposes an International Tribunal. How can women ask to be consulted as to its decisions unless they also are ready to do their best to make the Courts of their own countries just, equitable and respected?

The honesty, insight and sympathy of women may well be the very qualities needed in order to enable the legal world to grapple with the promises of to-morrow, and an education in the duties of a juror may teach the women of to-morrow to avoid the stupid enthusiasm for war which animates so many of our sisters. Justice is blind, while women are enslaved.

Watching the Courts

by Mrs E. Sanderson

19 JUNE 1915

To-day, for the first time, I made acquaintance with the inside of a Court of Law, and a very interesting and educative place I found it. Three of us went to hear a seduction case against David Donnelly, of Bray, in the King's Bench Division, Four Courts, before Mr Justice Boyd. A very curious case, as was pointed out by the defending counsel, as never before had a seduction case been brought where the injured girl was dead!

The case was opened by Mr O'Connor, and was rather a variation of the old story. The defendant (who did not appear) was a married man, well off, and had three shops in Bray and one in Greystones, tobacconist, hairdresser, etc. Mr O'Connor said there was no room for the plea that might have been accepted on behalf of a young unmarried man – that of 'human nature'! This had been an affair of months. There were witnesses to prove that this man visited the shop – which the girl ran for her mother – almost daily, and was seen on many occasions in a small parlour with her; wrote her suggestive postcards, and followed her down to the country when she was on holiday. Not until the day of the birth of a child and her own death were any of the girl's people aware of her condition; and then she made a dying declaration (to which the defending counsel objected as not evidence) to the effect that Donnelly was the father of her child. Her brother Michael, in the witness box, recounted the conversation he had with the defendant on the morning following his sister's death, when he taxed him with the seduction of his sister and the paternity of the child, which Donnelly admitted. Defending counsel again objected on the score that no man could admit what he couldn't know! Only the mother knew who the father was.

This was practically the case for the plaintiff. Mr Dickie, the counsel for the defendant, rather waived the seduction side of the case, and laid himself out to prove that, as the girl Agnes was not the servant of her mother, no damages could be claimed. This struck me, as a suffragist, as a shockingly derogatory position – a seduction charge cannot be brought by the wronged girl, but by her father, her guardian, or her 'master' (as the defending counsel put it). Loss of service must be proved before redress can be obtained – if one can speak of redress in such a case when it must be in terms of L.S.D.!

Mr Lynch, in addressing the jury for the plaintiff, pointed out that the defendant had admitted his paternity, and yet the girl's mother must support the child, as the father was under no legal obligation to do so. The only way this woman, who had had to close her shop since her daughter's death, could reach the father was to send this poor unwanted baby to the Union, and then the Guardians could sue him.

Mr Dickie, with great ingenuity, tried to prove that the girl Agnes was the owner of the fruit and florist business, and, incidentally, that Donnelly was a friend of the family; and, again, that the mother was to blame for allowing the intimacy between the two.

Mr Justice Boyd, in addressing the jury, was indignant, and pointed out that the least loss of service entitled plaintiff to damages, and that the mother of the deceased girl had said in the witness box that she was the owner of the business which her daughter managed for her. He characterised as disgraceful that the defending counsel should base his defence on 'legal fictions'!

The jury filed out, were absent for some ten minutes – I sincerely pitied the pathetic row of witnesses, the mother, sister, brother and friends of the dead girl – then they filed back, with a verdict for the plaintiff – damages awarded, £500!

It was all over, and I came away feeling rather depressed – damages for the loss of a daughter, a sister, a mother!

It struck me how appropriate a jury of men and women would have been on this and on many a similar case. Women, even the most sentimental, can only, like men, judge on the evidence before them, and in many cases are in a better position than men to judge fairly. No mention was made of the amazing self-repression practised by the dead girl in concealing her condition. Only a woman could visualise and sympathise with that nine months' torture.

About women as jurors, I think more than ever that it is only a natural sequence of other justices to women that we should take our share in administering justice. Perhaps it is not too much to hope that someday, in those brighter days to be, we may not only have women jurors, but women counsel and women judges, too.

The Girl Mother and Kindred Problems
by M.E. Duggan, LLB
4 SEPTEMBER 1915

I recently read in an English anarchist newspaper an interesting criticism on the Militant Suffrage Movement.

First the writer said that its supporters were out to govern other people, a statement with which I entirely agree; secondly, that the militants (and non-militants) object strongly to, and are horrified at, 'Free Love'. This latter fact may also be true, but is it a ground for reproach? When the advocates of any movement carefully ignore the most important facts bearing on their subject, one cannot doubt where truth lies. The literary supporters of 'Free Love' never, by any chance, allude to the fact that dangerous disease is the inevitable result of sexual laxity.

Again on another side we find writers, like W.E. Norris in 'Clarrissa Furiosa', scorning the movement for the emancipation of women because it does not make a woman happy to speak at public meetings, or to object to her husband having done what other men do. Acquiescence brings happiness, he urges, and carefully fails to mention that this happy submission also brings physical suffering to the wife and death to her children.

Irish suffragists are faced with the fact that reforms in the law relating to unmarried mothers and illegitimate children are needed, and must be discussed now if they are to be remedied as soon as possible at College Green or at Westminster. The Watching the Courts Committee hope to hold a small conference towards the end of September, dealing with various problems of this kind. A little discussion beforehand is essential. In what spirit are Irishwomen to approach the question of immorality? Are we to say that motherhood without marriage is good or bad for the woman? I unhesitatingly say 'Bad'. It is a thing we want to stop, and we deplore its prevalence.

But another question comes up: Is immorality in men a sin or physical necessity? Does man's nature compel him to live a life that brings pain and degradation upon himself, his wife, and family – and, above all, ruins, morally and physically, the women whom his bodily needs employ. Men's answer through the ages has been that men must yield, but that the women who comply are vile sinners. This is most unfair. Two remedies suggest themselves: one is, that men should lead moral lives, trusting to Christianity to enable them to resist temptation; the other is, that prostitution should be recognised by those who believe in immorality as an honourable profession. The wife who does not mind what life men live ought logically to admit fallen women to her friendship. Suffragists must either check vice in men or raise the social status of the prostitute to whom, on their own showing, men ought to be most grateful. It is just because men are considered sufferers and women sinners that the girl-mother is left to battle alone with a hostile world. In Ireland two remedies are open to her. She can enter the Workhouse and get the Guardians to sue for the maintenance of her child. Perhaps she objects to Workhouse life? What can she do? Or, if she lives at home with her people, her father or nearest relative can take an action against the man for loss of the girl's services. Thus, the mother of a factory girl living in Dominick Street recovered £35 damages, with £60 costs, against a clerk earning £2 10s. weekly. The 'services' need be nominal only, but they must exist. Suppose a girl or widow living alone, or in her employer's family, is seduced, the employer can sue. Imagine, Mrs _____ of Rathmines, suing Private Murphy for seducing Mary Anne! Worse still, if Mary Anne is seduced by her employer, or one of his relatives, she has no remedy. A servant girl is defenceless.

I always think that the results of our legal system might be classified as follows:

Towards Rich Men it is absolutely satisfactory.
  " Rich Women generally satisfactory.
  " Poor Men unsatisfactory.
  " Poor Women very unsatisfactory.

If, as we often hear in Court, men should be excused for sexual crimes, let them pay the women who helped them, honourably and well. If both are sinners do not let the woman bear all the punishment. But will not a cheap method of procedure encourage women to be immoral? Not if the child is made our chief consideration; every illegitimate child should be made a ward of the State, and have official guardians, who would see that the father's contributions went to its maintenance.

On the criminal side, we must enlist the doctors to help us.

I am convinced that certain forms of sexual immorality and madness are near akin. One would like to know a great deal more about the mental family history of men who outrage children. If they are lunatics, they must be treated as lunatics! Men regard inability to resist temptation with pity, and give light sentences. But is it right to send those who cannot control themselves back into the world? The asylum, not prison, is the best place for those who feel irresistible impulses. Viewed as a part of the mental deficiency problem, outrage cases lose their worst horrors, and suggest hope of future improvements.

Current Comment: Drugged Sweets

AUGUST 1917

The daily press contained recently brief accounts of an episode in a well-known Dublin suburb, when two little girls returning from one of Dublin's 'Schools for the Daughters of Gentlewomen', were stopped by a man in a quiet side-road, who offered them sweets, and when they refused them he attempted to force them into the mouth of one of the children. Frightened by his manner they ran away. Some of the sweets found in the child's blouse were given to the Chief of Police, tested, and proved to contain morphia. It is an extraordinary thing that this incident has raised no public outcry, no demand for some better system of safeguarding our streets from crime. We know too well how widespread in England is the unspeakable crime of assaults upon children: surely the women of Dublin ought to make the most vigorous efforts to prevent its insidious entry here.

Such cases though not numerous here, do occasionally occur.

In the last few years some of them have been noted in the *Irish Citizen*, although ignored by the Press generally.

The children in these cases belonged to the poorer classes, and we were disposed to attribute public silence to that fact. But here is a case where a child of the richer class seems to have had a narrow escape from an appalling experience – and still the public are dumb! We protest against the silence. And we assert that it is time some new system of guarding our streets was devised. We doubt if women police meet the need. We would prefer to have women inspectors appointed for preventive and helpful rather than for punitive purposes. And we would make the care of the children the chief duty of these inspectors. One of the most lamentable evils in Dublin is the conditions under which the children of the poorer classes grow up. Every stranger coming to Dublin comments on the tragedy of child life here. A well-chosen body of women inspectors could do much to improve those conditions in individual cases, and also collectively by recommending and promoting methods by which permanent reforms could be effected.

We suggest to the Dublin Watch Committee, by whose efforts the case of the drugged sweets referred to was taken up and made public, that they make it a special duty to secure some more adequate guardianship of Dublin's children.

Morality – Conventional or Otherwise
by M.K.C.

NOVEMBER 1917

In all ages men have been great sticklers for the observance of a code of conventional morality – on the part of women. An essential feature of this code has been a secret conspiracy against our common Mother Nature to conceal the fact that she has endowed women – in common with other bipeds – with a pair of legs! This terrible fact is still sought to be shrouded in darkest mystery, and is considered extremely bad form, if not bordering on downright indecency, to mention the matter of a woman's limbs at all, or recognise their baneful existence, in the view of some of our modern priests. The standard bearers of this modesty cult proceed from one extreme to another, and now the fact that women possess necks – 'glad' or otherwise – is become a matter of grievous offence. A Revd clergyman preached in Co. Sligo recently in a whirlwind attack on the 'glad neck' and the 'pneumonia' blouse, and declared 'It was appalling to see Irish girls parading their nakedness in this way, and he was inclined to think they should be refused Communion when they came to the altar dressed in this way.' These are extravagant and provocative sentiments well calculated to arouse resentment in the minds of self-respecting and spirited women. It is manifestly unfair to assail the character of women from the privileged position of the pulpit where those who are being assailed are powerless to defend themselves. Hitherto the cure of souls and the cure of pneumonia have been recognised as belonging to two distinct and well-defined professions; and there seems to be a great deal to be said in favour of the good old saw which advises 'the cobbler to stick to his last.' It is a thousand pities the Rev. lecturer was not endowed with a sense of humour which would have saved him from raising this very futile storm in a tea-cup.

His Eminence Cardinal Logue has recently expressed himself in a somewhat similar strain to an audience composed entirely of men – the shortness of women's skirts and the density of their stockings being held up as an outward and visible sign (especially in the case of stockings!) of the decadence of their morals.

That his Eminence, engrossed in the manifold activities of his high calling, should deign to notice such mundane things as skirts and stockings is a reassuring indication of his essential humanity. Nevertheless, one would think that the length of the European war (with all the multiplied horror and tragedy it connotes) would present itself as a more urgent human problem to set before Irish Catholics than the length of women's skirts, especially in view of the impassioned appeal to end the horrid strife so recently made by his Holiness, the Pope.

In Ireland, as elsewhere, public morals must continue in an unhealthy state while we tolerate the shameful double-moral standard, while we have the crying evil of the sweated wages paid to our women workers, and while for thousands of our Catholic citizens life means the indecent herding of a number of persons of both sexes and all ages into one room where every function of humanity has to be performed.

Modesty under such vile conditions must be a difficult virtue to practice! The ventilation of these evils has hitherto been left mainly to groups of women – suffragists and social reformers, and the Church which could wield such tremendous power in grappling with these festering social sores, has stood coldly aloof from the struggle. Women have now outgrown their swaddling clothes, and they decline to be scolded and put to stand in the corner like naughty children.

Lately Irishwomen were treated to a tirade on their morals by that eminent pillar of society, Mr Nugent, M.P. In England Father Bernard Vaughan, who some time ago urged upon Catholic Englishmen that their supreme duty was to kill as many Germans as possible (a new departure in Christian ethics!) has a well-defined place, and periodically reveals the ennui of fashionable English society by his rhetorical denunciations against the sins of women. In America Billy Sunday gaily fills the role of modern King's Jester, but it occasions no surprise in the general mind to behold these various gentlemen don the motley.

This latter-day attack on women suggests a final despairing attempt on the part of the old Adam in man to assert its ancient dominion over women's lives before it is finally swept away before the onrush of new ideas into the limbo of forgotten things.

A 'Light' Offence

MAY 1919

Recently in the Dublin Courts the foreman of a jury declared that the list of criminal offences was very light, there being only one 'light' offence on the calendar, 'that of indecent assault upon a child'. Imagine the mind of a man who describes such an offence as trivial. Unfortunately, this mentality is by no means uncommon both in juries and on the bench. We believe that men as a rule are disposed to be over lenient to such offences, which to women are far more revolting than attacks upon property. It is but another instance of the need of women lawyers, women jurors, women on the bench.

Wife-Beating

by L.A.M. Priestley-McCracken

(author of *The Feminine in Fiction*)

SEPTEMBER 1919

An age-long tradition prevails that in matrimonial affairs what transpires in the home must be carefully concealed from the world without. The quarrels and differences, ranging from 'incompatibility of temper' and wrangling, to physical violence and giving of 'black eyes', must be kept strictly secret, particularly on the wife's part if she is the one ill-treated. Now, in a sense, it is a proper and natural course to keep home life inviolate. George Eliot inculcates the sacredness of home life in various memorable phrases, and reticence is an admirable veil to drop between the domestic hearth and the curiosity of the outsider. But like many other virtues, it has the defects of its quality, and there is no doubt this natural shrinking from exposure gives a sense of security to the stronger, fiercer, and more dominant partner – the husband – in ill-treating his wife, if so minded. I fear there is no gainsaying the fact that wife-beating is of common occurrence, and is suffered for the most part in silence by the victim for the sake of her social or financial position, or for the sake of her children. The husband's power is buttressed by every pitiful attempt of the wife to keep up appearances. The first blow struck most likely in a sudden gust of passion, possibly unintentionally, and repented of in cooler moments, furnishes a vicious precedent, and the argument of the fist comes easier on every subsequent occasion when the angry husband wants to repress, control or bully his wife.

It is noticeable that when a downtrodden wife summons courage to carry her grievance to Court there is a marked tendency on the magistrate's part to let the aggressor off with a light fine or very short imprisonment; the reason usually assigned being that the wife and family cannot live without his earnings. Here again is tacit encouragement to the wife-beater; his importance as a bread-winner is set off against his cruelty. If we are to stamp out this hateful form of oppression we should insist on 'a punishment to fit the crime' – a long term of hard labour, and, if necessary the family and wife to be maintained out of public funds, till the recreant is released. What touches the public purse stamps itself well upon the public imagination, and if the community pays in this way there would be more hope of working a reformation in husbands. Unhappily there are subtle influences towards condoning the dastardly offence of wife-beating. Let me give an example or two. At the hearing of a recent divorce case in Belfast brought by the wife for cruelty and misconduct, the defendant's Counsel sought to excuse the man's cruel treatment by saying 'the woman provoked her husband beyond measure' and also by proclaiming the strange doctrine that 'some women by reason of their conduct did not deserve anything but harshness'. How would this learned K.C. like such rough and ready justice meted out to himself? In the same case the Judge summing up remarked that 'it was very trying to a man's temper when his wife turned out drunken or troublesome, or a hindrance in his business. 'Still,' he added, 'it took a good deal of that to justify personal violence.' Are we to infer from this that provided the wife is 'provoking' or 'very trying' to her husband he has a right to inflict upon her corporal punishment? The mere stating of the question makes one feel as if we were back in the Dark Ages of barbarism, and not in the presumably enlightened 20th century. And let me give yet another example of that trend of thought that assumes a man can treat his wife in a way he dare not with impunity treat any other living creature. Judge Granger, at Southwark County Court, is reported as saying to a man who pleaded his wife when drunk was awful, but when sober was thoroughly good: 'If you had given her a good thrashing it might have effected an improvement.'

Could we imagine a wife being recommended by one of these Solons of the bench to try giving her husband a sound thrashing to effect his moral reformation? No, patience and tenderness and tears over the dear prodigal's sins would be the course recommended to the wife. But these and such-like *obiterdicta* from legal luminaries leave a most displeasing impression upon all humane and right-thinking people, and worse, have an injurious effect in creating in the minds of cruel and tyrannical men an idea that it is the male prerogative to beat wives who are 'provoking' to their husbands, or 'who deserve nothing but harshness'. Of all forms of physical violence, this of wife-beating appears to me the most monstrous and revolting. For a man to woo and win a young, trusting girl with honeyed words, and offering her in alluring terms a future safeguarded by his love and care, and then after marriage to beat and bruise the soft, warm body his hand had caressed and fondled – turning happiness and joy and love into a hideous spectre of devil-tainted, brutality – seems the very negation of personal honour and morality.

We have heard a good deal about the atrocity of the Hun inside the last five years, but what atrocity of an enemy in warfare can equal the atrocity of a lover – transformed into a husband – raining dastardly blows upon the shrinking defenceless woman he has sworn to love, honour and protect.

No wonder married life, domestic peace, the sanctity of the home, and the well-being of its children are imperilled when lawyers and law-givers make light of this horrible offence of wife-beating. It is surely the duty of enfranchised women to seek to have the personal safety of the wife adequately and effectively secured, and every deterrent that an educated and Christian opinion, and heavy penalties upon the offender can enforce, imposed upon ill-tempered and brutally disposed men until the relation between husband and wife shall be that of civilised and independent human beings not that of ruthless tyrant and hapless victim. We have a society to prevent cruelty to children at the hands of their natural guardians, why not one to prevent cruelty to wives at the hands of their natural protectors – their husbands?

CHAPTER 3

Feminism, pacifism and the war

The impact of the First World War on the suffrage movement is a
fascinating topic and reveals many of the challenges and divisions within
the movement, not just in Ireland but internationally. As Margaret Ward
notes, the reaction of Hanna Sheehy Skeffington to the declaration of war
sums up the view of many suffragists, who felt like 'aliens in our own land,
powerless to stem the tide of barbarism' (2007: 136).

In studying the Irish suffragists' reaction to the First World War it is
important to locate the suffragists within the specific context of Ireland in the
early 1900s. The Irish suffragists' views on war were formed within the
particular political, economic and cultural contexts of their time. Mary Cullen
(1985), in posing the question 'How radical was Irish feminism?', says that the
suffragists can only be understood using a culturally sensitive perspective.
Although she uses a cross-national comparison of suffrage groups, she is aware
that the specific situation of Irish society in the early twentieth century needs
to be appreciated (see also Cullen, 2007), a point we will return to in chapter
5 when we explore the national context in more detail.

While agreeing that cultural specificity is important, my work has sought
to highlight the Irish suffragists not only within the context of Irish society,
but also within a more international setting (Ryan, 1997; Delap et al., 2006).

Using the *Irish Citizen* we can explore how the suffragists analysed war and
worked for peace. In order to do this it is necessary to place the Irish suffragists
in the broader context of international pacifism (see Delap et al., 2006). In this
way one can see how the suffragists were not only influenced by the dynamics
of Irish society, but also how they engaged with suffragists in other countries,
exchanging shared experiences (Candy, 2007).

The *Irish Citizen* was not only a force for feminism in Ireland; it was also
a staunch advocate of peace. Its editorial policy was strictly anti-war, and
throughout the First World War kept up strong criticism of war and
militarism and, as we shall see below, clearly linked the war to male dominance
in politics. There were regular contributions by pacifist suffragists such as Lucy
Kingston, Margaret McCoubrey and Meg Cousins. In addition, there were
contributions by international pacifists such as the American Jane Addams,
Dutch activist Aletta Jacobs and British suffragist Emmeline Pethick-

Lawrence. The debates in the *Irish Citizen*, however, also illustrate the divisions within the suffrage movement, as pacifism was by no means the only stance taken by suffragists in Ireland (Ward, 2007). In addition, the attitudes towards war expressed in the paper are important for another reason. They illustrate some of the suffragists' taken-for-granted ideas about the innate differences between men and women. On first sight some of these assumptions may appear ill-informed and even naive. But as this chapter will illustrate, suffragists drew on a varied mix of assumptions and theories to analyse women's position in society.

In an early editorial on the subject of the war in Europe the glamour and heroism of war were firmly debunked. There was nothing glorious about war, the editor asserted. It was the destruction of life, stability and economies, leading to deprivation of every kind. War, claimed the editorial, came about as a result of male dominance in government, 'making property their god and cultivating a steady disregard, in comparison, of the value of human life'. Male governments did not have an appreciation of human life itself. But women, precisely because of their role in giving life, had a different view, a different value system. The editor said that feminism proposed to bring these values into public life, and this explained why feminism was the polar opposite of war (8 Aug. 1914).

As mentioned above, Hanna Sheehy Skeffington was equally critical of war and especially of the suffering endured by women. Writing on 15 August 1914, she stated that war was a favourite method employed by governments who were hard-pressed at home and eager to shelve their responsibilities. The press, which only weeks previously had advocated lynching suffragists, was now pleading with them to join in the cause of war to support the men. She deplored women who dropped the suffrage cause in order to help the war effort. These women, she argued, were traitors to the cause. The fact that society now desperately needed women should in no way be seen as a recognition, on the part of men, of women's importance. Hanna accurately forecast that when the war was over, and women were no longer required in the labour force, governments would revert back to their old antagonism towards them. Women, she stated, should not be prepared to help by mopping up the blood and, in effect, prolonging war, but should instead clear 'away the whole rotten system'. She acknowledged the importance of 'the fine solidarity of organised womanhood' that raised a voice of protest against the 'devilry' of war. She argued that Germany was not women's real enemy. Women must join together internationally and recognise their common enemy – war-mongering governments. Indeed, Hanna saw the international peace movement among women as a positive sign that this was starting to happen (15 Aug. 1914).

Hanna's viewpoint is interesting because: (a) she recognised that women have a common enemy; (b) she advocated international cooperation among all women; and (c) she realised the consequences of the war for women. Obviously Hanna's main aim in this article is to emphasise women's common cause, but in so doing she perhaps overstates the degree to which women shared experiences. Hence, her article fails to adequately explain why so many women, including British suffragette leaders Emmeline and Christabel Pankhurst, did not join the international peace movement.

Why, in fact, were so many women willing to join the war effort? Hanna's husband Francis, probably the writer of the first piece cited above (8 Aug. 1914), shared her views on war. He saw war as barbarous and a very primitive solution to social problems. War, he claimed, perpetuated oppression and reinforced the kind of mentality that kept women in subjection. The notion of war as a method of controlling population growth was, he argued, typical of this ideology. It reduced women to a mere appendage of the uterus. However, he also seemed to suggest that 'artificial restrictions' on reproduction were immoral. This suspicion of artificial birth control was not unique to Irish suffragists (Bland, 1995). Francis suggested that the emancipation of women was a more effective form of population control. Once women had attained their full human rights, 'the nightmare of over-population' would be over. At present, all of women's energy and time went into reproduction. Once released from that role, women's vital energy would be spread over all fields of constructive human thought and action: 'humanity can then proceed to construct its utopia, to organise a social system based on peace and cooperation'. But this could never happen, Francis claimed, until women were emancipated. Therefore, the emancipation of women was the greatest world question for humanity (12 Sept. 1914).

Undoubtedly, Francis Sheehy Skeffington was one of the most outspoken pacifists in Ireland. His vocal opposition to British army recruitment during the war resulted in his imprisonment. As mentioned earlier in this book, his execution in 1916 has been linked to his pacifist activity (Roper, 1987). He was described as 'a born rebel, a questioner of ancient traditions, a shaker of ancient tyranny' (Roper, 1987: 51). This article from 12 September 1914 gives a very clear insight into his analyses of militarism and feminism. The article drew on a very evolutionist approach to social change. In attempting to explain population growth and the role of women in society he verged on a rather racist view point. He spoke of 'lower races of mankind', who, being further down the evolutionary scale, had large numbers of children, fearing that many would not survive through childhood. 'Races' higher up the evolutionary scale had relatively few children, as these had a very good life expectancy.

Despite the racist tones, there are many useful and enlightening aspects to Francis Sheehy Skeffington's analysis of war. He illustrated that war was 'the product of a system' that deliberately accepted war as a part of international relations. There was an acceptance of war, a continual readiness to fight. Government bureaucracies created wars and then played on people's fears by claiming the country was in danger. Francis argued: 'What is in danger is the governing bureaucracy, which tries to identify itself with the nation.' He totally refuted the argument that 'now we are in it, we must go through with it'. He argued that one way to stop war was to refuse to enlist. If men and women simply refused to support the war then the government would be unable to continue military operations.

However, Francis' arguments about the value of feminism are underpinned by the key assumption that an emancipated womanhood would really make a difference to the running of society. We will return to this point again later. But first let us consider how suffragists' reaction to the First World War fractured the movement.

Irish suffragism and war-relief work

On the question of British suffragettes who abandoned the suffrage cause during the war, Francis Sheehy Skeffington was drawn into debate with Miss E.A. Browning of the Irish Women's Reform League (IWRL). While the *Irish Citizen* and leading members of the IWFL took a pacifist stance and opposed the war, it would be wrong to assume that other suffrage groups in Ireland agreed with them on this point (Delap et al., 2006; Ward, 2007). While Francis Sheehy Skeffington was particularly critical of the Pankhursts' 'sellout', Miss Browning wrote to the *Irish Citizen* to say that Irish people should respect Christabel Pankhurst's love of 'her Empire'. Browning further accused Irish militants of inconsistency in using militancy for their own ends but condemning men for using militancy to preserve the nation (10 Oct. 1914). Francis Sheehy Skeffington quickly responded that so long as Irish and English women remained voteless, they did not have a nation to defend. They would, therefore, have nothing to lose under a German invasion. He also added that while militant suffragists only destroyed property to gain basic human rights, the war was destroying human life to gain property. He accused Christabel Pankhurst of hypocrisy because while she had condemned the Irish 'home rule first' movement, she was now advocating war first and suffrage second. By so doing she was betraying women (10 Oct. 1914). In a subsequent issue of the *Irish Citizen*, we read that Miss Browning will have nothing more to do with the paper because of its anti-war stance (31 Oct. 1914).

While the IWFL and *Irish Citizen* stood firm and never became involved in any war-relief work, other suffrage groups took a different approach. Although the pacifists were significant, it is important to realise that they were outnumbered by suffragists who accepted that the First World War was necessary (Hearne, 1992; Ward, 2007). Thus it is clear that the paper, while allegedly representing all suffrage groups in the country, was, in fact, out of step with most of the other suffrage societies on the subject of the war. Nevertheless, the paper continued to provide a platform to all suffragists even when they firmly disagreed with *Irish Citizen*'s policy. All articles submitted by suffragists were published regardless of their position. This is what makes the paper such a valuable source of material for historians and other scholars interested in women's movements.

Dora Mellone, based in Co. Down and secretary of the Northern branch of the Irish Women's Suffrage Federation (see Watkins, 2014), wrote to the paper on behalf of the Suffrage Emergency Council, a group set up by the IWSF to carry out relief work. Mellone admitted that relief work was taking up much of the suffragists' time and so could prove a risk to the campaign for enfranchisement. However, she defended relief work by saying it was not aimed at helping the government but the ordinary people, men and women who were experiencing hard times. She took the attitude that suffragists could not ignore the suffering caused by the war (1 May 1915). However, one week later, writing in response to Francis Sheehy Skeffington, she offered a clearer insight into her attitudes on the war. In her letter she displayed some quite anti-German feelings, declaring that the Prussian ideal of military domination must be defeated. She expressed her hope that 'this ideal' would not be allowed to enter 'our system'. This attitude may partly explain her support for relief work and may suggest that she had been influenced by the British government's fierce anti-German propaganda.

Those involved with the IWFL and other concerned individuals were particularly worried about the effects of war on women. For them the war was exposing all that was really wrong with the system. Plans to reintroduce the Contagious Diseases Acts (CDAs) during the war years caused outrage among many suffrage groups. In some ways the campaign against these acts brought many of the scattered suffrage groups together (Cullen Owens, 1984). Writing to the *Irish Citizen*, Margaret Connery of the IWFL saw the CDAs as attempting to make sex safe for men, especially soldiers and sailors, by regulating and degrading women. Under the terms of the act, the police had the power to arrest any woman on suspicion of having venereal disease, and subject her to enforced medical examination. The woman had no say in any of this procedure. There were no checks for infected men. These CDAs had been repealed in the nineteenth century after decades of feminist campaigning by women such as Isabella Tod and Anna Haslam (Watkins, 2014; Cullen, 2007), but now, during the war, a similar practice was to be introduced under the Defence of the Realm Act. For Connery this simply proved that women could not trust men in government to make decisions for them. Any concession granted to women could be revoked at any time that the all-male government deemed it necessary. She regarded this as the ultimate proof that women must have the vote to protect their own interests (21 Nov. 1914).

The international peace movement

As previously mentioned, pacifist suffragists saw the only hope for peace resting with the women's movement, especially the international women's peace movement (see Delap et al., 2006). The *Irish Citizen* gave its full support to Mrs Pethick-Lawrence's Peace Party.

Emmeline Pethick-Lawrence, who was a major financial supporter of the *Irish Citizen* and owned the English paper *Votes for Women*, was an English militant suffragette who, unlike the Pankhursts, totally opposed the war. She helped form the Peace Party, which was a militant, international suffrage group. The main aim of the group was to improve democracy not only by enfranchising women but also by giving the ordinary people more control over all international treaties and alliances and in the manufacture and export of arms.

Louie Bennett, founder of the Irish Women's Reform League and Irish Women's Suffrage Federation, also helped to set up the Irish Women's International League, which was dedicated to peace, opposing war and militancy of every kind (see Cullen Owens, 2001). Louie herself had always opposed militancy as part of the suffrage platform. However, while opposing the war, she did support relief work as necessary and practical. She was not a nationalist, in fact she saw both nationalism and patriotism as barriers to internationalism and, therefore, to world peace (Hazelkorn, 1988). She did not believe that the suffrage should be postponed until after the war. That would, she argued, only prolong the war. Through the *Irish Citizen*, she reiterated that suffragism went across all national boundaries – it was above any war because it was the cause of all humanity. She recognised militarism as the most dangerous foe of suffragism. The suffrage movement could not join hands with that which sought to destroy it, she said. She gave her full support to the Peace Party and while she was sympathetic to the National Union of Women's Suffragist Societies (the largest British suffrage group, which was non-militant and led by Millicent Garrett Fawcett), Bennett saw their pro-war stance as misguided (27 Feb. 1915).

The *Irish Citizen* fully endorsed the International Women's Peace Conference, which was held in the Dutch city of the Hague in 1915. The paper attempted to give it as much publicity as possible, since the national press was boycotting the conference. Louie Bennett, in supporting the conference and its efforts to promote peace, internationalism and suffragism, described the feminist movement as a powerful international force. Women, she said, were more sympathetic to internationalism than men because of the 'bond created by the special function of motherhood'. But why then did so many women actually support war despite such a common bond of motherhood? These women were, according to Bennett, 'the lingering result of centuries of subjection by brute force'. She went on to say that the pillars of constructive peace were equal citizenship of men and women, and the democratic control of foreign policy and armaments (10 Apr. 1915). These ideas were very much in line with those of Mrs Pethick-Lawrence.

This article indicates that suffragists were aware of how social structures influenced the attitude and behaviour of people through 'socialisation' processes. However, Bennett seems to be saying that while the natural biological drives in women are good, the attitudes into which they have been socialised by society are bad. This argument could be interpreted as biological determinism taking precedence over wider social influences.

The general tone of many articles in the *Irish Citizen* during the war years assumed that if women were to occupy positions of power in society then war would be avoided. Several articles frequently resorted to a kind of biological determinism to explain women's 'natural' aversion to war. Women, it was assumed, would bring such virtues as caring and nurturing to the public sphere. Women, because of their biological capacity to produce life, would never set out to destroy life through war (Aug. 1914; Dec. 1914; Mar. 1915). However, as Jo Vellacott (1993) has argued, it is all too easy to dismiss pacifist feminists as merely indulging in biological determinism. Similarly Karen Offen (1992) has argued that what may appear as simple biological determinism is often complex and multifaceted. Offen points out that feminists are frequently eclectic in their approach and may use a variety of arguments including both the equality of men and women and also the differences between men and women. Valerie Bryson's detailed study of the development of feminist political theories (1992) indicates that feminists have always used a mixture of theories and analyses. Those who drew on biological determinism may also incorporate some social learning or socialisation theories in their feminist analyses. To dismiss their biological determinism out of hand is to dismiss a central tenet of feminism going right back to the 1700s (Cullen, 2007).

In addition, as I have argued earlier, feminist assertions about the public value of women's positive, maternal characteristics, may also be interpreted as an important counter-narrative. Feminists sought to challenge many of the commonly held, negative stereotypes about women at that time. Instead of being silly, vain, emotional and irrational creatures, unfit for public office, feminists argued that women would bring much-needed humanity and a caring ethos to political life.

A very clear example of a suffragist who made these arguments through combining a variety of social theories was Margaret McCoubrey. Born in Scotland, she was a socialist and a member of the other militant suffrage group in Ireland, the Belfast Irish Women's Suffrage Society, and would later be elected to Belfast corporation as a labour councillor. In a two-part article in the *Irish Citizen* newspaper of 1915, she analysed the First World War from a socialist and feminist perspective. She accused the government of feeding people silly sentimentalism in the form of patriotism. As a socialist she interpreted the war as the working class being used like cannon fodder to protect upper-class interests.

In this article she demanded political freedom and economic equality for women: 'We have shouted ourselves hoarse on the question of equal pay for equal work' (6 Mar. 1915). However, at the same time she highlighted the differences between women's and men's views on war. McCoubrey claimed that the thoughts of a woman looking down on a battlefield would not be 'there lie so many Germans, so many British, so many French'. It would be 'so many mother's sons! All our service of motherhood gone for naught ...' (27 Feb. 1915). McCoubrey argued that when women took their rightful place beside men in the government of affairs, war would become a thing of the past. Why? 'because women all appreciate at its highest the value of human life'. She concluded her two-part article on 6 March by declaring: 'For only with the help of women dare you dream of true Internationalism only with the help of the world's womanhood can the Ideal of a true and lasting Peace be realised' (6 Mar. 1915). This article illustrates very clearly what Offen (1992) has already suggested: that feminists draw on both individualist arguments of equality and freedom as well as more essentialist arguments relating to motherhood and biology.

It was generally agreed by those contributing to the *Irish Citizen* that the war brought to light all the ways in which women were being exploited in society, ways which had been so carefully masked by such false notions as chivalry. The double standards in morality were also brought up during the war, especially with regard to sex, alcohol and dress.

The British government made serious efforts to stop women from drinking during the war, even going so far as to officially ban them from public houses. While the *Irish Citizen* and many of its regular contributors supported temperance and considered women to be the 'temperate sex' (in fact, several Irish suffragists were teetotal), nonetheless, many opposed the double standard in banning only women from drinking in pubs.

Margaret Cousins, writing from England, tried to be slightly more optimistic about the effects of war on women. War had, she argued, demonstrated the value of women in society. Economic necessity had forced a complete rethinking of women's role – no longer confined to the home, but desperately needed in the workplace. But, like Hanna Sheehy Skeffington earlier, she also realised that women could not merely be happy with this arrangement but they must seize the opportunity and demand equal rights, equal pay and trade unionism (1 May 1915).

Those Irish suffragists who opposed the First World War also, in principle, opposed the use of violence in relation to Irish freedom. In his 'Open Letter to Thomas MacDonagh', Francis Sheehy Skeffington argued that all violence was wrong. While he supported Ireland's right to self-determination, he said threatening violence would only lead to violence and would result in Irish people killing Irish people (22 May 1915). This article is particularly poignant given that both MacDonagh and Sheehy Skeffington would die violently just one year later.

In May 1915 the IWFL organised a protest meeting in response to the government's tactics in preventing women from Ireland and England attending the Hague peace conference. By closing the North Sea route in the days just prior to this international event, the British government prevented all bar a very few English women from reaching the Hague. No Irish woman was able to attend. The protest meeting in Dublin was very well attended by women and men, and Louie Bennett was among those who addressed the audience.

A full account of the meeting was carried by the *Irish Citizen*. The report pointed out that while the women 'groaning under the yoke of German tyranny' were given permission to attend the conference, the British government saw to it that no Irish woman was there. Thomas MacDonagh, commandant of the 2nd Battalion, Dublin Brigade of the Irish Volunteers, addressed the crowd and offered his complete support to the women's struggle, adding that he believed women could solve such issues as war.

But Meg Connery, chairing the meeting, quickly reminded him that suffragists could never condone the use of violence by the Irish Volunteers (the complex relationship between suffragists and nationalists will be discussed in chapter 5). She went on to say that it was a far better thing to live in one's country than to die for it. The world must be constructed on love not on hate, she said, echoing the sentiment of the Hague conference (22 May 1915).

'Questionings' headed an interesting editorial on May 1917 on the subject of the ongoing war. While the editor admitted that many women had remained servile during the war, she hoped that women would soon assert themselves. During this period, following the execution of Francis Sheehy Skeffington, the editorship of the *Irish Citizen* was taken over jointly by Louie Bennett of the IWRL and by Miss Bourke-Dowling of the IWFL. It is likely that this particular editorial was penned by Louie Bennett, as the ideas expressed here are similar to those expressed by her in earlier articles. The editorial went on to argue that women and men were not entirely equal. Their differences were important and complemented each other. Women, she claimed, should not imitate men in dress, ideas or behaviour. Instead, women should follow their true instincts, developing and preserving life. This is somewhat different from the ideas put forward by Francis Sheehy Skeffington when he wrote that women should be released from their breeding function and devote their energies to public life. However, the editor went on to clarify her point. Her views on the differences between the sexes did not mean an acceptance of separate spheres for men and women. On the contrary, she recommended that women should enter public life and occupy such professions as medicine and teaching:

> An emancipated womanhood can only find full and free expression in a world where physical force is subordinated to moral, where power and materialism are dominated by spiritual impulses, where competition is superseded by cooperation. (May 1917)

She also acknowledged the influence on her thinking of that veteran suffrage campaigner Mrs Annie Despard.

This debate on the war brings to light many suffragist attitudes not only towards violence and killing but also towards the essential nature of women. A close reading of suffragist writings reveals the wide range of political theories that they employed, from liberal theories of equality to socialist analyses of class conflict to more essentialist theories of biological determinism and female superiority. This mixture of complex and even contradictory theories was not unique to Irish suffragists (Bolt, 2014; Hall, 2004). Like feminists in many other countries, Irish suffragists were eclectic, and rarely propounded any single systematic political theory.

It is clear from the discussion so far that most of the suffragists associated with the *Irish Citizen* were not simply after 'the vote' as such. Some wanted a fundamentally different type of social system where the 'womanly virtues' of peace, love and cooperation would replace war, hate and competition. Though many certainly supported Irish self-determination, the internationalists were quite vocal within the movement too (Ward, 2007). Indeed, the *Irish Citizen* served an important function in keeping Irish campaigners in touch with suffragists worldwide, and frequently carried reports from the USA, Australia and India, as well as other European countries. Thus the Irish movement was certainly not isolated from what was going on in suffrage movements in other countries (Delap et al., 2006).

For that reason it is important to compare the Irish suffragists with their closest neighbours, the British suffragists. Such a comparison illustrates the similarities between their arguments and ideas. But the great differences are equally as important and should not be underestimated. The attitudes of the Irish suffragists towards the First World War are just one example of the differences between the suffrage movements in Ireland and Britain. Many Irish suffrage groups became involved in war-relief work. The IWSLGA gave itself up almost entirely to helping Belgian refugees (IWSLGA, 1919). However, the out-spoken pacifism of a significant proportion of the Irish suffragists stands in sharp contrast to the British suffrage movement. Only a small proportion of the movement in that country openly denounced the war. One possible reason for this was that the British suffragists feared incurring the wrath of the British government, and of the people generally, by openly condemning a war that involved almost every household in Britain. In contrast, to condemn the British government in Ireland was a little more acceptable, especially with a nationalist uprising brewing. It seems that one of the primary differences between the Irish and British suffragists was national/political background. The political question in Ireland provided an important backdrop to the suffrage/feminist movement. The influence of the home rule and nationalist struggle on the women of Ireland, be it positive or negative, cannot be underestimated.

As I have argued elsewhere (Thapar-Björkert & Ryan, 2002), the Indian women's movement provides another interesting example of the influence of nationalist politics on the campaign for women's rights (see also Cousins, 1950; Jayawardena, 1986; Liddle & Joshi, 1986; Haque, 2013; Banerjee, 2012). Both the Irish and the Indian examples show that feminism and the women's movement are not isolated from other political, economic and social events in a society but are, in fact, highly influenced by what is going on in the society around them.

This highlights the point made at the outset of this chapter that suffragist activism needs to be understood within the context of its own society. However, that is not to say that comparisons are unimportant. Comparisons between the Irish and Indian suffrage movements, for example, may prove very useful. The Irish suffragists, although influenced by events in Irish society, were not internationally isolated. And, as the extracts illustrate, they believed very strongly in the international community of women or, as Hanna Sheehy Skeffington called it, 'the fine solidarity of organised womanhood'.

The following extracts are selected from the period 1914–15 and reflect some of the feminist analyses that took place in the *Irish Citizen*. However, these extracts do not represent all suffrage viewpoints. Because of the enormous number of articles written during the First World War, I have had to omit many fine pieces, some of which have been mentioned in this introductory discussion.

Suffrage Week in Dublin.

DO NOT FAIL TO ATTEND THE
SUFFRAGE CONFERENCE

IN THE

ROTUNDA CONCERT ROOMS, DUBLIN, DECEMBER 9th to 12th.

DECEMBER 9TH, AT 3 P.M.—*PRESENT POSITION OF WOMAN'S SUFFRAGE.*
Speakers: Miss S. R. Day; Mrs. Carson, B.A.; Miss Courtney (N.U.W.S.S.); Mrs. Tanner (Women's Freedom League); Mrs. Kineton Parkes (Tax Resistance League).   Chair—Mrs. Maude.

DECEMBER 10TH, AT 3 P.M.—*CONDITIONS OF WOMEN'S WORK IN IRELAND.*
Speakers: Miss Mellone, Miss S. R. Day, Miss Morony, Miss Browning, Dr. Edith Badham, Dr. Ella Webb, Rev. Dr. Denham Osborne.   Chair—Sir William Barrett, F.R.C.Sc.

DECEMBER 11TH, AT 8 P.M.—*WOMEN'S TRADE UNIONS AND THE VOTE.*
Speakers: Miss Marion Phillips, D.Sc. (National Women's Labour League, London), Miss Cahalan (Drapers' Assistants Association), Miss Euphan Maxwell, M.D.; Miss Eleanor Rathbone (N.U.); Mrs. Cope, Rev. R. M. Gwynn.   Chair—Conal O'Riordan, Esq.

DECEMBER 12TH, AT 3 P.M.—*IF WOMEN HAD VOTES.*
Speakers: Miss Gladys Potts (N.U.W.S.S.), Mrs. Cowan, Mrs. Webb Smithwick, Miss Stack, Rev. Savell Hicks, Miss Palliser (N.U.W.S.S.)   Chair—Miss Hamilton.

All Suffragists must support the Cause at the *Debate with the Antis* on Thursday, December 11th, at 3 p.m.   Miss Mary Hayden, M.A., will speak for the Suffragists. Chair: MRS. MARCUS GOODBODY.

HALF AN HOUR ALLOWED FOR OPEN DISCUSSION.

See Ibsen's Remarkable Play, "Rosmersholm,"

Produced by MISS ELIZABETH YOUNG at the Theatrical Club, 40 Upper Sackville Street, December 8th and 9th, at 8 p.m.

MRS. DUNCAN has arranged a fine programme of music, recitations, and short suffrage speeches, concluding with the production of a play, *Not Made in Heaven*, by Miss Costello, for the evening of Wednesday, December 10th, in the Rotunda Concert Room. Good Music.   Clever Artists.   A really entertaining programme.

A CONVERSAZIONE to conclude the week will be given at Mills' Hall, Merrion Row, on Friday, December 12th, at 8.30 p.m.   MISS LANDER and MR. J. M. KERRIGAN, Abbey Theatre, have kindly promised to contribute items to the programme.

MR. LEGGETT-BYRNE will give two Tango turns.

Every day Light Luncheons and Afternoon Tea will be served in the "Tea and Lounge Room" at the Rotunda.

Every day a GREAT CHRISTMAS FAIR will be carried on.   Fancy Articles, Books, Xmas Cards and Calendars, Suffragist Turkeys, Suffragist Sweets, Suffragist Flowers, Suffragist Toys, Suffragist Dolls, and Suffragist Homes,—all can be bought at this Fair.

SUFFRAGISTS! BUY YOUR XMAS PRESENTS ONLY AT THIS FAIR!

Notes for Delegates attending the Conference:

MEETINGS OF THE FEDERATION COUNCIL will be held on Tuesday, Wednesday and Thursday, at 11 a.m., at the Rotunda.   All members of the Council are requested to attend.

THE ANNUAL MEETING OF THE FEDERATION will be held on Friday, December 12th, at 11.30 a.m., at the Rotunda.   All members of Societies affiliated with the Federation are urgently begged to attend.

Season Tickets for the Conference ...	...	...	... Price	2/6
Tickets for the Debate with the Antis	...	...	... „	2/- & 1/-
Tickets for "Rosmersholm"	...	...	... „	2/6
Tickets for the Conversazione	...	...	... „	2/6

Can be had at 29 South Anne Street, Dublin.   Ribbon Badges for Delegates—price 1d. —will be on sale.   All Delegates visiting Dublin for this Conference are specially begged to buy and wear one.

To promote suffragism, many events were organised, including concerts, plays and fairs.

Extracts from the *Irish Citizen*

Editorial: The Writing on the Wall

8 AUGUST 1914

The terrible war into which we are now plunging marks the Nemesis and the doom of the man-made state and of the purely male ideal of government and polity. Blind to spiritual forces, devoting themselves to the building of a civilisation on a purely material basis, making property their god and cultivating a steady disregard, in comparison, of the value of human life, the rulers of Europe have gone on complacently in the belief and confidence that their system of society was destined to endure, and that they represented the final triumph of civilisation. Amid all the outward splendour, all the conquests of commerce, of science and of industry, the penetrating eye of the seers of this and the last generation have long foretold collapse. At the top, excessive arrogance, boundless ambition, unscrupulous exploitation; at the bottom, destitution, crime, and shame – thus did the Cassandras of our day depict the fabric of civilisation, permeated, in spite of its overwhelming appearances by a rottenness that sprang ultimately from one cause – an insufficient appreciation of the sacredness of human life and personality – that is to say, a lack of precisely those thought-elements which it is the special function of women, in public as in private life, to supply.

It has long been predicted that the sex-bias of the modern civilisation would lead to its overthrow; that the anti-feminist canker in its heart would fester, breeding war or revolution, ruin from above or ruin from below. These predictions, scoffed at so long, are on the verge of fulfilment. War has come; revolution at least in the countries which suffer most heavily, cannot be delayed. All that delicate network of civilisation, of human brotherhood and international amity, which artists and scientists and philosophers have been patiently weaving by their accumulated work for decades, has been swept aside at one blow at the command of the unreasoning blood-lust and thirst for domination. Those who yesterday, were horror-stricken at the destruction of a stained-glass window, a racecourse stand, or a picture, are to-day contemplating without protest and in some cases with joy, the wholesale destruction of ships of war, the bombarding of cities, the burning of thousands of houses, accompanied by the inevitable loss of millions of human lives – lives every one of which has cost some woman the agonies of the Valley of the Shadow to produce. Bombs dropping from the sky, tearing up the ground, hurling hundreds to death, destroying blindly the most precious products of human industry and artistic skill, as well as the human beings themselves;

great ships, the work of thousands of hands and brains, manned by hundreds more, ramming each other in the deep, and plunging together to annihilation; blazing cities, thousands of destitute wanderers, mobs fiercely fighting for bread, soldiers aflame with passion wreaking their cruelty and their lust on the defenceless – these are some of the horrors that are now, in the true sense of a much-abused word inevitable; for once the demon of war has been unleashed, nothing can control him.

We are clearly of opinion that the root cause of this appalling dissolution of society is to be found in the same spirit that engenders contempt for women and denies them a place in the state. War and anti-feminism are branches of the same tree – disregard of true life-values. It is not a coincidence that all the countries concerned in the war are countries which do not recognise women as citizens and that those which are most aggressively and unscrupulously war-like are precisely those in which women are held in least regard.

It is no mere coincidence that it is those who support women's claim to freedom who are, in every country, the most active in trying to prevent war or to limit its consequences. And the one ray of hope in the darkest international situation within living memory is, that when the lurid and unimaginable sequel has burnt itself into the brains and bodies of humanity, a new Europe may arise, with a new spirit, determined to build no more unstable and lop-sided foundations, but to erect a new society based on the divinity of humanity, without distinction of physical sex. But before that day can dawn, Europe will go through the valley of agony.

The Duty of Suffragists

by Hanna Sheehy Skeffington

15 AUGUST 1914

The present situation offers many lessons to suffragists. There are many pitfalls at our feet. The women of Europe, whose motherlands are engaged in strife, are all alike in their voteless condition. Like us their hands are clean; they have no responsibility for this war. Like us, they have to pay the price none the less to the uttermost farthing. They have to deliver up the sons they bore in agony to a bloody death in a quarrel of which they know not the why or wherefore, on the side of the particular ally their Government has chosen for the moment; they have to face starvation at home for themselves and their children meanwhile; many of them are exposed with their helpless daughters to the lust and outrage of a war-maddened soldiery. That is what in cold fact war means to women. It is an aspect that the world's press disregards, because it would make war unpopular.

There is one 'bright spot' – and it is a real one, not a will o' the wisp – in this, namely, the fine solidarity of organised womanhood. With one voice at the International Suffrage Alliance and through the entire suffrage Press it spoke bravely and firmly against the 'insensate devilry' of war. When the Churches of the Peacemaker were silent, womanhood, standing for civilisation and progress, lifted a voice of unanimous protest. But her appeal was as usual disregarded by male statesmen, eager to let loose the yelping dogs of war at one another's throats. Still the protest has been registered: united womanhood has intervened for the first time on a great issue and her message will be remembered when the shouting is over.

At every crisis suffragists must be alive to insidious dangers that threaten to swamp the cause. War is the favourite method employed by governments hard pressed at home and eager to shelve their responsibilities. The rock of party politics, on which so many suffragists in the past suffered shipwreck, they now, thanks chiefly to the militants, have learned to avoid. We smile now when we are told to put the needs of the party first, not to embarrass the Government or Home Rule or the Union by pressing our claims 'at this crisis' (and this 'crisis' is a chronic state). We now know by bitter experience that the women who heed these cries are traitors to their cause, and that it is their supineness which is largely responsible for our voteless condition.

Now the 'wreckers' are at work again. This time attempts will be made to induce women to abandon propaganda, to roll up the map of suffrage with the map of Europe, to forget their own pressing economic and political grievances (now more acute than ever) because of the 'national crisis'.

Now will the test-stone be applied to the soundness and sex loyalty of every one of us; do we really put Votes for Women above everything, or does it fall into second rank? Are we women first of all? Note how we women are being worked upon by a Press that advocated lynch-law for us but a few weeks ago. We are inundated with invitations to be up and doing 'to help the men'. They have not yet forced Conscription upon us, not because they desire to spare us the horrors of war – for these we suffer as non-combatants to the full – but because it is our function to replenish the nations decimated by fire and sword, to continue to supply 'food for cannon'.

But short of facing the enemy's guns in actual warfare, every other duty is expected from us. Here is a list compiled from the daily Press of things that we may do to show 'we are not unworthy of our soldier brothers'. We are to knit 'soft woolen comforters' for the departing soldiers, to replenish their cigarette-cases from our pin money, to see to food supplies at home, so that no unseemly riots take place among the starving poor to disturb the progress of affairs, to accompany the troops as Red Cross nurses, helping to patch up the shattered victims of machine-guns and torpedoes, to fill the places of reservists and conscripts at a lower wage at home, to till the fields and garner the harvests left by the labourer, and contrive the weekly budget on a diminished allowance so that our menfolk may not have cause to grumble at their dinner, though society totter. Some of these tasks are noble, some ignoble, but all end for suffragists in a cul-de-sac. When the war is over we shall be gently but firmly put back in our place once more – on our pedestals.

While some invitations to suffragists are a flattering admission of the efficiency and public spirit of organised women, they constitute none the less a grave danger. How often have we been invited to drop our troublesome propaganda, to show our fitness for citizenship by 'being good', by slumming, by playing at municipal reform, by devoting ourselves to poor-law work, by any and every imaginable side-issue. Anything but Votes for Women!

Again it behoves us to reply to all those who would enlist our services – Suffrage First! Every suffragist will take to heart the lesson of present happenings. We see more clearly than ever what humanity loses by refusing to enfranchise women throughout Europe. May Europe's, England's, difficulty be Womanhood's opportunity! A truce to tinkering with reform while the very bulwarks of society are being swept away. It is not for us to mitigate by one iota the horrors of war; such attempts, however laudable, are but 'casting snowballs into hell to lower the temperature'.

To humanise war is to perpetuate war: once seen in its naked hideousness, the glamour of romance gone; its sway is over.

Women are eminently practical: they realise the futility of fiddling with symptoms while the disease rages unchecked.

If male statesmanship after all these centuries has nothing better to offer by way of adjusting differences than a universal shambles, then in heaven's name let men allow women to lend a hand, not at mopping up the blood and purifying the stench of the abattoir, but at clearing away the whole rotten system. Until then it is our duty to press on with unabated energy, to increase our activities at this crisis, to preach peace, sanity and suffrage.

War must not devastate our ranks: this at least it is in our power to prevent. Our guns must be directed not against the Germans (from whom, by the way, we have much to learn) but against our common enemy – the warmongering politician, the pledge-breaking Government, now so sentimental over the wrongs of oppressed nationalities, while it continues to sweat and bully with impunity the women of the land. These are the enemy: it is these upon whom we wage war until they offer terms. The suffragist who turns aside from the cause of Votes for Women at this hour is, indeed, helping to put back the clock. By redoubling energy in pursuing our propaganda, in war as in peace, we suffragists shall find ourselves when the war is over – and may it be sooner – not in the position of a disbanded army for whom there is no more active service, but as eager and strenuous in our campaign as before, as determined to have a voice in the councils of the nation in order to avert in future the evils of a Man-run State. All the rest is vanity; it is but pandering to the war fetish. Retro Satanas!

War and Feminism
by Francis Sheehy Skeffington
12 SEPTEMBER 1914

That the logical and necessary antithesis between War and the Woman's Movement is not clearly recognised is due to a want of consistent and penetrative thought as to the bases of these two antipodal factors in human affairs. I propose to demonstrate, first, that war is necessarily bound up with the destruction of Feminism; secondly, that Feminism is necessarily bound up with the abolition of war.

I

In the course of the evolution of Life on this planet, we observe a steady replacement of the ideal of quantity of life by that of quality. The lowest forms of life spawn freely, produce an enormous number of seeds or eggs. Concurrently with this stage, we find that the progeny thus prolifically produced are subject to wholesale destruction from co-existing natural causes. The individual life has very small chance of survival; it is only by producing it in overwhelming quantities that the low-grade animal can hope to escape the entire destruction of the species.

As we proceed up the line of evolution, we find this prolific spawning and wholesale destruction gradually giving way to a life-cycle in which less fertility, with increased chance of survival, is the rule. It is generally true that, the higher an organism is in the evolutionary scale, the fewer individuals of the species are born, and the greater proportion of these survive to complete the full life-cycle.

Mankind, at the top of the scale relatively to other living forms, repeats within its own evolutionary ascent the features of biological evolution in general. Lower races of mankind – and lower types among the higher races – are very prolific; but only a small proportion of the progeny survives. The others are weeded out by the natural forces co-existent with a low state of civilisation; by famine, by pestilence, and above all by war.

Following the analogy of other forms of life, we might expect two related phenomena to present themselves in the evolution of human society – a greatly reduced fertility, and a greatly increased chance of survival.

The diseased state of modern civilisation arises mainly from the fact that the latter phenomenon has presented itself without the former. Pestilence and famine are of increasingly rare occurrence; the progress of science makes life day by day easier, lessens hardship, lengthens the average duration of individual life. The result is that the world is 'filling up'. Mankind, having become the dominant form of life on the earth, finds itself confronted with a condition of affairs – not too remote for the earth as a whole, and immediately pressing for certain portions of its surface – in which the resources of the planet may prove insufficient to nourish its human colony. It is this fact, the despair of believers in human perfectibility, which has hitherto proved an insuperable stumbling block in the way of the creators of utopias.

They, and other philosophic and scientific minds, have wrestled with this problem and attempted its solution along many different lines. Crude theorists have advocated infanticide as a solution – only a few months ago a bulky volume, seriously propounding this 'solution' appeared from the London press. Devotees of science, agriculture and land reform point with enthusiasm to the as yet unexhausted possibilities of the earth. But to these there must be some limit; postponement, not solution, is the most that is to be looked for in that direction. Certain misusers of the name of Malthus advocate artificial restrictions on population. But the instinctive aesthetic repugnance which these evoke in normal minds is shown by experience to be justified by the grave physical and moral evils which they bring in their train. No healthy solution can be found in that direction.

II

The systematic upholders of war as a beneficent factor in human affairs (and they are not by any means confined to Germany) declare that not only is war a tonic to prevent mankind from growing torpid and slothful, not only is it valuable as a 'shaker-up', but that it presents the only practicable solution of the population question. Like the older school of surgeons, they think the occasional blood-letting, as a matter of deliberate policy, is the proper cure for the congested social system. Whenever the pressure of excessive population becomes too great, war will automatically reduce the numbers of mankind, and at the same time – so say war-mongers – provide for the survival and dominance of the 'fittest' race.

This is a simple, blunt, and logical theory. But it is based on the logic of barbarism. It implies that war is to be retained as a permanent factor while its old co-partners, pestilence and famine, have been weeded out by science – except in so far as they are again and inevitably brought back in the train of war itself. It implies that the qualities which lead to success in war are those which ought to be perpetuated in the race. With the present revelation of what success in war means before our eyes, the falsity of this theory needs no demonstration.

This theory implies that, ever and anon, the fabric of civilisation, so painfully built up by generations, is to be overturned in catastrophe, and a fresh start made. It condemns mankind, at best, to a wearisome treadmill; at worst, to the total decay and disappearance of civilisation and human society. For in every such outbreak of barbarism something is lost; mankind is left several steps nearer to the primeval beast at its conclusion than at its commencement. This theory renders impossible the emancipation of women.

By the war-maker, woman is, and must be, regarded merely as a breeding machine. No escape is possible along the line of 'quality rather than quantity'; in war it is the quantity that counts, the overwhelming numbers of human beings wantonly flung to slaughter. Moreover, the increasing destructiveness of modern weapons renders this slaughter greater in every war than in the preceding one. Men, and more men, is the cry of the warlords. Women count only as producers of men. Woman must remain, as one writer of this school has coarsely put it, 'an appendage of the uterus'. We should be thankful to him for his bluntness. Woman as a human being disappears; she is of value but to produce 'food for powder'.

III

Start now from the other theory – the antipodes of the war-theory of society; start by assuming the emancipation of women. This, in its broadest aspect means that woman must cease to be 'an appendage of the uterus'. Woman must count in and of herself, as a human being, with the human rights of an individual. Woman's vital energy, hitherto dammed up into one channel – that of reproduction – will be spread over all the fields of constructive human thought and action. And automatically, by the quiet action of the conservative processes of nature, the amount of woman's vital energy available for reproduction will diminish.

The ideal of 'quality not quantity', will prevail; the nightmare of overpopulation will disappear. Humanity – man and woman – can proceed to construct its Utopias, to organise a social system based on peace and cooperation, without being haunted by the dread of an overcrowded and starving world. War, which is in ultimate analysis the expression of the savage competition of the hungry for food – 'commercial competition' is the polite term – will be generally recognised as the crime and madness it always is, and will cease to trouble the earth.

This is the line of true human progress – the only possible line of human progress. The Emancipation of Woman is the essential condition of progress in that direction. That is why the Emancipation of Woman is incomparably the greatest World-Question for Humanity.

IV

So much for general principles. In the application of them to contemporary circumstances, one runs some risk of provoking disagreement among those who have followed the argument thus far. Nevertheless, I shall proceed to show how, in my opinion, these principles ought to be applied at the present moment by those who accept them.

If we want to stop war, we must begin now. This war is the product of a system – a system for which every statesman in Europe must bear his share of the blame. All deliberately accepted war as a permanent factor in the adjustment of international relations. All prepared to be as strong as possible against the day of the 'inevitable' war. None took any sincere or effective steps to make Peace inevitable.

Pacifists were fooled by the pretence that great armaments would maintain the peace. We now know the folly, or the hypocrisy, or both, of that presence. But we are insensibly yielding to a new cant, preached by Mr H.G. Wells and others of his school – that this war will make an end to war. It is false. War can breed nothing but a fresh crop of wars.

By accepting this war, in any degree whatever, we are helping to perpetuate war. If we want to stop war, we must begin by stopping this war. The only way we can do that is to hamper as far as possible the conduct of it. The best way to do that is to stop recruiting.

We shall be told, of course, that 'the country is in danger'. What is in danger is the governing bureaucracy, which tries to identify itself with the nation. No conquest can possibly be as disastrous as the continuance of war.

We cannot admit that 'now we are in it, we must go through with it'. That is the argument of all tyrants and evil-doers. We must simply say to the governing bureaucracy, 'You have brought on this war. If you say you could not have prevented it, you stand condemned as incompetent. It was your business to prevent it. We cannot allow you to use the weapon of war, any more than we could allow you to use the weapon of forcible feeding under plea of necessity. Stand aside and let us start on a better path.'

Nothing that has been alleged of 'Germany atrocities' in the hot blood of war exceed in horror the callous brutality of forcible feeding, in cold blood. And the man that is guilty of that crime is on a recruiting mission – to get more men to strengthen his hold on power.

The woman who does not, in the measure of her opportunities, discourage recruiting, has an imperfect understanding of the basis of the feminist movement. The woman who deliberately encourages recruiting is betraying that movement – though her name be Christabel Pankhurst.

ISF and Relief Work

by Dora Mellone

(Secretary, Suffrage Emergency Council)

12 SEPTEMBER 1914

It seems to me time that the position of the Irishwomen's Suffrage Federation should be explained in the columns of the *Irish Citizen*. The Emergency Meeting of the Federation Executive Committee was held on August 15th. It was then decided the Federation should include among its activities the prevention and relief of distress during the present crisis. The decision was submitted to all the Federated Societies for ratification. This having been obtained, the Federation is now taking an active part in the support of the Suffrage Emergency Council, an account of which is contained in last week's issue of the *Irish Citizen*.

Now, for what reasons did the Federation adopt this course? It is perfectly clear that to divert the energies of suffrage workers into other channels may involve a slackening of the ordinary suffrage propaganda: it may be easily urged that this is no moment for such a course. The present crisis supplies the clearest evidence of the urgent need for the enfranchisement of women. Had women been given their fair share in the management of European affairs during the last twenty years the probabilities of this war would have been greatly lessened. The pitiful difficulty experienced by the average 'womanly' woman in finding scope for her energy in the present crisis supplies another argument for the need of that education in citizenship, which the use of the vote can alone afford. Only grave reasons can justify a suffrage organisation in slackening its propaganda for the sake of relief work.

In enumerating the reasons, which in the view of the Irishwomen's Suffrage Federation justify such a course, the less important may be mentioned first. It was felt that Suffrage societies should act as units as far as possible.

It was not desirable that Suffragists should lose their identity and be swamped in the flood of workers; also, the work of suffrage organisations follows different lines from that of the ordinary relief committee. The latter simply carries out a propaganda of work settled for it by the Government, the Central Relief Committee, or some other body. The former initiates schemes of work and concentrates its energies in the prevention rather than the relief of distress. As an example may be instanced, the efforts of the Suffrage Emergency Council to secure contracts for local firms, and to open up new channels for employment. Further details of work in this direction will be forthcoming in the next issue of this paper.

Our principle justification for undertaking this work was our deep conviction that it is necessary. The question whether the war is justifiable or unjustifiable we do not discuss, any more than we discussed the question whether Home Rule was good for the country or bad for the country; I may say in passing, the opinion on the former subject is very strong, but I have no wish to enter into a discussion on it here. The war is here. If the nation is to be saved women must help in the saving. It may be argued that this is only a stronger reason for holding back; the 'difficulty of the Government is the opportunity of the Suffragists'; we ought to refuse all assistance to the Government until we have obtained a pledge for the early introduction of a Government measure enfranchising women. To do otherwise, it may be said, is to haul down the flag of suffrage first, and hand over our fighting forces to the enemy without conditions.

Our answer is, we cannot do this, because we might destroy the nation. How often we have heard doctors say 'I cannot operate the risk is too great.' It is so with us. We are deeply convinced this war will be fought out, not only by the grim lines of guarding ships and thousands of armed men, but by the so-called non-combatants at home. We have always held the argument: 'Women cannot fight, therefore they should not vote' as being worthless.

We have always argued a national success in war depends as much on the courage, wisdom, and endurance of the men and women at home as on the courage of the soldier on the trenches, and the wisdom of the General in command. We hold that view still: we believe success in this war depends upon the exertions of women as well as men. It must be 'fought to a finish' and women take their share in this fighting, though the weapons used are neither rifles nor bayonets. In view of the danger that threatens us, we dare not risk our national existence by refusing our help. We might so refuse did we value women's health and women's work less highly. But we believe this work and help is absolutely necessary, and therefore, we give it in full measure. There is another reason: we ask for the vote on the same terms as it is or may be given to men. Just now voters and voteless are in the same position. We are on equal terms with men. For the moment voters have no control over the methods used in the prosecution of war or for home administration during the war. They and we alike can only work to mitigate the suffering produced by the war. It will not be so later when conditions of peace can be discussed: we shall then feel once more how our hands are tied. But for the moment we can do all that men can do, therefore, to save the nation we take our share in the war.

And when it is all over will our services be recognised?

When medals are given and rewards distributed, will it be remembered that women helped to save the nation? Perhaps not. It would be no new experience to find ourselves set aside, ranked again with the pauper, the criminal, and the lunatic, unfit to take any share in the government of the country, though proved fit for the heaviest and most responsible work. We recognise these probabilities without bitterness. For the present our duty is to help to save the nation by lessening its suffering: in the future our duty will be to help to save it by lessening the dangers of another such catastrophe as the present. In other words, for the present we will organise relief work – in the future we will again throw our whole energy in the work for votes for women.

Irish Militants, the War and Relief Work

by M.K. Connery

19 SEPTEMBER 1914

Whatever else may be said of the war we must admit at once that it has proved a tremendous testing time for individuals and organisations no less than for nations. We rejoice that once again the I.W.F.L. has proved the soundness of its metal by the way in which it has stood this fiery ordeal and resisted the manifold efforts made to seduce it from the cause of its true allegiance. Our position is simple, and scarcely needs explaining. We have adopted the only attitude consistent with womanly dignity and self-respect, based on our conception of what are the true and real interests of the nation in this crisis.

We are never without a crisis of one sort or another. Men take care to keep us plentifully supplied with them in order to divert our attention from our own wrongs and grievous disabilities as a sex. Are we weather vanes then that we turn about with every breeze that blows, or are we serious human beings with a serious purpose in life? The present state of affairs will furnish the answer to each of us. A few months ago we were in this country faced with a crisis which touched us far more nearly – we were faced with civil war.[1] We did not on that occasion haul down our flag, suspend our activities, range ourselves on the side of the respective combatants whose cause we personally favoured. We refused to split our forces on that rock; we still more emphatically refuse to split them on this one.

In the autumn of last year there was wide spread suffering and want in Dublin. Gaunt famine stalked through our streets. Thousands of people were thrown out of employment; thousands of men, women and children were hungry, and cold and ragged and friendless. There was urgent need for relief works. The health and well-being of the nation was threatened through famine and disease, yet we did not witness any wild stampede of women to grapple with this national problem. Individuals amongst us were free then as now to give what aid we could to lessen the general distress, but we recognised clearly that relief works, however, praiseworthy and necessary, were outside the scope of our organisation.

Our movement was founded with the definite aim of securing the political freedom of women. To this work we have pledged ourselves, and to no other. Nothing has occurred within the last few weeks to justify us in turning aside from our life's purpose. The European war has done nothing to alter our condition of slavery. It has only served to make us realise more deeply and poignantly than ever the utter helplessness and defencelessness of our position as political outcasts in attempting to stem the tide of masculine aggression and brute force.

We stand now where women all down the ages have stood – without the pale of citizenship and human fellowship with man – a state of things so intolerable, so morally indefensible, so disastrous to our national well-being and so gross an offence against the spirit of liberty that we dare not at this juncture turn aside from our great crusade against the forces of evil lest the principles and ideals on which alone true nationhood are founded be wholly swept away and the nation itself destroyed.

There is profound truth behind the old saying that 'a rolling stone gathers no moss'. The need of the moment for women is to concentrate. We have always held the view that success in this women's war – against male

---

1 This probably refers to conflict between the Ulster Volunteers and the Irish Volunteers prior to the outbreak of the First World War.

dominance and chattel slavery – depends on the tenacity of purpose, the singleness of aim and unswerving devotion to principle of the women engaged in it. It must be 'fought to a finish'. We are neither going to bury the hatchet nor yet to resurrect the domestic mop (true emblem of our enslaved condition)! What possible affinity between women struggling for freedom and the forces responsible for precipitating the present horrible catastrophe? Let those who have plunged the nation in war be made to shoulder the full responsibility for their deed. This is the duty of the State. If the State must drive men forth like 'dumb driven cattle' to be slaughtered, let it at least have sufficient humanity to make provision against want for the homes it has desolated, for the widows and orphans its policy has made. For groups of private individuals to attempt to cope with a condition of distress so far-reaching and complex is on a level with the labours of the historic lady who strove to keep out the tide with a broom.

We are opposed to this war, as we are opposed to all war, because we are profoundly convinced that war is in itself an unmitigated evil and the greatest existing menace to true human progress. It is anti-Christian and anti-social, and is only calculated to foster the lowest and most bestial passions of mankind. Further, it is our conviction that feminism and militarism are natural born enemies and cannot flourish on the same soil. As the spirit of militarism (based on brute force) grows and triumphs so must decay the spirit of comradeship, human co-operation, and sympathy for which our woman's movement stands. Let us consider the calibre of those individuals who are behind the war and satisfy ourselves if they are deserving of the confidence or respect of women. There is Lord Kitchener – the ruthless despot, the notorious woman hater. There is Mr Asquith, 'a grey old wolf and a lean', the fanatical bigot who has stubbornly blocked the way of woman's emancipation for years, under whose government and sanction suffragists have been subjected to every conceivable form of insult, personal injury, calumny, mob violence and prison torture. There is the whole tribe of harpies who follow in their train, and there is the corrupt Press which is their mouthpiece. Behold, then, the new saviours of humanity – the champions of freedom and civilisation! Ah, do we not know them of old, and shall we not refuse to be beguiled from the path of honour and righteousness by the false doctrine of these political mountebanks!

Let us clear our minds of the cobwebs of sentimental humbugs and cant and consider well under what banner we shall serve.

All the old, evil problems of a corrupt and decaying civilisation are with us to-day, even as they were yesterday. Woman slavery, the double moral standard, the sweating and exploitation of women, the violation of children, vice, intemperance, political corruption, and the loathsome disease – these are the real dangers which threaten the nation's life. How often and how vainly have we appealed to the people to come to our aid and help us in the struggle to save the Nation from destruction; but men refused to leave their work or their play or their political squabbles to listen to our cry. Now that the nations are at war, blinded with fury and mad, unreasoning rage against one another, these things and every other rank and poisonous weed will flourish exceedingly and take on a new lease of life because some who might have protested against wrong and roused the public conscience have proved false to their trust and abandoned their posts to pursue some worthless will-o'-the wisp. This nightmare of horror shall pass, but the grim realities and tragedies of life will remain; we shall continue to cry out against them, even though we stood alone in a world gone suddenly mad. Already a new generation of women come thronging behind us. We must not lay down our arms now and pass on to them only a heritage of failure and defeat. To us they look for guidance and inspiration. We must not fail them, we dare not fail them!

Editorial: War upon War

5 DECEMBER 1914

Of the many movements towards peace which have been started in different quarters since the war began, that initiated by Mrs Pethick-Lawrence seems to be the most fruitfully active. Setting out from one of the belligerent countries, Mrs Lawrence recognised that the idea required to be transplanted to a neutral country before it could develop and grow. In the United States she has found the needed seed-plot for these ideas, which will be again transplanted to Europe as soon as they are sufficiently developed to stand the frosts of belligerency. While other suffrage leaders were allowing themselves to be stampeded into mere relief work, or even into active participation in the crimes of the war-mongers, Mrs Pethick-Lawrence has maintained the true path of the organised suffrage movement – to preserve neutrality as between the combatant nations, but to wage war on War itself and the spirit of war. Last week and this week we publish some accounts of her American tour, and further details will appear in further issues. We hope Irish Suffrage Societies will associate themselves with this campaign.

It differs from former peace movements in two main points. First, that it is militant in spirit. Hitherto, the war-mongers have had things pretty much their own way. They have set war before themselves as a desirable object; they have spared no pains to prepare for it; and in preparing for it they have made it inevitable. The pacifists, on the other hand, have for the most part contented themselves with deprecating talk; they have trusted to the spread of an educated public opinion to put an end to war; they have not realised the necessity of vigorous action to prepare peace, and they have accordingly been swept aside with ease by the war-mongers when the critical moment came. The new movement is to be militant against war; it is to set about creating and constructing Peace, and placing it on a sure and permanent footing. To this end – and here is the second distinguishing point – it proposes to call in the forces of organised womanhood, everywhere the greatest sufferers by war, the most opposed to war, and the least consulted as to war. Women's equality with men in all public affairs is an essential of the new movement. Its motto is 'Suffrage First'; but it proposes to show women how, with the weapon of the suffrage, they can sweep away war – just as of recent years much of the suffragist propaganda was (rightly) devoted to showing how the vote would aid women in dealing with prostitution.

The movement initiated by Mrs Pethick-Lawrence is making headway in the United States. Apparently it is being organised not as a new society of individuals but as a grouping of societies – this saves energy and gives power; no Woman Suffrage Society, whatever its precise shade of policy, need hesitate to link itself up with the principles embodied in this movement. There are to be three definite stages in the campaign, starting from the Convention to be held in January. First, a campaign to be held throughout the United States (here the great strength of the women's organisations, especially in the states where women vote, will be used to advantage), culminating in a delegation to President Wilson. Secondly, a delegation to visit all the neutral States of Europe, urging them to co-operate, through their Governments, in carrying out the principles of the movement. Thirdly, a direct appeal, backed up internationally, to the belligerent Governments, with suggestions as to the principles on which peace may be based and maintained.

As it is important to keep before us the principles of the movement we reprint the propositions in which they are embodied. These have been received with enthusiastic approbation at Mrs Lawrence's meetings in New York, Boston, and Washington, and groups have been formed to carry on the work. The Washington papers in particular have taken up the scheme warmly, and have given great prominence to Mrs Lawrence's ideas. We invite the opinions of our readers on the scheme, and on the part which Ireland can play in furthering it.

'To organise public opinion and bring its pressure to bear upon the Governments of the world to the following ends:

1. The reinforcement of democracy by the inclusion into the articulate ranks of citizenship of the mother-half of the human race.
2. The construction of some constitutional machinery (where none exists) by which the democracies can exercise some control over foreign policy.
3. The ratification by the representatives of the people of all Treaties and Alliances with foreign Powers.
4. The nationalisation of all manufacture of armaments, and a veto on the export of ammunitions from one country to another.
5. The holding of the Allies to their slogan that this is a War to end War. Insistence that no province shall be transferred from one Government to another, without the consent of the population concerned, to be obtained by plebiscite – women as well as men to be included.
6. Representation of women as well as men at the Hague Convention.
7. The furtherance of International agreement that will put all the Powers back of any law-abiding nation that is aggressively attacked.
8. The furtherance of the construction of some form of European Senate of Nations, by which Nationalities can conduct negotiations for concessions or rights, and can bargain and exchange for necessary outlets, without being driven as the only alternative to seize what is vital to their development by slaughter and looting.'

The Chivalry of War

(An address delivered to the Ulster Socialist Party, Belfast)

by Margaret T. McCoubrey

27 FEBRUARY 1915

I

We live in an age in which sentiment rather than reason largely controls our standards of morals and behaviour. This sentimental value attaches itself to certain words or phrases and is accepted unthinkingly by the multitude.

Since the outbreak of the present war we have had endless instances of this. The word 'Patriotism' has been used daily with but the loosest of meanings. We have talked vaguely about the 'Rights of Small Nationalities', 'Belgian Neutrality', and so on ad infinitum, and at least the masses of the people – those whom Nietzsche would designate the rabble – have little or no conception of all that lies hidden in a deep analysis of such words and phrases. Of course we have with us also the aristocracy, whose function it is to keep the rabble in subjection – the Supermen. This type at the moment is portrayed in such characters as that of the Prime Minister, the Secretary of State for War, and the First Lord of the Admiralty, a triumvirate inside the Cabinet who have assumed dictatorship and are now conducting and controlling the affairs of the country. The House of Commons at the present time is reduced to impotence.

They are part of the rabble, but being directly in touch with the Supermen they are entrusted with a mission, and that mission is to see to it that the rabble thinks as little as possible; to see to it that all the energy and life force of the rabble shall be used up in the struggle for existence, and that, therefore, the parrot cries of 'Patriotism', of 'Your King and Country Need You', shall be accepted without question and at their sentimental value.

The old satire said that in Napoleon's time the House of Lords did nothing, and did it very well. That reasonably expresses the function of the Parliamentary representatives of the male electorate at the present time. I should not, perhaps, think it worthwhile mentioning the fact, were it not that at the moment every woman in the country is, to some extent, contributing to that £8 a week which men's representatives are receiving for doing nothing, and doing it well!

Around no word in the English language has greater sentimentality gathered than around the word chivalry. Chivalry has been made an excuse for all sorts and conditions of injustice and barbarity. It is a word that is still used to gloss over and to hide the real crimes against womanhood. It is often said in laughing jest that the days of chivalry are dead and gone, and a superficial study of present day conditions would almost imply that the likely spoken words were in some measure true; but to those of us who believe that nothing in man or nature can be satisfactorily or reasonably explained except by the processes of evolution, that is not the case. Our standards change with changing years. Chivalry had its roots far back in the feudal system. It was an Ideal of Knightly behaviour, casting around womanhood (within certain limits, of course) a delicate halo of mystery. In the days of feudalism this ideal did much to counteract the contempt for womanhood encouraged by monasticism and the ascetic over-estimate of sex. True, in those days the fair lady, for whose favour the Knight would embark on the high adventure in which life itself might possibly be forfeited, generally belonged to the nobility. Chivalry then – no more than now – did not extend to the common women, the daughters of the people. But 20th century chivalry is hardly in a position to cry 'black' to the chivalric conception of feudal times on this account. To-day in good society we have the sugared despotism, the false heroics of a cheap politeness – supposed to be a tribute to true womanhood – supposed to be chivalrous – but in the underworld, amongst the women who earn, amongst the women whose sons are the food for cannon, the defence guard of the well-to-do and upper classes – amongst our women – the sugared despotism and cheap politeness are often dispensed with, and, as in the old days of feudalism, our mission on earth – in common with the mission of the husbands, fathers, and sons of our class – is to be the hewers of wood and drawers of water. Ours not to reason why. Ours simply to work – to bear unquestioningly more sons of empire, and to dream not of a civilisation which shall be a reality and not the mere surface varnish which present-day civilisation has proved itself to be.

The standard will change again. The time will come when chivalry will mean the care and the protection by the strong for all who are weaker either physically or morally. This new conception of chivalry will utterly abolish our existing systems for the maintenance of law and order: our gigantic farce called Courts of Justice, with their unjust administration. In those days there shall be no need for charitable organisations, for prisons, or for rescue homes.

This may seem to you like a dream of a tired present-day socialist. To me it is with equal certainty a vision of the standard which shall exist when women get their chance of wiping false ideas of chivalry forever off the slate – when women get their chance of being men's comrades and equals – not playthings, to be treated indulgently, nor yet economic slaves to be exploited and taken advantage of.

But to leave alone the past and the future, let us consider the present. I want to-night to talk about the chivalry of war – or, perhaps, to be more accurate – the chivalry of the war – as it is not my intention to refer to any but the present war. We have heard much and read much on the questions of Britain's obligations to take part in this great European carnage. Arguments – both pro and con – have not been wanting. But one argument which has not been voiced to the extent it ought to have been, which has not been considered at all by those superior beings, those Supermen – the diplomats who made the war, but who are not the men found in the front fighting line – is the argument that with anything like a true conception of chivalry, war would not have been declared by any civilised country without first of all consulting the womanhood of that country on the question.

In the past women have always borne part of the weight of war, and the major part. In primitive times women suffered for the destruction of the fields they had tilled and the houses they had built. In more modern times women, in taxes and material loss and additional labour, have borne equally with men the cost of war; and I need hardly refer to what women as nurses have done –

since the days of Florence Nightingale until now – to alleviate suffering and pain, and to preserve, if possible, that mysterious force called life which, at times and seasons, men value so lightly. Women's relation to war is so intimate, so personal, so indissoluble, that had chivalry existed at all she must needs have been consulted. Men have made the boomerangs, the maxim guns, the Zeppelins, and the other murderous appliances of modern warfare. Women produce the primal munition of war, without which no other would exist. Women pay the first cost on all human life.

What, think ye, would be the thought of a woman who looked down on a battlefield of slain and wounded? It would not be 'there lie so many Germans, so many British, or so many French'. It would be 'so many mothers' sons! All our service of motherhood gone for naught – that an acre of ground may be manured with human flesh where next year the green grass shall grow and the red poppies gleam redder than before!'

On the day when woman takes her place beside man in the government of affairs, shall be heralded the death of war as a means of settling human differences. In the manhood and the womanhood of the future no tinsel of trumpets or flags will seduce into the insanity of recklessly destroying life, nor gild the wilful taking of life with any other name than that of murder, whether it be the slaughter of the million or of human beings one by one. Not because women lack courage, not because we admit even physical incapacity, not because we assume higher virtues than men, will women declare against war, but solely and simply because women alone appreciate at its highest the value of human life.

As Olive Schreiner so aptly says: 'To the male, the giving of life is a laugh; to the female, blood, anguish and sometimes death. Here we touch one of the few yet important differences between man and woman.' The war to my mind indicates clearly our false ideas of chivalry, and emphasises the fact that the sentimental value put on the word means nothing.

During the past six months, in which the war drums have rattled us back to barbarism, let us examine the chivalry of war. I am not in a position to deal adequately with what has happened in neighbouring countries. We hear tales of atrocities too sickening to repeat. We hear of outrages of all kinds on women and on children and helpless non-combatants. 'This', says the War Lords, 'is the chivalry of war'; and the War Lords, by the way, are not all in Germany. No doubt German soldiers have perpetrated atrocities on the weak and helpless.

But, with even a limited store of knowledge of what happens within our own borders, I am not prepared to take a brief for the stainlessness of the honour of all British, French and Russian soldiers. I shall not, however, attempt to deal with the fate of women and children – under the chivalry of war – in countries where actual fighting is taking place.

The Chivalry of War
by Margaret T. McCoubrey
6 MARCH 1915

II

Of what has happened in our own country we may speak with certainty. The first striking event is, that after war had been declared without women being consulted, there went up a chorus of supplication from Church and from State, from landlord and from capitalist, to women to come and help. Our many avenues of usefulness were even detailed. The woman of means, the woman of leisure, the woman with no money, the poor and rich alike must needs throw themselves into the breach and help men in their muddle. And women, even some of the finest, the best, and the most intellectual, were overwhelmed by their country's calamity.

With that spirit of self-sacrifice, which in many ways has been woman's undoing, just as it has been her crowning glory, women gave and are giving ungrudgingly and spontaneously the service demanded – not the least of the sacrifice being the fathers of their children and the sons of their own body.

One would have imagined that the chivalry of war would have been such that never in the history of the world had women been so honoured. But was it so? Think back to those early days of the war. Recollect all the fuss and trouble there was over separation allowances. Think of the pressure that had to be brought to bear ere the amounts were raised a fraction above their original disgraceful scale. Think what they are even now, after all the agitation, after all the pressure. The wives and children of the men who have responded to the call that their country needs them are receiving allowances proven to be utterly inadequate to maintain physical fitness. Nor is that all. Another triumph of war chivalry was the War Office circular empowering the police to supervise the women receiving allowances – because, forsooth, so much unaccustomed wealth might be squandered! To save women from themselves, the public-houses also are closed to the temperate sex at certain hours of the day. Not content with that, the chivalry of war has allowed the capitalist to take advantage of the exigencies of warfare to raise the price of every necessity of life. What does that mean? Simply slow starvation for thousands, mainly for little children.

Julia Dawson tells us that 'Two ounces of mother's milk a day will enable a child to grow strong'; but because of existing conditions – because many women have to go out to work instead of nursing their babies, thousands must die for want of those two miserable ounces of milk. And many members of the Labour Party have gone recruiting; and Christabel Pankhurst has gone to America to tell the people there how bad and wicked the Germans are; to explain that Britain, France and Russia are the countries where flourishes the Higher Civilisation and a fine Idealism; and the Union of Democratic Control believes women ought to help to bring about a constructive and lasting peace – and later on in the never, never land, and the never, never time, when there is nothing more important to be done, 'we will give you the chance to fight for those two miserable ounces of mother's milk'. That is all part of the chivalry of war.

We have had, too, quite a serious proposal to revive the C.D. Acts and State Regulation of Vice. Plymouth Town Council occupies the proud position of making this chivalrous suggestion. Mr Asquith hastened to assure women that no such Act of Parliament would be passed during the war. And immediately after the pledge had been given, there was the disgraceful occurrence at Cardiff. Of course, we are under martial law, and Colonel East, Commander of the Severn Defence, was quite within his rights when he prohibited certain women to be out of doors between the hours of 7 p.m. and 8 a.m. Under the Defence of the Realm Act, five women were court-martialled by the military authorities.

Why should the chivalry of war decree that those women should be victimised and harried when the men who make their existence possible are not checked or restricted in any way. If some of our gallant defenders are found to be unable to control themselves, why not confine them to barracks, instead of penalising and court-martialling women? The commanding officer's plea was the health of the troops – not, mark you, the morals. Dare we even whisper 'German atrocities'? Our regiments evidently have at least a sprinkling of this sensual type of manhood.

If he cannot be trusted in our own towns to behave properly, what do you expect from him when the dogs of war awaken the beast and lust runs riot in his veins? Since the outbreak of the war many of our magistrates have been so chivalrous (to men) that they have acquitted perpetrators of shameful assaults on little girls, on the grounds that the man had joined, or would join, the Army.

In the good old days, when people had nothing else to talk about, we were told – 'Well, you know, if you women got the vote you'd lose a lot. Men would not get up and give you their seats on the tram-cars – not pay your fare – nor lift their hats – nor put you to the inside of the pavement – nor open a door for you – nor let you enter a room first.' Let us get away from this mawkish sentiment. From it springs this chivalry of war, which you will agree with me, is damnable. And it is high time Socialist and Labour men did more than avow their belief in the equality of the sexes.

The fight that we women should be waging to-day is not the fight against German militarism – it is the fight against militarism at home. That is our nearest enemy, and as dangerous to childhood and womanhood as is the German Hun.

Let us look at the chivalry of war from the economic point of view as it affects women. It is, of course, beyond dispute that thousands of women are out of employment owing directly or indirectly to the war. That in itself involves suffering and want. During the past fortnight much controversy has taken place over the agricultural labourer.

In some places there is a shortage of labour. But instead of allowing this to be an opening for some of the women thrown out of work, forcing the farmer to give them the same wages as the men, there is a shameful proposal that the tragedy of child-labour shall again be re-enacted in this country. Happily, the agricultural labourer, in some places, is waking up. He knows what life on the land has meant to him – endless toil, absolute lack of opportunity, and wages which don't in many cases keep body and soul together. And some of the men are objecting to their sons following in their father's footsteps.

The Trade Unions are also up against the problem of allowing women to come into trades which have up to now been considered the province of the skilled workman.

The whole question is fraught with difficulty from the point of view of the men. By steady, slow degrees the strong Unions have bettered their conditions. They have not, however, had foresight and vision. Their leaders have not concerned themselves with the wages and conditions of the unskilled worker, and the labourer, whose position is in many cases irrevocably bound up with that of the skilled artisan. During recent years Trade Unionists have stood aside and allowed women to fight a strenuous battle for political freedom, which we firmly believed would make for better economic conditions. We have shouted ourselves hoarse on the question of equal pay for equal work. We have pointed out that where women had been forced to come in and do work previously done by men at a lower rate of pay, it was the employer who benefitted – not the women. And if the suggestions made by Mr Tennant are carried out, and women are employed at a lower rate than men, Trade Unionists have themselves to blame, in that they have failed to fight for the principle of equal pay for equal work. Suffragists, at any rate in this matter, have clean hands.

We have denounced a Government which sees to it that the fair wages clause is observed where men's labour is concerned, and allows women to be sweated iniquitously on Government contract work. Judging from the experiences of the past months, one can hardly imagine that the chivalry of war will demand for women equal pay for equal work. It is quite possible that their labour may be used in the interests of the Government, and incidentally (of course) to the benefit of the capitalist. That is conceivable. But I am more and more convinced that so long as we are hampered by a political disability, so long will present ideas of chivalry and fair play be the guiding standards of politicians and employers. Were there no other reason, that alone justifies a suffrage policy which, in time of war no less than in days of peace, demands Votes for Women – and Votes for Women Now! For only with the help of women dare you dream of true Internationalism; only with the help of the world's womanhood can the Ideal of a true and lasting Peace be realised.

Editorial: The Hague Congress

8 MAY 1915

Further information as to the circumstances in which the Government issued permits to twenty-four women to travel to Holland for the Hague Congress fully confirms our view that the permits were deliberately withheld until there were no boats running. The best public exposure of the Government's action was made in the Herald, where it was pointed out that while all permits issued were for the Tilbury route, the mails continued to run all through the week from Harwich. The British Committee seems to have taken the Government's action altogether too quietly. We are glad to learn that a protest meeting is to be held in Dublin. We publish a special article by Mrs Sheehy Skeffington on the subject and also the text of the questions asked in the House of Commons.

Of the Congress itself very little news is to hand. The Irish Press virtually ignored it. The reports in the English Press were of the most meagre character, and written with an evident bias against the objects of the Congress.

No official report is yet to hand. From these reports, supplemented from the French Press, it is possible to give merely an outline of proceedings. Miss Jane Addams presided and the total attendance of members and visitors is estimated at between 1,000 and 2,000, mostly Dutch. There were 44 (some reports say 48) delegates from the United States; the number of German delegates is variously given at 28 and 35; there were 15 Austrians (another report says 4 from Austria and 16 from Hungary), 16 from Norway, 10 from Sweden, 7 from Denmark, 4 or 5 from Belgium (who were permitted by the German authorities to attend, on condition of returning at the close of the Congress), 2 from Italy, one each from Russia, Poland, Spain and Brazil. There were none from France; but the French women interested in the Congress sent an important message of sympathy; it would appear that travel facilities were denied to them as to the British delegates. Miss Chrystal Macmillan and Miss Courtney represented the British Committee, and Mrs Pethick-Lawrence was also present. It would seem that, in addition to these, a British follower of Miss Christabel Pankhurst obtained entrance into the Congress in order to disturb it.

This conclusion is suggested by the fact that, on the closing day of the Congress, a British 'delegate', whose name is given in one report as Miss Amy Lillingston, made a Jingo speech, declaring that for every woman in England who wanted to attend the Congress a thousand wanted to go to France and fight! One report states that the Italian women were prevented from coming through Germany; but one of the two Italian delegates present said that the women were 'fearful' of coming owing to the possibility of Italy becoming involved in the war.

On the first day (Wednesday April 28) the Congress adopted resolutions (1) protesting against the madness and horror of war; (2) protesting against the wrongs done to women in war, and against the assertion that war means the 'protection' of women; (3) demanding equal political rights for both sexes, as one of the surest means of preventing future wars; (4) advocating the promotion of mutual understanding and goodwill among the nations; (5) urging the education of children should be directed towards the ideal of constructive peace; (6) demanding that future international disputes should be referred to arbitration or conciliation.

On the second day, two important resolutions were carried; one demanding democratic control of foreign policy (by both men and women) and declaring that all secret treaties should be null and void; the other declaring that no transfer of territory should take place without the consent of the inhabitants. Under this heading, some attempts were made to discuss the particular cases of Belgium, the Trentino, Finland, Poland and Alsace, but these references were ruled out of order. To this resolution the words were added 'and the Congress demands the autonomous democratic representation of the people'.

On the Friday the Congress came to grips with the question of the present war. A resolution was adopted, expressing sympathy with all who were suffering from the war, 'because all the peoples engaged in the present war believe they are not waging an aggressive war, but one in defence of their national existence'. The resolution went on to call upon the various Governments 'to end this bloodshed and open peace negotiations'. It was declared that peace, to be lasting, should be based on the general principles already accepted by the Congress; and, on the motion of one of the Belgian delegates, the phrase 'peace with justice' was incorporated in the resolution.

On Saturday, May 1st, the Congress closed with an important decision, which appears not to have been adopted unanimously. It was decided to elect an International Delegation, composed of women representing both neutral and belligerent nations, to convey personally to the heads of all the neutral States of Europe, and to President Wilson, the Congress Resolution calling for the termination of the present war. It would seem (though on this point we have only a casual allusion in one French paper to guide us) that arrangements were also made to keep the machinery of the Congress in existence, as the nucleus of the Women's International Peace Party.

CHAPTER 4

Women, work and class

It would be easy to dismiss the Irish suffragists as a group of well educated, middle-class women who wanted the vote for themselves and paid little attention to the needs or rights of ordinary working women. Certainly some of the most famous suffragists were middle-class women who were brought up in Dublin's genteel suburbs. They perhaps had little contact with working-class and rural women, with the exception of their own servants. Nonetheless, having such a background did not necessarily make them insensitive to the plight of the working classes. As Rosemary Cullen Owens says of Louie Bennett: 'Despite her solid bourgeoisie background, there can be no doubting her commitment to promoting the status and conditions of women workers' (2001: 59). Here we will examine in detail suffragists' attitudes to work, class, wages and trade unions, as discussed through the lively debates in the *Irish Citizen*. And as we shall see, their perceptions of issues around class and waged work were by no means clear cut.

There was great division among the suffragists. As we have already seen in earlier chapters, some, such as Margaret McCoubrey and Marion Duggan, held radical socialist attitudes towards class and sharply criticised the middle-class prejudices of their fellow suffragists. However, the pages of the *Irish Citizen* also offer hints of more patronising attitudes towards the working classes and attempts to justify the middle-class base of the suffrage movement. These debates, recorded for posterity in the pages of the *Irish Citizen*, provide us today with a good insight into the varied kinds of women who were active in the suffrage movement.

We can see that while appealing to working-class women for support, some suffragists failed to understand the problems experienced by Irish working women. These debates also enable us to come to a better understanding of feminism within the suffrage movement. A close reading of the *Irish Citizen* suggests that many suffragists not only called themselves feminists but believed that their movement, far from being a simple campaign for the vote, was actually a feminist movement. However, this brand of feminism may not always have accommodated the needs of working-class women.

This analysis by the *Irish Citizen* is important and informative not simply because it tells us about the suffragists but also because it offers an account of

Irish society in the early 1900s. Accounts of factory conditions, rates of pay and trade union campaigns provide an unusual insight into an aspect of Irish history that has been understudied (for a discussion, see Ferriter, 2010).

The extracts that I have chosen from the *Irish Citizen* provide a good indication of the problems faced by women in factories in Belfast and Dublin, and perhaps go some way to challenging the myth of Irish women as primarily wives and mothers in cosy homesteads (Clear, 2000). In Belfast, for example, by the early 1900s, over 50,000 women were working in the linen industry in conditions that were described by contemporary observers as 'horrendous' (Kleinrichert, 2007: 191–2).

But the *Irish Citizen* extracts also indicate the gaps that existed not only between the middle-class suffragists and working-class women, but between the middle class and working class generally in Ireland at that time. In the years before Eamon de Valera's Ireland came into being, and images of small farmers came to dominate the Irish imagination and national identity (see Ryan, 2002), class divisions did exist (Ferriter, 2010). Contrary to the myth, our foreparents were not all people of no property who 'endured the same hardships, ate the same food, feared the same landlord' (Cronin, 1985: 37). Class divisions in early twentieth century Ireland need to be taken more seriously and, in particular, the gendering of that class experience needs more research.

The extracts in this chapter from the *Irish Citizen* reflect the views of suffragists from a range of suffrage societies, many of whom were also active trade unionists. Their articles are interesting, therefore, because they draw links between feminism and class politics. For example, Louie Bennett, who spent some time as editor of the *Irish Citizen*, became general secretary of the Irish Women Workers' Union (IWWU). Winifred Carney, perhaps best known for her work with James Connolly in the 1916 Rising (see McAuliffe & Gillis, 2016), was also a suffragist and trade union organiser among the mill workers of Belfast. Along with other Northern women such as Mary Galway and Marie Johnson, Carney saw suffrage and trade unionism as key ways to overcome the exploitation of working-class women (see Kleinrichert, 2007). Marion Duggan, whose efforts to publicise the sexual abuse of women and girls were discussed in a previous chapter, was not only an active suffragist but also a member of the Labour Party, and her feminism had strong socialist overtones. Before presenting the extracts I wish to highlight some of the key arguments, raised by suffragists, concerning class and workers' rights.

Class bias and the suffrage movement

From the very beginning, work and the plight of working women were major concerns of the *Irish Citizen*. Articles, editorials and letters regularly addressed these topics. For example, on 28 December 1912 Meg Connery wrote to the paper claiming that suffragism was only one aspect of feminism. She argued that while the campaign for votes was perhaps the most visible manifestation of the movement, all over society women were revolting against conventions and against employers. This movement was, according to Connery, based on the great ideal of the 'unity of humanity'. In this lengthy, two-part article, which was originally a speech to the Dublin branch of the Independent Labour Party of Ireland, Connery asserts that she has been to tenements in the city and witnessed the poverty and hardship endured by families. She wonders how husbands can bear to see their wives so over-burdened and worried by the 'crowd' of 'puny' children they have to feed and care for. Why, she asks, do husbands continue to inflict this repeated suffering on their wives with no thought for their health or the well-being of their growing numbers of children?

This question can be viewed in several ways. It could be seen as an argument for some form of birth control and thus a snipe at church doctrine on family planning. However, it could also be interpreted as a plea for self-control and the need for more self-discipline among the lower classes. In either case, her observations about the living conditions of families who shared one, over-crowded room in a Dublin tenement may well have been quite shocking to middle-class readers.

Connery agreed with the accusation that the women's movement was predominantly middle class. She justified the predominance of middle-class women in the movement on the grounds that it was these women who were denied any useful occupation, and so they were the ones most immediately threatened with 'social extinction'. Working-class women, on the other hand, being closest to oppression, were most overwhelmed by it. They had neither the time to think about it nor the freedom to do anything about it. She saw the working-class woman as the most oppressed and 'exploited slave on the face of the earth'. While this sounds rather patronising, her point of view is clear. Women must organise and demand change in society. But it is middle-class women whom she felt were the best equipped to take on this struggle.

This article illustrates the view that the vote was not an end in itself but only one aspect of a wider feminist movement, a subject already explored in chapter 1. In addition, this article shows the way in which some, at least, of the active middle-class suffragists perceived working-class women. Indeed, the whole issue of class is one that has plagued the history of the suffrage movement. In her autobiography, Margaret Cousins claimed that the IWFL, of which she was a founder member, included people from all classes and helped to break down social barriers (Cousins, 1950: 166). However, Meg Connery, also a leading member of that group, claimed it was predominantly middle class. Meanwhile, Helena Moloney of the IWWU claimed that the suffrage movement was elitist and had little appeal to the majority of Irish women (cited in Fox, 1935). In her research on suffragism and trade unionism in Belfast, Denise Kleinrichert (2007) has explored the challenges of mobilising women mill workers in the early twentieth century. Despite the best efforts of campaigners like Mary Galway and Winifred Carney, women factory workers were wary of participating in any organised movements. In the words of Mary Galway: 'so many hundreds of women and girls, knowing that their weekly wage is all that stands between them and starvation, are terrified to do anything that might deprive them, even for one week, of that wage' (cited in Kleinrichert, 2007: 196).

The socialist Marion Duggan also had some interesting points to add on the subject of class. Writing on 8 August 1914, she said that the furious debate between militants and non-militants within the suffrage movement was misleading, as this was certainly not the main dividing issue within the movement. The real split was between 'universal suffragists', who wanted votes for all women, and the 'high-franchise suffragists' who wanted votes for middle-class women. The main body of this article has been discussed in the chapter 1, but for our present discussion a few points are important. Duggan argued that if only middle-class women got the vote then working-class women would be dependent on the bounty of these women to make fair decisions and influence fair laws concerning working conditions, wages and other issues. Duggan feared, however, that such 'ladies', once enfranchised, would only seek the aggrandisement of their own class. Instead, she asserted: 'I would like to see the forward suffrage policy of tomorrow decided by Labour suffragists, militant and non-militant' (8 Aug. 1914).

In addition to her membership of the Labour Party, Duggan also played an active part in the Irish Women's Reform League (IWRL), which was especially concerned with class politics and trade unionism. It was this group that kept the *Irish Citizen* readership informed of labour and class issues by its regular reports on these topics. In August 1913, Miss E.A. Browning reported on the findings of a study carried out by the IWRL on women's wages in Dublin. She was particularly concerned by the high level of ignorance among middle-class women concerning employment issues and wage rates. She hoped to begin educating such women about the appalling exploitation of working women in Ireland. She described the policy of the IWRL: 'all women are sisters with common interests and common aspirations' (9 Aug. 1913).

Browning gave accounts of a number of strikes by women in Dublin and examined the working conditions and low wages that had prompted strike action. She concluded that working conditions would only improve if pressure was brought to bear on employers by women factory inspectors, women politicians and women in the legal system: 'Women everywhere, that is the need of our country ... Rise! You must free all others to be free.'

Marion Duggan returned to this subject on 20 February 1915. She claimed that some working-class women might see the suffrage campaign as a distraction from their aim of getting together with working-class men and forming a cooperative commonwealth. While arguing that women workers needed the vote, she recognised that it would do them little good unless they organised collectively. That would enable women to pursue the joint tactics of demanding wage increases by pressurising employers as trade unionists, and also by lobbying government as voters. Furthermore, Duggan returned to the thorny issue of class within the women's movement. Working-class women, in demanding the right to vote, cannot simply be led by middle-class women, she asserted. Working women had the right to make their own choices and fight their own campaign. Therefore, Duggan argued, suffragists must adopt: 'the staple basis of the thorough education of women workers themselves – to do things by themselves for themselves' (20 Feb. 1915).

This attitude is quite different from Meg Connery's 'profound pity' for the over-burdened working-class women, and it suggests that Duggan, Browning and the IWRL had a more sensitive approach to issues of class, which is unsurprising, given their involvement in the trade union movement.

Of course, it would be inaccurate to discuss women's work without addressing housework. The lot of the housewife in early twentieth-century Ireland, especially among the more disadvantaged classes of society, involved the gruelling effort of 'making ends meet' on a meagre income, as well as back-breaking domestic chores without the advantage of any labour saving devices (Clear, 2000). The *Irish Citizen* carried a number of articles on this subject.

For example, Meg Connery was very critical of those who saw house-keeping as a woman's primary duty. She argued that there was no reason why women were better suited to such work than men. The notion of housekeeping as a particularly feminine occupation had been used to justify the relegation of women to the domestic sphere. Women, she asserted, were subsequently denied education and professional training on the grounds that such were not required by mere housekeepers. Connery was particularly concerned about the isolation of women working alone within the home. She pointed out that women workers in every other area were increasingly organising into unions and demanding change. But houseworkers were forced to carry on alone. Her solution to the slavery of the housewife was collective housekeeping. Connery was especially critical of those feminists who had appointed themselves experts on the subject of housekeeping and yet had servants to do such work. She concluded her article by citing Oscar Wilde, who said that 'human beings were made for something better than disturbing dust' (July/Aug. 1920).

In the same issue of the paper, the editor, Hanna Sheehy Skeffington, also entered the debate. She argued that housework was not mindless drudgery and should not be undervalued. She said that domestic science must be accepted as a really important pursuit. If housework was done in an intelligent and practical way it could be just as attractive as any other job. In reply to the idea that women should be paid for housework, Hanna said that women were currently paid in kind for their work within the home. Houseworkers had more freedom than factory and shop workers. However, she then went on to address the 'servant problem' and women who grumble over their 'daily help'. This suggests that she was addressing herself to middle- class women. Judging by the some of the commentaries and advertising which regularly featured in the paper, it seems that the *Irish Citizen* frequently addressed a middle-class audience.

In August 1913 the paper published a short piece giving tips on addressing the public at outdoor meetings. According to the article one thing which all suffragists should avoid was that terrible admission: 'she knows nothing about working women'. Does this mean that middle-class campaigners generally did not know anything about their working-class sisters? Certainly, this was the view expressed by Miss Browning in her article cited above (9 Aug. 1913).

Undoubtedly, most of the paper's advertising was aimed at middle-class women with money to spend on expensive clothes. Prices of the goods advertised ranged from 10 shillings and 6 pennies for a pair of shoes to 63 shillings for an 'autumn costume'. At the same time, the *Irish Citizen* informed readers that the average weekly wage for a working woman was 4 shillings (2 Aug. 1913). However, it should also be acknowledged that the paper relied on the core support of some regular advertisers. Given its precarious position, decisions about advertising may have been driven by financial expediency.

While considerable space was devoted to working-class and trade union issues, working-class women were often depicted as 'other'. For example, there was a tendency to present them either as victims or as being dependent upon middle-class women for guidance and leadership. Having said that, however, it is necessary to acknowledge shifts in the paper's content and tone through its history.

Women, economic justice and trade unions

Over the years, the *Irish Citizen* gave increasing coverage to trade union issues. The paper also supported the 'equal pay for equal work campaign' (Aug. 1917; June/July 1919). For example, in the 'Current Comment' section of August 1917, the paper used the example of teachers doing the same work with the same qualifications to show the disparity in pay between men and women. The paper observed, somewhat humorously, that men and women do not pay different prices for food, according to their sex, so their pay should be equal for equal work. In other articles, the paper also tackled the common argument that women did not need as much pay as men because women, unlike men, were not supporting dependents. The paper challenged this view by citing evidence from Fabian Society research which found that over 49 per cent of women workers were using their income to support dependents (19 July 1913).

In January 1918, Louie Bennett wrote to the paper about the dramatic increase in the numbers of women active in the trade union movement. She remarked on the significance of this high level support for trade unionism among working-class women. Bennett urged the paper to devote more space to union matters and less to suffragism. By this time, the Representation of the People Act (1918) had granted limited enfranchisement to women.

Bennett went on to argue that there should now be more concentration in the *Irish Citizen* on 'the broader aspects of feminism'. While praising the paper for maintaining a pacifist stance throughout the First World War, she added that it should now realise that feminism and peace were not possible without economic justice. In reply to this article, the editor, Hanna Sheehy Skeffington, wrote that the *Irish Citizen* had 'always been the organ of economic justice for women', and added that the paper would be happy to publish any reports sent in by women's trade unions.

By 1919, the paper had all but become the organ of the women's unions, and Louie Bennett even suggested that the *Irish Citizen* would become their official organ. This never happened for various reasons, including financial problems and policy clashes between Louie Bennett and Hanna Sheehy Skeffington (see Levenson & Natterstad, 1986: 145). Nevertheless, in November 1919, the issue of working women and trade unions was receiving full coverage in the *Irish Citizen*.

This time it was a debate on the question of women-only trade unions versus mixed trade unions. Louie Bennett believed that a women's union was essential because mixed unions were dominated by men and male interests. Bennett argued that men, all men, from dukes to working men, shared the same human weaknesses. Therefore, women must unite to safeguard their personal and public interests. Bennett seems to be suggesting that men were innately different from women and that this difference made all men, regardless of their class background, similar to each other, while all women, regardless of class, shared similar interests. This argument appears to go against a class analysis of society that underlines the shared interests of working-class men and women. Instead, Bennett implies that women cannot rely on working men as allies who share their concerns or represent their best interests in mixed-sex organisations. Bennett has been described as 'a woman of great determination and strong character, with firm ideals regarding pacifism and women workers' (Cullen Owens, 2001: 59). However, her ideas on the women's trade unions were not shared by all women activists at that time.

Bennett's suggestion of women-only unions was challenged by Cissie Cahalan of the Linen Drapers' Assistants Association. She argued that the continued separation of the sexes would only lead to more antagonism (Dec. 1919). She believed that only capitalists would gain if men and women were divided into separate unions, because employers could then play one group of workers off against the other. It was through unity, not division, Cahalan argued, that a workers' republic could ever be achieved.

In understanding these differences, perhaps we should consider the backgrounds of these two women. Cahalan was one of the few working-class women who played an active part in the suffrage movement (Cullen Owens, 1984). As a working-class woman, Cahalan was perhaps more concerned with the class struggle than was the middle-class Bennett, who called for unity among women across class lines.

The *Irish Citizen* reported, with interest, the struggles by women to gain admission to all professions. As we saw in chapter 2, the paper was especially concerned about women gaining access to the legal profession. In addition, the paper supported equal pay and the rights of working women, be they married or unmarried (29 May 1915). It would seem that some feminists did not see any problem with married women being in paid employment. However, during the 1920s, the IWWU showed itself to be quite ambiguous on this contentious issue (Jones, 1988; Cullen Owens, 2001).

In January 1920, an article was printed in the paper entitled 'Duties of Women'. By this time a number of professions were beginning to admit women. The article argued that, as so many doors were opening to women, it was their duty to take advantage of these opportunities and not shrink away 'like violets'. Women, especially those who were well educated and had leisure time, should come forward and take up public office. Again the hint of class bias is apparent in such a statement.

In its latter days, when the paper came close to being the organ of the unions, it may well have had a significant readership of working women. But one cannot deny that most of those who wrote for the paper were middle-class, and had university degrees. The problem for researchers today is that, while Margaret Cousins assured us that working-class women were active in the IWFL, these working-class women have not left any accounts of themselves. It is usually middle-class people who write autobiographies or, at least, leave biographical material behind after their deaths. Unfortunately, if working-class women were involved in the suffrage movement, with a few exceptions like Cissie Cahalan, they have remained silent and been lost to history. However, there is some evidence that working women and poor rural women did attend suffrage meetings and did express their support for the cause (see Day's reports of tours in Kerry, 20 Sept. 1913, in chapter 1).

This discussion on work and class has attempted to further illustrate the diversity and range of suffragist viewpoints. As was discussed in chapter 1, suffragists did not all agree on who should be enfranchised. This chapter has suggested that there was some uncertainty about the precise role that working-class women could play in the campaign for enfranchisement. In addition, this uncertainty was underlined by a deeper disagreement about the relationship between class politics and gender politics. In other words, should all women unite as sisters sharing common goals? Or should working-class women join working-class men in pursuing common class interests? These difficulties and contradictions around 'sisterhood' were not unique to Irish women (Burton, 1995). Indeed, the notion of sisterhood, women's shared experiences across class and national boundaries, remains contentious for feminism today.

"The people that walked in darkness have seen a great light."—Isaiah ix., 2.

"Though few, we hold a promise for the race That was not at our rising."
—Meredith: A Ballad of Fair Ladies in Revolt

Extracts from the *Irish Citizen*

Editorial: The Sweated Women Workers of Belfast

28 DECEMBER 1912

We have received from Miss Winifred Carney, Secretary of the Irish Textile Workers Union, which has its headquarters at 50 York Street, Belfast, a copy of a manifesto addressed to the sweated women workers in the Belfast Linen Industry, with a request that we give it publicity. We gladly do so, to the extent permitted by our space. The manifesto begins by recalling to the women workers the admitted facts that:

> 'the conditions of your toil are unnecessarily hard, that your low wages do not enable you to procure sufficiently nourishing food for yourselves or your children, and that as a result of your hard work, combined with low wages, you are the easy victims of disease, and that your children never get a decent chance in life, but are handicapped in the race of life before they are born. All this is today admitted by every right-thinking man and woman in these Islands. Many Belfast mills are slaughter-houses for the women and penitentiaries for the children.'

It then appeals to the women who suffer from this slavery to do something to help themselves.

> 'Especially do we appeal to the Spinners, piecers, layers, and doffes. The slavery of the Spinning-room is the worst and least excusable of all. Spinning is a skilled trade, requiring a long apprenticeship, alert brains and nimble fingers. Yet for all this skill, for all those weary years of learning, for all this toil in a super-heated atmosphere, with clothes drenched with water, and hands torn and lacerated as a consequence of the speeding up of the machinery, a qualified spinner in Belfast receives a wage less than some of our pious mill owners would spend weekly upon a dog. And yet the spinningroom is the key to the whole industry. A general stoppage in the spinningrooms of Belfast would stop all the linen industry, factories and warerooms alike.'

The demands put forward by the Irish Textile Workers' Union are next enumerated:

'We demand that the entire Linen industry be put under the Sweated Industries Act, which gives power to a Trades Board, on which employees and employers are requested to fix the minimum wages for the whole. Under that Act the wages of women in the Clothing Operatives Trade has been already fixed at a minimum wage of 3d per hour. Until the extension to the Linen Industry or that Act, we demand and pledge ourselves as a Union to fight for a Minimum Wage of 3d per hour for all qualified spinners, proportionate increases for all lower grades in the Spinning-room, and increases in the piece rates for the Reeling-room and all departments in piece work; abolition of fines for lost time; all stopping to be at the same rates as the daily pay per hour. We also demand from Government the appointment of a competent woman Inspector for the Belfast District exclusively, in order that the inspection of our mills, factories, and warerooms may be a constant reality instead of the occasional farce it is today.'

When the manifesto goes on to claim that 'united action can secure every point in this modest programme within less than a year', we demur. We dislike any disencouragement of optimism, but we cannot shut our eyes to the fact that without political power to enforce their economic necessities, the sweated woman workers of Belfast are virtually powerless to secure the legislative changes which they demand.

Women and Labour
by Margaret K. Connery
28 DECEMBER 1912

I

Being portion of an address delivered to the Dublin Branch of the Independent Labour Party of Ireland.

What is called the Votes for Women movement is but a side-issue of a much greater and more far-reaching problem. It is true that the Votes for Women movement is the chief manifestation of Feminism in these countries, but, though public attention has been particularly focused on this one phase of Feminism, the girl who first defied the conventions by riding a bicycle, the most obscure girl student in the humblest back-room who is today struggling to fit herself for something better than being a shop assistant or a domestic drudge, the poorest and meanest woman anywhere who is revolting against the conditions of her life and longing for a chance to relieve its monotony – all these are part and parcel of the great uprising amongst women, just as much as is the most ardent Suffragette, although they may themselves be quite unconscious of the fact. I propose to consider some of the underlying causes of this revolt and social unrest amongst modern women.

The great ideal towards which all the best minds and hearts of this age are striving is an ideal of this unity of humanity; an attempt to substitute harmony for discord, love and help for hatred and distrust; in a word to aim at establishing the Kingdom of Heaven upon earth by recognising the divine principle of the universal brotherhood of man.

It must be obvious to every thoughtful mind that no serious realisation of these high aims is possible so long as one half of humanity (the woman half) remains sunk in servitude and degradation. Consciously or unconsciously, woman is being propelled forward by the mighty, unseen forces guiding and controlling humanity. She feels, sometimes dimly sometimes with startling vividness, that the future teems with great promise of splendid achievements for humanity, and that, however great the sacrifice and suffering it may involve for herself and others, her most urgent duty is to fit herself to take her full woman's share in the activities and possibilities unfolding themselves before the children of men.

It is as if the human race had suddenly come to a halt – a stopping place where it has got to decide finally whether it will go forward to the Promised Land, or sit down by the roadside and stagnate and die within sight of it. And it seems as if fate had decreed that to Woman it shall be given to make the choice; and Woman feels that she is called upon to make a decision of transcendental importance, not for the sake of her own sex only, but for the sake of the future of the Race whose guardian she is. It is only when man and woman stand side by side, helping and not hindering one the other, that the world can ever realise its dream of progressing upwards and onwards.

In primitive times when man and woman first wandered together, 'naked, newly erect savages', the labours of life were divided between them. The man hunted and fought; the woman bore the race, carried it on her shoulders, raised the rude dwellings within which it was sheltered; each had a share of labour, both were content. For a long time this division of labour continued. The woman hoed the earth and reaped the grain, shaped the dwelling and wove the clothing, studied the properties and uses of plants, so that the old women of primitive times were the first physicians of the race, as often its first priests and prophets.

Then changes began to take place. Men had become more numerous and more powerful, and it was no longer necessary that they should all devote themselves to hunting and fighting, so they began to take a share in woman's particular 'sphere' of labour. They built the houses and tilled the fields, and slowly but surely the hoe, the potter's tools and the grindstone, began to pass from woman's hands into man's till at length woman moved completely within the house walls, and left all things without to the care of men. But still in these days she had ample scope for all her energies; she wove the clothes of her household, baked the bread and brewed the ale, prepared simples and medicines; and her numerous children, from birth to manhood and womanhood, lingered around her fireside and kept her fully occupied.

In the course of ages another change came, vast and revolutionary, leaving nothing as it was. In modern civilised communities, machinery has everywhere taken the place of crude human labour. This is true of the country no less than of the city, of the arts of war as well as the arts of peace. Hence the most far-reaching changes in the field of human labour, and the present day male unemployment problem. For the man to-day who has nothing but the crude unskilled labour of his hands to offer to society there is practically no market. The demand of the twentieth century is no longer for brawn and muscle, but for brain and nervous force and mental capacity to do the world's work. But though man's field of labour has thus undergone a change, it has not contracted; on the contrary it has been infinitely extended. 'Never before', in the words of Olive Schreiner, 'in the history of the earth has man's field of remunerative toil been so wide, so interesting, so complex; never before has the male sex, taken as a whole, been so fully and strenuously employed'.

How has woman fared through all these changes? As the old forms of labour have grown obsolete or departed from her, has she found new outlets for her energy? Has her sphere of activity grown and developed side by side with man's? The opposite has been the case. Wherever the condition which is known as modern civilisation obtains, woman has been robbed of almost all her ancient field of labour, productive and social. Man has entered 'Woman's Sphere' and transferred almost all that was valuable and honourable in her domain to the world outside, and left to woman, his partner and fellow labourer from time immemorial, only the dregs and drudgery for her portion. And every attempt she has made to win her way into the new field of human endeavour to take her place again by man's side has been met by him with the most strenuous opposition. This is the modern Woman's Labour Problem.

The view is held by some that the labour problem confronting the modern woman and that before the unemployed modern man is identical. I have heard such a sentiment expressed by people in the Labour movement, who urged that women, instead of agitating independently, should throw in their lot with the men, or remain passive, and that the men in solving their own labour problem would at the same time solve the woman's. Mr Ramsey MacDonald's paper, the *Daily Citizen*, preaches some such fatuous doctrine; it amounts to this: 'You women, cease your clamour and put your trust in me and the other men; that way only salvation lies for you.'

But there is little or no resemblance between the male and the female labour problem. As the old fields of labour close up behind man, he has only one problem and one choice – he must find new fields of labour or die. Society will refuse ultimately to support large bodies of men in a condition of idleness or parasitism. If they cannot fit in with the new order of things, they must make way for a more skilled and intelligent type of man. The woman's problem on the other hand is not merely to find labour but to win the right to labour. 'The choice before her as her ancient fields of domestic labour slip from her is not often the choice of finding new fields of labour or death; but one far more serious in its ultimate reaction on humanity as a whole – it is the choice between finding new forms of labour or sinking slowly into a condition of more or less complete and passive sex-parasitism.' We have two examples of sex-parasitism before us to-day; namely the woman of the aristocratic class and the woman of the street. These two classes are really only divided from each other by a very fine line. They are alike in this; that they are denied all useful, honourable and remunerative occupation, and are maintained by men through the exercise of their sex-functions alone.

The wholesale parasitism of the Roman women was a fundamental factor in the decay of the Roman Empire. In European Turkey to-day we behold the same drama being played out. The women of the Turkish Harem are condemned by religion and custom to a life of odious inactivity and dependence; and the effete sons of these helpless parasites are to-day being swept away by men sprung from a race of active and courageous labouring women. Again and again successive societies of men have deluded themselves with the fallacy that it was only necessary to train and educate one-half of the race to play an honourable part in human affairs, and that it did not matter in the least if women were left to lag behind in a state of ignorance and incompetence; the growth and development of the male was all sufficient to guarantee the progress of humanity. Vain hope! 'Only an able and labouring womanhood can permanently produce an able and labouring manhood.'

Women and Labour

by Margaret K. Connery

4 JANUARY 1913

II

It is interesting to note in passing the curious tendency there is among some people in the Labour movement to fall into the same pitfall. They fancy they can go forward and scale the highest altitudes of human endeavour quite independently of women; and when they have themselves attained those giddy heights, they will graciously reach down a hand and lift woman out of the abyss to take her place beside them. These are the people who, confronted with such vast problems of our modern civilisation as poverty, drunkenness, vice, lunacy, disease, and every other symptom of race degeneracy, think that the reversal of the Osborne Judgment, or the Nationalisation of Railways, or some other pet scheme of their own, is charged with more vital importance to the nation than the emancipation of its womanhood.

We have seen that, owing to the invention of machinery, man's field of labour has been revolutionised and infinitely extended, and in the course of this process man has absorbed practically all woman's field of labour and denied her the right to advance side by side with him. We are all familiar with the parrot-cry of the anti-feminist who declares that woman must confine herself to her own proper sphere – that her place is the home; and that in the rearing and caring of children she has full scope for all her powers of heart and brain. The assertion that woman's sphere is the home, and that she need not go outside it in pursuit of honourable occupation, though profoundly true of the women of past generations, is when applied to the women of today, simply an antiquated lie.

Even in that sphere of work peculiarly and organically hers, the bearing and caring of children, Time has wrought changes. In the old days, the children grew up around their mother's knee till adult years were reached. Large masses of people were constantly demanded to perform severe physical labour, as every kind of work was done by human hands; and so very large families were the rule, and women were actively employed during the greater part of their lives in caring for, clothing, or feeding their families.

The introduction of machinery affected the position of woman in this her last great stronghold – her relation to the family. To-day there are thousands of women debarred from having any children, and many more who are restricted to having very few children, because the cost of rearing and training the modern child, if he is to survive and succeed, has increased enormously. In this matter of training, the individual mother has been deposed by central educational bodies, Boards of Education, and other authorities, mainly if not wholly composed of men. Amongst the wealthy classes the boy usually leaves the home at a very early age for the public school and the University; and thus passes wholly beyond the circle of his mother's influence. In the homes of the poorer classes, too, scarcely has the child passed beyond the first stages of infant life ere it is transferred from the mother's care to the teacher's, and gradually comes to be more and more withdrawn from the mother's control.

Viewed in the light of these facts, it becomes clear that woman's 'sphere' of domestic labour, once ample and all-sufficing, has contracted almost to vanishing point. For increasing numbers of women to-day there is no such thing as a domestic sphere: for those women engaged in the domestic sphere there is little left to accomplish that is either useful, beautiful or permanent – nothing save the sordid, soul-wearing drudgery of housework – and even this will be taken from them in course of time with the introduction of additional labour-saving devices. So that the woman at last becomes deprived of every form of honourable toil, and must inevitably sink into a condition of helpless dependence upon man – in a word, must develop into the human female parasite, 'the most deadly microbe that can make its appearance on the surface of any social organism'.

This then is what underlies the modern woman's passionate pleading for labour and the right to labour. If she may not grow and develop, and exercise all her powers of body and mind, she, and the race through her, are threatened with ultimate extinction.

Sometimes one hears the woman's movement sneered at as being a 'middle-class movement' by persons who appear to hold very advanced democratic theories – generally typified by the wearing of a very fierce red tie. It is quite true that the woman's movement had its rise and inspiration amongst the women of the middle classes. There are many good reasons for that. In the first place; this is the class of women most immediately threatened with social extinction, through being reduced to a parasitic condition for lack of useful occupation. These are the women who have been loudly knocking at the doors which debar their sex from the arts and sciences and the learned professions. From this class came the pioneers who bravely faced insult and violence in order to study medicine and open up this avenue of honourable work to women. Several other doors they have forced open, but many yet remain fast shut.

Is it likely that the inspiration and courage to found a great movement for liberty could have its beginning amongst the poorest, most ignorant, and most subject of all classes of women – the charwomen, the sweated factory hand, the labourer's wife? These poor slaves are bowed down too close to earth even to think of lifting their faces to the sun, until some who are given a little more room to grow, and a little more light to see the evil of woman's position, should loudly proclaim a message of hope and redemption to stir their heavy hearts. Many indeed are so bent beneath the yoke of their servitude that the very trumpet of the archangel could not arouse them. The same phenomenon may be observed in the male labour movement, some of whose most brilliant exponents are drawn from the middle classes – men like Bernard Shaw, H.G. Wells, Masefield, Galsworthy, and others – men of imagination and ideals.

The condition of the working woman to-day fills one with a sense of burning indignation and profound pity – especially the condition of the working-class wife and mother. Her life is one long-drawn-out chapter of suffering and privation, with scarcely even a gleam of joy or hope to brighten her dull horizon. I sometimes think the men of that class must be strangely lacking in humanity and tenderness towards the patient drudges who toil painfully through life beside them. I have been in a great many tenement houses: I have seen white-faced, over-worked, underfed women, living in one room, with a crowd of puny, ragged, half-starved children. And the thought would rise in my mind: had the man no pity for this poor, exhausted woman, that he should impose on her so much physical torture and sorrow; had he no pity for the hapless children he brought so recklessly into the world, for whom there was no welcome and no place prepared – to whom he had nothing to offer but cold, hunger, hardship and disease? Every child has the right to be well-born and well cared for; and every child's mother has the right to be well-trained and well-fitted physically and mentally for her tremendous task. The woman of the labouring class to-day, whether as industrial worker or as wife and mother, is the most exploited and overdriven slave on the face of the earth.

The need of rising her up and making her hard lot easier is the most pressing need of our day. The lower and more degraded her condition, the lower sinks the race she bears.

If the position of modern civilised woman be as I have tried to outline it, it may be asked, what is the remedy for this state of things? – what is the woman's demand? The reply may best be given in the words of Olive Schreiner, to whose pages I have so frequently been indebted in the preparation of this paper:

'We do not ask that the wheels of time should reverse themselves, or the stream of life flow backward. We do not ask that our ancient spinning-wheels be again placed in our hands, or our old grindstones and hoes be returned to us; or that man should again betake himself to the ancient province of man, the chase, leaving to us all domestic and civil labour. Neither do we ask that the children whom we bear shall again be put exclusively into our hands to train. This we know cannot be. The past conditions of life have gone forever; no will of man can recall them; but this is our demand: We demand that in the new, strange, world that is arising alike upon the man and the woman, where nothing is as it was, and all things are assuming new shapes and relations, that in this new world we also shall have our share of honoured and socially useful human toil – our full half of the labour of the children of Woman. We demand nothing more than this; and we will take nothing less. This is our Woman's Right.'

Editorial: Why Working Women Need the Vote

19 JULY 1913

The scandalous underpayment of women as compared with men for precisely equal work is mainly justified by a prevailing opinion that men do, whereas women do not, support dependents. In this connection the *Manchester Guardian* of July 4th contained an article from a correspondent embodying the results of an inquiry conducted by the women's group of the Fabian Society in England. The investigation, which was a summary of one thousands replies, ranged impartially over every variety of women worker, from 'the university graduate earning 500 pounds a year to the sweated industrial worker earning 6s. a week' and dealt alike with 'a rural district, a university, and the large and lesser manufacturing and country towns'. A conclusion, therefore, which seems to give a fair average for the whole country, is reached, 'that of the employed women in the United Kingdom rather over 49 in every hundred are spending part of their earnings in the maintenance of some other person or persons'. More especially does this appear to be true of the women in the poorer groups, among whom the average of such cases is, as might be expected, far higher than among the middle-class professional women, teachers, etc. Among laundresses in particular, the percentage reaches 86.2. The theory, therefore, so complacently accepted without examination by employers, headed by the

Government, 'that the needs of an individual woman form the proper basis of a woman's wage', is out of accord with the facts. The fallacy is symptomatic of the way in which the peculiar point of view of the unenfranchised is bound to be ignored to suit the convenience of those who have a vested interest in the established state of things. The Government and the employers will refuse to see the reason and the truth of the matter until they are forced to do so by the only pressure which counts, the pressure which makes an opinion a driving force, the pressure of the vote.

A particularly glaring instance of the truth of our contention is afforded by the Government's attempt, by an order issued on July 1, to cut down the wages of skilled tailoresses in the Pimlico Factory by about 1s. 6d. a week.

Last week's *Votes for Women* informs us that there have been already five successful attempts in two years to cut down the wages of the women, who are picked workers, and treating the moral of such phenomena in a leader remarks: 'No Minister of the Crown would dare to reduce … the wages of men in the employ of the Government, for they would alienate the whole of the Labour vote.'

It is, however, worthy of note that this scandalous bullying by a democratic Government provoked no protest from the Labour Party in the House of Commons. Of course not. The Labour members do not represent women, they represent men. And yet people can be found who say that votes have nothing to do with wages!

Women's Work and Wages in Dublin
by E.A. Browning
(Hon. Press Sec. Irishwomen's Reform League)
2 AUGUST 1913

I

It has been said that one half of the world does not know how the other half lives, and this is certainly true of the women of Dublin. What the eye does not see, the heart does not grieve for, and, so far the eye of the woman of the leisure classes has not seen, for instance, how the factory girl, in our own town, lives, or how she works, what in fact life means to her; and so the heart has not sympathised, and the head has not troubled to do more than accept without challenge, the first casual information that comes to hand.

The time for social apathy is past, and now that we are claiming to be citizens we lose our small individual sense of ease or dis-ease (as the case may be), and we assume the civic sense – the civic eyes and ears the civic heart and head – the civic consciousness in fact which registers the pulse of every member of the State. How we each live ourselves is no longer of sole and supreme importance, for we have become sensitive to the common needs and satisfactions, and find that the joy of one is a gain to all, and the suffering of one an injury to all.

True, we women are denied, so far, the hall-mark of citizenship, but what of that. Should not the stigma of exclusion rather make us eager to prove ourselves worthy citizens in all but name? What is happening in our town is ours to know, above all what is happening to our women, the voiceless members of our state, is even crying out for a hearing.

Recent articles in two of our daily papers – records as they are, or should be of our civic doings – brought to our notice that labour strikes had reached, in Dublin, the proportions of an epidemic, and that these disturbances were no longer confined to men, but that women workers were also affected. It was further stated that the discontent of these latter was most unreasonable, as the women had no real grievance, and that they were well paid, and that greed alone was urging them to demand an advance of wages. One of these strikes is being carried on in connection with Messrs. Somerset and Co.'s factory in Golden Lane, and from the *Irish Times* and the *Independent* we were supplied with the following details:

The factory, we were told (presumably Mr McKeefey, the manager, is the authority), was opened three or four months ago to carry on a fancy linen manufactory (embroidered linen cushion covers, cloths, bedspreads, etc); about 100 girls, quite ignorant of this work were taken on, taught and paid (piece work) so handsomely that quite a beginner earned 16/9 in a week, and – granted a girl was 'smart enough and clever enough' – she could earn 30/- a week; then an advance of over 50 per cent was demanded by the workers, and Messrs. Somerset and Co., 'thoroughly tired, no doubt, of the interminable vexations of conducting business in Dublin, have decided to close down their business and leave the city.' Bear the situation well in mind. Here is a city – a poor city – full of girls who need employment; they are taught a business at which they can earn up to 30/- a week, and do earn 16/, and yet after three months they strike for twice that amount; they expect an actual 30/- a week, and a potential 3 pounds! To anyone who knows anything of the Dublin working girls it is not convincing. From where has she imported such 'dreams of avarice'? Certainly they are not indigenous, for wages are lower here than in almost any other city, and 30/- a week is an unheard of sum for a factory girl anywhere. Can it be that the Dublin girls' expectations have been raised by what she hears from Belfast? There Messrs. Somerset and Co. pay their embroiderers 9d. a day for what they here pay 2 1/2d.

Be that as it may, the Irishwomen's Reform League came to the conclusion that the tale, as told by the Press, did not satisfy in the telling; the picture drawn of the factory was too rosy; the grasping nature of the factory girls too overdone it seemed likely that this question, like most others, had, at any rate, two sides to it. We had the manager's story, and, therefore, it could do no harm to try and hear what the discontented female striker had to say.

The information gathered is scrappy, but to the point.

Messrs. Somerset's factory is not a new establishment. The business has only passed into new hands; for many years it had been known as Taylor's. Mr Taylor was a Jew, and paid his girls fairly well as things go – but he got into bad health, and sold the business to the Belfast firm, Somerset and Co. The girls, therefore, were not raw hands; they did not require, and certainly there was not provided for them, the experienced teacher we read of. Four kinds of workers are employed – Needlewomen, embroiderers, pressers and clippers (who clip off the ends of the coloured thread), and it will be understood how the work of the latter must depend on that of the former.

Taken on an average 4/- a week is what many of the girls got, though a forewoman may rise to 10/-, and a typist to 12/6. On the other hand, one girl received 9d. for three week's work, another 11d. for 12 days' work, and another 6d. for a week, while three girls refused to return because of what they earned in a morning's work, namely 1/2d.

This more grim picture of the factory in Golden Lane goes on to show how pressure had to be brought to bear on the manager before the windows were even opened, or lavatories washed out, etc., and how the language – 'brutal' it had been called – of the manager towards the girls showed what he thought of them – a subject race who dare not rebel – wage slaves.

So the case stands – the women on strike demanding twice 4/- a week – Messrs. Somerset and Co. offering good employment with a wage of 16/- a week, or perhaps 30/-, and no one accepting it!

Let the civic consciousness decide: let it 'look on this picture and on that', and then may its voice be heard!

Women's Work and Wages in Dublin
by E.A. Browning
9 AUGUST 1913

II

The Irishwomen's Reform League has only one reason for bringing the labour disputes between women and their employers before the readers of the *Irish Citizen*, and that is a desire to help.

Trade Unionism, now an old weapon in the hands of men, is only just coming into existence as a power for good or evil in the working life of Irishwomen; and it would be a pity if the newer organisation had as long a battle before it as the older has had, without victory even yet in sight, either for masters or men – or, let us rather say, for the establishment of justice.

We are inclined to think history need not repeat itself; that there is no reason why the new broom of awakened womanhood should not sweep so clean, that the dust of slumbering ages will be brushed away, and that false relations between employers and employed will become first of all intolerable and finally impossible. And that result, we trust, will not long be delayed now that the suffragists have proved that all women are sisters with common interests and common aspirations.

Last week an account was given of a strike in Messrs. Somerset and Co.'s embroidery factory, and this week attention is drawn to another small woman's labour war. The trouble this time is between the Proprietor of the Savoy Cafe in Grafton Street and his chocolate makers.

These girls have most of them worked for Mr McMurty for some years, have been invaluable to him in helping to build up his confectionery business, and in spite of unpleasant conditions, such as an over-preponderance of rats, were fairly well satisfied with their employment. But lately Mr McMurty wished to introduce a new system which, as well as we can understand it, necessitated the making of three small chocolate centres at the same cost as one. The girls are paid by piece-work, and say the small centres would take as long to make as the large, and therefore their earnings would be cut down very considerably. Therefore they refused to work on the new terms. Subsequently they returned under an agreement which recognised and remedied their grievance; but then, under plea of slack trade, these girls were gradually weeded out, and new ones taken on who did not come under the agreement. The strike began again, and still continues, and is, we presume, one of those referred to as quite unreasonable in some recent articles in the daily Press.

The trouble has grown more serious lately, because the girls have joined a trades-union, and not only will they be therefore able to hold out longer, but the overcoming of their independence becomes a more serious matter. A manager may very likely dismiss a few unorganised girls, but it is quite another thing to face a labour union. Women's unions, however, being young, are consequently weak, and to come to satisfactory terms would encourage them. Here is where the need of some third and quite disinterested party is required to make public the facts on both sides, and state the most just solution; here is where public spirited women have their opportunity. The manager of the Savoy, or any other like concern, could not withhold from an influential board of women the full facts of his business, nor could the girls refuse to show why they were discontented.

The employers of female labour must be held responsible in any town to the rate-paying women of the town, and then the employed would soon learn to reflect credit on their sex should they not be doing so already.

But not only does this dispute bring prominently before us factory conditions, but it is making public some facts regarding the making of confectionery and the great need there would seem to be for a woman inspector to oversee and certify the cleanliness and purity of even the most expensive chocolates. It is scarcely fair to those who enjoy their 'candy' to repeat the details we have heard, and, besides, we hope they are exaggerated. We only want to emphasise how much there is to be learnt, how much to be done, that is already within our compass.

Factory inspectors – women factory inspectors – women law makers, women police, women on the jury, women lawyers, women everywhere that is the need of our country, that is the obvious explanation of the so-called superfluous woman – we need her!

'Rise! You must free all others to be free!'

Women Workers and the Vote

by M.E. Duggan, LLB

20 FEBRUARY 1915

I do not think I am saying too much in praise of the great majority of Suffragists – nay, even of some Antis as yet unconverted – in stating that they are most of them earnest seekers after truth and do not desire to back up their cause by doubtful facts and hazy generalisations. Of course we all know the type of person (sex indifferent) who, having made an assertion – say, that Votes and Wages have no connection – regards any attempt to alter his (or her) opinion a personal insult. In vain might authority after authority be cited. A self-willed person will stick to a bad argument, though Aristotle himself rose to confute it.

It would be derogatory to his or her own dignity to admit a mistake. That is why one so greatly admires a person who says frankly, 'I was wrong' or 'I don't seem to convince people; can you tell me why?' Now, I understand that some Irish suffragists are just a little perplexed about votes and wages. The arguments in favour of the theory that 'the Vote' could alter wages seem unanswerable; yet Trade Unionists don't seem quite convinced as to the immediate necessity of extending the franchise to women. Why so?

For this reason, Votes without Industrial Organisation are of little use to workers as workers. If you have sufficiently strong industrial organisation, the Trade Union and Co-operative Congresses will supplant Parliament as the place for settling Labour questions. As far as working-women go, see to it that they are well organised, and take advantage of their right to be represented at Congress.

Parliament is a worn-out, dying institution. (Those who heard Mr Tom Mann a year ago in Dublin will recognise whence I derived this point of view.) So reason men. But working-women, their leaders still think, need the Parliamentary Vote. Men's Parliamentary votes have protected and helped forward their Unions. Also, women must ask for every kind of vote that men have. Men do not admit women into all trades. This is due less to antifeminist prejudice than to a fear of being undercut. Women's low wages are bad for both men and women. To get admitted, women must first be strongly organised, so as to show men that they will not be undercut. The question of payment for wives will have to be settled, and there are other 'women's questions' which must, in the near future, come before Parliament. If Parliament is to dictate to women, women in turn must be the electors, not the serfs of Parliament.

The argument from expediency is often a low one; but I just want to point out that there are large numbers of 'Conservatives', 'Anti-Socialists', 'Employers', or what you will; to tell this kind of people that 'Votes' will alter wages is, to them, an argument against extending the Parliamentary franchise to women! They do not desire to see wages increased, or to take working women 'out of their station in life'. 'What!' cries an indignant suffragist, 'am I not to tell these people the truth?' To this, a trade unionist – at any rate a follower of Tom Mann – will point out that it is a big mistake to let Conservatives think that by refusing the Parliamentary Vote to women it is possible to keep back and destroy the hopes and aspirations of the working classes. Leave to the anti-social reformers their dear old Parliament run by peers and millionaires! The workers will all the more turn to Parliaments of their own. If they cannot vote, they will strike! In co-operation lies the possibility of transferring industry from employers to workers. Capital and land are essentials, but capitalists, employers and landlords are gradually being dispensed with. Think of the revolution to be caused by all dressmaking being done in Co-operative workrooms run by Trade Unions.

Of course, if working men had not the Parliamentary vote, trade unions, cooperative societies, strikes, might all be completely illegal. This is what, I think, Anti-Suffragists mean when they say that men's votes protect working women i.e. women can avail themselves of the right to strike, won by men's votes. When an Anti asserts this truth, admit it, but suggest that women may not want to strike, and ask where was that particular Anti during the Dublin Labour troubles. It's mighty easy for comfortably off Anti-Suffragists to talk about 'trade unionism', but it's a long, long way to Liberty Hall; and, in practice, the Anti stays at home, reads leading articles about 'paid agitators', and abuses the 'ignorant, uneducated girls', quite forgetting that she herself has told the universe that votes were useless, and that workers must rely on organisation!

Some trade unionists (mostly French) deny the need for the Parliamentary Franchise. I myself understand English and Irish leaders to think it is necessary, but that in future, owing to stress of Parliamentary business, power will pass more and more into the hands of organised workers. 'The Vote' really means 'the right to vote', and that right must be claimed, and is actually needed in respect of any kind of 'Parliament' or Congress dealing with human affairs. As the years go by, men and women learn from past experiments.

To quote Tom Mann again: the first boat in which our ancestors ventured from the shore was a poor affair compared with a modern liner. But it was not a failure. In making it and its successors, the art of shipbuilding was discovered. Repeated trials made for success. Workers in the past may have tried in vain for shorter hours, for wage boards; may have had sectional strikes and isolated co-operative workrooms. These failed in a way, certainly but they have shown the need for federation; for co-operative rooms not for some, but for all dressmakers; for the abolition of private ownership of the means of production. To sum up:

For women workers, Parliamentary votes without organisation are of little use. (Organisation here includes voting together.)

If organised, they can do a great deal, some say all, without votes for Parliament. Votes for Congress they must have. A Mohammedan would deny this!

When organised, women will be fit to use the Vote, and will appreciate the need for it.

When enough women ask for the Vote, many believe they will get it. In the last ultimate bed rock of things women must be consulted somehow, because their consent is necessary in order to continue the race. Our habit of not speaking plainly has caused us to not think plainly. Women cannot be governed by force, because as a medical fact, force applied to an expectant mother will kill her child.

You can kill women by force, but you cannot thereby prevent them killing their children and themselves.

When women have recognised the need for the Vote, they themselves must decide how best to get the Vote, by full, frank, free discussion.

Some working-class representatives object to the modern movement, more especially militancy, because it tends to divert and side-track the attention of women-workers from their ultimate end – the establishment of the Co-operative Commonwealth! You must go straight for the big thing.

(The suffrage movement might be to rich women what the Unionist cause is to Ulster employers.) But in this Commonwealth women are to be in every way equal (i.e. having equal opportunities with men). Again, whatever their theory, workers' representatives in Parliament must vote for practical reforms, of which 'the vote' is one. To some of us, Trade Unions seem the right place to go in order to work for suffrage. It seems better to stick to the right way, though seemingly slow, than to be attracted by the excitement and glamour of new remedies, which are not founded on the staple basis of the thorough education of women workers themselves – to do things by themselves for themselves.

Current Comment: A Boom in Trade Unionism

AUGUST 1917

Presently we shall see emerging into public life in Ireland a class as yet unheard in this country, the women workers.

The last six months has seen a growing sense of independence and of 'push' amongst the women workers. Long held down by fear and miserable conditions, they have aroused at last to the realisation that their fate is in their own hands and that they have in trade unionism a force to control it. Consequently, they are organising now with all speed. The Irish Women Workers' Union is increasing its membership in leaps and bounds. The

Amalgamated Society of Tailors and Tailoresses have the splendid help of Mrs Pete Curran in organising the tailoresses and dressmakers for the past few weeks and have added 500 women members to their Union in that short time. With equal enthusiasm the Munition workers have rallied to the Women's Federation. Obviously these women are going to prove themselves a new force in Irish affairs which no class of politicians can ignore. They have intelligence and ideas: they are gaining courage. In a little while Irish life will feel their influence.

Current Comment: Treatment of Women

AUGUST 1917

In the findings of the Commission of Enquiry into Industrial Unrest one cause of unrest is given as 'the inconsiderate treatment of women whose wages are sometimes as low as 13s'.

But in Dublin 13s. is regarded as good pay for a factory worker, although food prices are as high as in England. Why are we content in Ireland with industrial conditions much more unjust than those which are threatening England with revolution? The determined blankness of the official mind on the subject of equal pay for equal work standard is amazing. The new scheme for increases of National School Teachers' salaries has directed some questions to us: 'If 127 pounds for men teachers in Grade 1 Division II is insufficient under present conditions, why is an increase leaving the woman teacher's salary at 123 pounds deemed satisfactory? Has there been some recent order, overlooked among the multiplicity of such decrees, by which the price of food varies according to the sex of the purchaser? If 63 pounds is too low a salary for a man entering one the lowest posts (Grade 3) is it satisfactory to increase the woman teacher, doing the same work with the same qualifications, to a salary of 64 pounds, while the man's pay is increased to 78 pounds?'

Women and Trade Unionism

by Louie Bennett

JANUARY 1918

The most notable development of the women's movement in Ireland during the past year has been the sudden growth of trade unionism amongst women workers. A year ago the members of the Irish Women Workers' Union numbered only a few hundreds: now they are over 2,000. The Munition workers are strongly organised under the National Federation of Women Workers; tailoresses, shirt-makers and other workers with the needle are enrolling in great numbers in all the big towns in the Society of Tailors and Tailoresses. Women clerks are now amongst the keenest and most active members of the Irish Clerical Union and the National Union of Clerks, although this time last year the women clerks of Dublin were still in doubt whether they were not too nice for anything resembling a Union! The most interesting point in regard to this rapid organisation is the spirit in which the women have come into the movement; this spirit promises to atone for their tardiness in entering. They are keen and progressive; quick in their grasp of the fundamental principles of trade Unionism, and loyal in adherence to them. The stand the women in the printing trade made during the recent printers' strike was a surprise to many people – not least, perhaps to the employers!

Do the women of other classes realise how significant and how far-reaching in effect this development amongst Irish women workers will prove? Hitherto, these women have spent their idealism and loyalty mainly upon nationalism. Now their nationalism promises to express itself in a practical direction, and women will find the best means of serving Ireland through the power of the trade union. When they have lifted themselves out of the sweated conditions under which they work at present, we shall begin to feel their influence in broader directions and stimulating the civic reforms which all classes' desire but which only the workers themselves will ever effectually achieve.

Is it permissible to suggest that the *Irish Citizen* ought now to formulate a definite policy in accordance with the new ideas of the day? It is time that it extended its attention from the purely suffrage movement to the broader aspects of feminism. The great merit of the paper since the war broke out has been its fidelity to the truth so clearly expounded by Mr Sheehy Skeffington, that Feminism and Militarism cannot work as partners. That truth is far as yet from general acceptance, and the *Irish Citizen* must still keep it in the foreground. But that truth in itself is but part of a greater truth: that Feminism and Co-operative Internationalism (the substitute for Militarism) are dependent upon economic justice. When we have won economic justice of the workers of the nations, we shall be able to secure it as the basis of relations between nations, and thus, and only thus, make the world safe for democracy.

Why should not the *Irish Citizen* make itself the organ for economic justice for women? What better service could it render to the whole cause of Feminism?

(The *Irish Citizen* has always been the organ of 'economic justice for women', and will, as in the past, be happy to receive and publish all matters relating to women's work. Should women's trades unions, therefore, see their way to sending us in reports of their activities we will be happy to publish them – Ed. *I.C.*)

Is an Irish Women Workers' Union Needed?

by Louie Bennett

NOVEMBER 1919

Did we dream that when we won the right to the Parliamentary vote we had finished with the woman's struggle for her place in the world? As a fact, the suffrage campaign was little more than a preliminary skirmish in a big progressive movement. And we are already launched upon a new development of the campaign – more active in the countries which were deeply involved in the war than in Ireland. But the conditions for it exist here too, and before long the issues will become clear. Women have yet to win equality of opportunity as workers, whether professional or industrial. We have heard in the past the catch cry many times repeated – 'Equal pay for Equal work'. The principle is acknowledged, though rarely acted upon. But the real crux arises over the equal work. The struggle for equality of opportunity in professions seems to be approaching universal success, but it has only begun in industry. And in industry the position is much more difficult and complicated for many reasons. The entry of women into skilled trades even on the same terms as men must inevitably mean some disemployment for men; and the fact that the majority of workingmen are the supporters of a wife and children and only a minority of working women have similar responsibilities, makes the most progressive amongst us hesitate to urge women industrial workers to invade men's trades. Already there is a considerable amount of antagonism to and jealousy of women's work in the Labour movement: in England the antagonism has become actually embittered. Here we may escape that embitterment – first, because the average Irish woman is not a feminist in the modern sense, and, secondly, because the stimulus which the war gave to the dilution of labour by women was not felt here. Irish women workers may progress more slowly towards sex emancipation, but they may travel on sounder and more harmonious lines. Personally, I think the 'class war' must be fought out, and the present industrial system revolutionised before women workers can, with just consideration for wives and mothers, make any real fight for equality of opportunity. In a society where the financial burden of keeping the home lies upon the male wage-earner, working under a system so heedless of human needs as the industrial system of to-day, it would be madness for women workers to attempt to disturb fundamentally the present distribution of industrial work. That distribution is stupid to the point of absurdity. When co-operation has superseded capitalism it must be completely re-adjusted, and it will be largely a women's task to compel and lead that re-adjustment. It is not one bit too soon for her to prepare for that task by building up a strong organisation. If women are to remain in industry – and all present omens point to that as a certainty – they will have to make a struggle for a place in the sun of industry. And meantime, a woman's organisation has much immediate work to do. There has hitherto been too facile an acceptance of the theory that women and men are best organised in the same Trade Union. It is noticeable, however, that woman's instinct – as a rule, a sound guide – drives her most often to a purely feminine organisation. That is her first tendency, although she may be easily led away from it by the advice and arguments of the men. Few people, however, have seriously weighed the pros and cons of organisation on the basis of sex, or the fundamental reasons demanding such organisation at the present time. I suggest that the *Irish Citizen* open a discussion on this problem, and I now put forward the reasons in favour of a woman's Trade Union.

Human nature is the same everywhere: the labouring man has the same human weaknesses as the duke. Which means that the women in industry have as much, or greater, need to safeguard and promote their personal and public interests as the women of political or professional aspirations. There is a disposition amongst men workers not only to keep women in inferior and subordinate positions, but even to drive them out of industry altogether. In this they are actuated by various motives – the very natural and reasonable fear of having their jobs taken from them or wages kept down by 'dilution'; the prevalent contempt of the male for women as workers, the old dream of woman on a pedestal above the world's turmoil, or woman as the cradlerocker. But whatever the motive, whether petty or idealistic, the result is dangerous for women workers, and clearly points to the need for a women's organisation for purposes of defence.

But it has a special constructive purpose to serve. In Ireland women in industry have been so badly paid that it has not been worth the while of employers or managers to organise their work on sound lines. Little trouble has been taken to establish conditions which will make them better workers and happier and healthier human beings.

Only a few women's trades have an apprenticeship system worth calling such. There has been no incentive to that self-respect as a worker which gives the note of happiness to any toil, however insignificant. Industrial women still have the great task before them of raising their whole status as workers, and certainly such conditions as will prevent them from remaining or becoming mere drudges. Even if they must to a great extent remain for the present in positions subordinate to men, they may still claim the rights and privileges to which every form of useful service is entitled. But they will have to secure these rights and safeguards for themselves. They will have to stand together in a solid block to win them.

It will be said – a mixed organisation can do that equally as well as a one sex organisation. I assert the contrary, because there is no real equality of men and women in industry. The men have already won a status to which the women are only now struggling. The women in a mixed organisation are as backward pupils in a school class: the teacher can't delay the forward march of the more advanced in order to push on the backward element. Moreover, the men have not the same aspirations for women as the women have for themselves, and in a mixed organisation much time and trouble would have to be wasted in securing the co-operation of the men in a demand for reforms for which the women may feel urgent need. For it must be borne in mind that in mixed Trade Unions the men are practically always the dominant element. It is not to be expected that a Trade Union Executive which draws its chief strength, numerically and financially, from men, will devote a large amount of time, energy and money to forwarding the interests of the weaker element, or will grant to that element any appreciable measure of control over the business and activities of the Trade Union. I know of no Trade Union or Labour Committee in England or in Ireland where women are represented in such a measure as to make their influence felt. This fact reacts badly in many ways – not least in its effect on the character of women workers, since it deprives them of responsibility and leaves them no power of initiative. And in England the women are now so alive to the handicap thus imposed upon them, that many are members of mixed craft Union, and of the Federation of Women Workers.

It is argued that this difficulty could be removed by giving a kind of Home Rule to women within the Industrial Union or the One Big Union. But this won't meet the case, except perhaps in industries where the theory of equal work for equal pay is accepted in full. (But where are those industries?) The Industrial Union is still almost as much an ideal as the One Big Union. Neither can be fully and successfully achieved unless they are based on the principle of equality of rights and equality of opportunity. There is no such equality, so far as women are concerned, in the Labour world to-day.

Therefore, working women must be extremely cautious as to the terms upon which they agree to surrender the authority and independence of action which a Trade Union composed of and governed by women gives them.

At the same time I grant the increased fighting and bargaining power of a broad-based Industrial Union, and I see the necessity for the close association of all the workers in movements for changes in working hours or wages.

But so long as women occupy a subordinate position within the Trade Union Movement they will need the safeguard of an independent organisation.

It is futile to deny a latent antagonism between the sexes in the world of industry. We want to obliterate that antagonism with the minimum of embitterment or injury to either side, and to pave a clear road for the transition stages of women's industrial emancipation. It is surely better to concede to the women now full freedom for self-government and self-development rather than have them rise later on (as they threaten now to do in England) in bitter revolt against the dominance of 'the stronger sex'. I have hopes that women workers, thinking of themselves and their place in industry from the sex standpoint, that is primarily as women, may eventually create great and beneficent changes in the world of industry. The true lines of progress for women may be parallel, but not identical with those for men. I am not satisfied that the reckless invasion of industry by women caused by the war means progress along the right lines. Our Irish women, proceeding more slowly, and one hopes more thoughtfully, may find for themselves a special place in the Co-operative Commonwealth, where their feminine aptitudes, physical and mental, may have scope for full expression, and prove a source of real enrichment to life. If they are caught up now in the industrial struggle merely as human units, irrespective of their potentialities as women, much promise of good and beauty may be crushed out of life. (Trade Unionism as advocated to-day by Irish Labour Leaders has this tendency.) I suggest that just here lie the strongest and deepest reasons for the separate organisation of women workers. The sphere of women in the world is still unexplored: her natural and true place is still undefined: her influence is still without a true objective. This is true in industry as in politics. I contend that whilst we thus lack vision it is unwise to yield without question or reflection to the superficial arguments in favour of mixed organisations, and to abandon the educative, inspiring and protective force of a women's organisation.

The whole problem is of vital importance, not only to women themselves, but for the human race. Its right solution lies with women themselves. Let them follow confidently the light that is within themselves rather than pursue distractedly the uncertain beacons hitherto held up to them.

Is an Irish Women Workers' Union Needed? A Reply
by C. Cahalan
DECEMBER 1919

I read Miss Bennett's article under the above title very carefully, but I was unable to decide whether the writer advocated one big Union for all women workers or a number of trade sections, each catering for its own particular trade requirements, independent of the Union for men workers in the same trade sections.

It is surprising to find such a good feminist as I know Miss Bennett to be proposing a line of action which would have the effect of perpetuating and keeping alive the very thing she complains of as existing in the Labour movement – viz., sex antagonism. The antagonism which Miss Bennett refers to is not, in my opinion, sex antagonism in the real sense of the word, but a very natural fear and dislike to anything or any person which might have the effect of lowering the standard of wages. It cannot be denied that the advent of women into industry has had this effect, hence the opposition of men to the entrance of women into their particular trade.

Women have allowed themselves to be used by the capitalists as a means of lowering the standard of wages. If women demanded equal pay for equal work we should not have had this antagonism. Men have been blamed for not 'seeing to it' that women received 'equal pay for equal work', but it is hardly fair to put the blame entirely on the men.

Women themselves must take their share of it. It cannot be denied that women were and are still very difficult to organise, and even when they are organised they seem to leave the management of the Union almost entirely in the hands of the male members.

It also cannot be denied that the mixed Unions that we know of here in Ireland were mainly built up by men. No doubt they had the loyal cooperation of the women members, but it must be admitted that the drudgery of carrying on the Union, committee work, etc., has been left to the male members to a very great extent.

In the mixed Unions women have the franchise on the same terms as men, but they (the women) are very often extremely reluctant to go forward as candidates at Election time, hence we find the branch and executive committees of these Unions almost entirely male.

I do not understand what Miss Bennett means when she refers to the subordinate position women occupy in the Labour movement. As I have already pointed out, women have the right to act as delegates and sit on the various Trades' Councils. There is at present a woman acting on the National Executive of the Irish Labour Party, and if there are not more women on Labour Councils, whose fault is that?

If women are not numerically strong on these bodies it is because women are not as class conscious as men are.

The position of women in the Labour movement is not subordinate. It may be a weak one, which can, when women wake up to their economic position, become very strong. But, unfortunately, women have been so apathetic and indifferent to their own interest that they are still in comparison to men very badly organised. Does Miss Bennett believe that the formation of One Big Union for all women will inspire these apathetic and careless women and girls into earnest apostles of Industrial Liberty? Organised women workers, even in mixed unions, have the power in their own hands to compel their union officials to attend to their needs and carry out their wishes. If they have not sufficient intelligence to do this, well they won't get very far, even in a separate union. Still less will they find their place and power in the cooperative commonwealth.

The dividing up of men and women in the same trade into two sections would be fatal in times of disputes. The bosses would find it a very effective weapon in their hands, and play off one section against the other. Even in peace times it would entail endless confusion and overlapping. We have plenty of evidence of the evil of two or three different Unions catering for the same class of worker.

In Ireland there are no less than seven different organisations catering for shop assistants and clerks, each having a different minimum wage scale. Only one of these organisations has demanded equal pay for equal work – viz., the Irish Drapers' Assistants' Association. The remaining six have accepted a much lower scale for their women members, which naturally makes it extremely difficult for the I.D.A. to establish their no sex difference scale. The employers point to the other Unions where the difference was allowed, and are seeking to make it the law. This is but one point. Space forbids me to give more. In conclusion, I would remind Miss Bennett that the pioneers of the Suffrage did not seek to establish a separate Parliament for women, but demanded a place in the Nation's Parliament. If women in the industrial world want a place in the Labour movement, they must seek it in the Labour Parliament, shoulder to shoulder with men and not in any separate organisation apart and isolated. It is only by closing up the ranks – by centralisation and absolute Unity – that the goal of Irish Labour – the Workers' Republic – can be reached.

CHAPTER 5

Feminism and Irish politics

When the young Maud Gonne expressed an interest in joining the Irish nationalist movement in the 1880s she encountered suspicion and resentment (Ward, 1990: 19). Hanna Sheehy Skeffington later wrote that even nationalist groups that subsequently admitted women, like the Gaelic League, relegated them to purely traditional roles (Innes, 1993: 139). Women's complex relationship with nationalism is well illustrated by examples from Irish history. This discussion seeks to contribute to the wider analysis of nationalism and feminism by using the *Irish Citizen* to explore some of the key debates between suffragists and nationalists.

Over the last twenty to thirty years, there has been growing interest among researchers about the relationship between women and nationalism in Ireland (Ward, 1989; Meaney, 1991; Coulter, 1993; Innes, 1993; McCoole, 1997; Ryan, 2002; Ryan & Ward, 2004; Steele, 2007; Valiulis, 2009; Matthews, 2010; MacPherson, 2012; Pašeta, 2013). In addition, the recent commemorations of the 1916 Rising have prompted several new publications on women's activist role in nationalist movements (see, for example, McAuliffe & Gillis, 2016; McDiarmid, 2015).

Internationally, the relationship between feminism and nationalism continues to stimulate research interest (Yuval-Davis, 1997; Banerjee, 2012). Of course, as Gerardine Meaney (1991) reminds us, it is necessary to locate nationalist policies and campaigns within anti-colonialism and the effects of centuries of British domination. A critique of nationalism should not overlook the underlying problem of colonialism. The experience of colonial domination moulds the form of nationalist opposition. As Meaney notes: 'Subject people, in rebelling and claiming independence and sovereignty, aspire to a traditionally masculine role of power' (1991: 7). As a result, within anti-colonial struggle, the rights of women and the rights of nations may be perceived as competing and conflictual (Jayawardena, 1986). In India, for example, nationalist movements used women to further the nationalist cause but were often resentful of any attempts by women to gain political rights (Liddle & Joshi, 1986; Thapar-Björkert & Ryan, 2002).

Against the backdrop of wider international scholarship on the complex and often tense interrelationships between feminism and nationalism, the Irish suffrage movement provides a fascinating case study. As played out through the pages of the *Irish Citizen*, suffragists' debates on nationalism not only illustrate the complexities of feminism and nationalism, but also offer insights that challenge any simplistic view of these two discourses as oppositional and competing. Far from being monolithic, suffragists reveal a diverse range of views on nationalism, which could be simultaneously supportive and critical. Neither were the suffragists' views on nationalism fixed and entrenched. On the contrary, there appeared to be a marked degree of fluidity over time (Ryan, 1995; Ryan & Ward, 2004).

Thus, the situation is not a simple, clear-cut case of two opposing ideologies. Many Irish feminists in the early decades of the twentieth century were nationalists and supported Ireland's claim to independence. However, they objected to the male-defined nature of the nationalist movement and to the way women were represented within much of the nationalist rhetoric. This added to the complex relationship between the two movements and also led to some fascinating debates as suffragists engaged in a war of words with nationalists. This war frequently took the form of battles waged through the pages of the *Irish Citizen*, although the disagreements had begun years earlier in the pages of the short-lived nationalist women's paper *Bean na hEireann* (Innes, 1993).

Throughout the history of the *Irish Citizen*, and, indeed, the suffrage movement as a whole, there existed an uneasy relationship with Irish politics generally. As discussed in the introduction to this book, the home rule bill and the Irish Parliamentary Party (IPP) that fought so hard to attain it were perceived by some people as a threat to woman's suffrage (Ward, 1982). Hostility towards female suffrage gained Redmond and his party the wrath of not only the British suffrage movement but also of many Irish suffragists (Cullen Owens, 1984).

Suffragists' views towards nationalism ranged from suspicion to sympathy. Some suffragists saw nationalism, and the radical forces associated with it, as the only true path to the emancipation of women, while there were many suffragists who saw the nationalist movement as yet another distraction from the cause of votes for women.

In October 1919, the editor of the *Irish Citizen*, Hanna Sheehy Skeffington, issued a policy statement clarifying the position of the paper: 'we recognise the right of the majority of the Irish people to mould its own destinies … we stand for self-determination for Ireland'.

This attitude is quite different from the one she had put forward a few years earlier. Reporting on the mass meeting of Irish women on 8 June 1912, which included unionists and nationalists (see chapter 1), she had written that party loyalties should be subordinated to the sex principle and votes for women must be the first priority:

> Home Rule or no Home Rule, Westminster or College Green, there is a new spirit abroad among women: whether the vote is reluctantly granted by a Liberal Government or wrested from an Irish parliament, to women in the end it matters but little. (8 June 1912)

How can this apparent change of attitude be explained?

Of course, by 1919 many women had already won the right to vote and this may partly explain the change in attitude expressed above. In addition, the events of 1916 had a significant impact on the women's movement in Ireland. Many loyal supporters of the women's cause died as a result of the Easter Rising, for example James Connolly, Thomas MacDonagh, Ernest Kavanagh and, of course, Hanna's own husband and the founder of the *Irish Citizen*, Francis Sheehy Skeffington. But the *Irish Citizen* did not merely undergo a simple transition from anti-nationalism to pro-nationalism. As the following discussion will indicate, the situation was far more complex and merits serious analysis. Between 1912 and 1920 the paper's coverage of Irish politics is fascinating and deserves attention not least because it is just about the only contemporary treatment of these issues in Irish history from a feminist point of view.

The extracts that follow this introduction are selected not only to reflect a range of viewpoints but also to represent the changing stance of the *Irish Citizen* editorials over the years. But before reading the extracts it is important to explore the context within which they were published.

On 8 April 1914 Louie Bennett, writing under the heading 'Modern Irish Women', made a very astute observation. Women in Ireland, she argued, had suffered more than most women because of the very male-oriented nature of Irish politics. She pointed in particular to home rule from which, she claimed, women were totally excluded. Thus, excluded from party politics, Irish women had, according to Bennett, put their energy into cultural and social movements including feminism.

However, although women were excluded from party politics that is not to say that party politics played no part in the suffrage movement. Suffragists were drawn from a range of political viewpoints and, as I have discussed elsewhere in an analysis of the suffrage campaign using social movement theory (Ryan, 2006), it was not always easy to overcome political differences and maintain unity among the various elements of the movement. Nationalism and unionism were always threatening to cause tensions and divisions.

But suffragists were quite aware that they could only achieve their goal if they presented a united front. They demonstrated this clearly at the mass meeting of women held in Dublin in 1912. The importance of unity was reiterated in a letter to the *Irish Times* reprinted in the *Irish Citizen* in June 1917:

> The great association of Irish Women Suffragists can provide members of all shades of Irish opinion. The women, at all events, have succeeded in all sitting round the same table without 'ramming each other's convictions down each other's throats'.

The letter was written by the novelist Edith Somerville, president of the Munster Women's Franchise League, a group with approximately 500 members, making it one of the largest non-militant suffrage groups. It has been described as a rather genteel group made up of writers, artists and society women (Murphy, 1989: 19). In the course of her letter, Edith Somerville described herself as a unionist. However, Gifford Lewis (1988) has argued that Somerville was much more amiable to nationalism than her cousin and fellow author Violet Martin (Ross), who was an outspoken unionist.

When one considers that these women were president and vice president of one the largest non-militant suffrage groups in Ireland, then the importance of maintaining unity across political divisions becomes clear. To date, limited research has been completed on unionist suffragists (though see Hill, 2007; Urquhart, 2000). However, there certainly were a number of ardent unionists in the suffrage movement not only in the North, but also in the South (Hearne, 1992; Cullen & Luddy, 1995).

Regarding suffragists' attitudes to nationalism, Francis Sheehy Skeffington is a particularly interesting case. On 13 July 1912, in an article entitled 'Home Rule and Votes for Women', he declared himself to be 'speaking as a nationalist'. Those who demand home rule for men only are not true nationalists, he added. Like so many other suffragists, he did not trust the men of the IPP to give the vote to Irish women after home rule had been established. He, therefore, insisted that votes should be immediately included in the home rule bill. He pointed to the open hostility of the IPP towards suffragists as evidence of their deep-seated opposition to female enfranchisement. The party had voted against the suffrage bill in parliament but voted for the notorious 'Cat and Mouse Act'. Sheehy Skeffington went on to say that:

> There is stronger and purer Nationalism in Mountjoy prison at this moment than any Mr Redmond's followers can boast … Mountjoy prison where women, Nationalist and Unionist, are sacrificing their

Liberty for the liberation of the human spirit and the enfranchisement of the entire Irish Nation.

At this time, Hanna Sheehy Skeffington and other members of the IWFL were in Mountjoy prison for the first militant attacks on government buildings carried out in Dublin by Irish suffragists. But in this revealing article, which is included in full in the collection of extracts later in this chapter, Francis Sheehy Skeffington illustrated not only the tensions between the IPP and the suffragists, but also the potential tensions between nationalist and unionist suffragists. By demanding that women's suffrage be included in the home rule bill, he revealed his own personal support for home rule. Of course, this would have been quite unacceptable to unionist suffragists.

However, being a pacifist, Francis would never support an armed struggle for the attainment of Irish self-determination. In a public letter to Thomas MacDonagh, later published as a pamphlet, Francis stated his opposition to violence (22 May 1915). As already mentioned in chapter 3, this letter outlined that while Sheehy Skeffington supported the objectives of the Irish Volunteers, he opposed violence of any kind. He also warned MacDonagh that the Volunteers contained quite a reactionary element. He was particularly suspicious of the Volunteers' exclusion of women. Instead of armed struggle, Francis suggested that Irishmen and Irishwomen should come together and demand equal rights and justice without threatening war and bloodshed. This, he said, was the only way to extricate themselves from the militarist tangle.

The home rule versus votes debate

As the discussion so far indicates, the issue of home rule was potentially divisive for the suffrage movement. In February 1913 the *Irish Citizen* gave extensive coverage to this question and invited the opinions of all interested parties on the matter of home rule and votes for women. In this way the paper could be used as a platform by women of all political ideas to discuss the challenges associated with home rule and recognise their differences of opinion.

Susanne R. Day, from the Cork branch of the MWFL, wrote to the *Irish Citizen* saying that, while home rule was a popular issue in Ireland, suffrage was not. 'There is no real hostility to women's suffrage as such in Ireland', she said. But if suffragists were actively to oppose home rule, she warned, it would result in alienating their cause completely. 'Let us, therefore, pursue a steady, quiet course of educational work throughout the country' (8 Feb. 1913). She concluded that only after gaining a mandate from the people should the suffragists go to the IPP and demand votes.

Margaret McCoubrey, the socialist from the Belfast-based militant IWSS, wrote that constitutional means of gaining suffrage had so obviously failed due to a lack of political will that the only policy to adopt now was an 'anti-government' one. Mrs Baker, also a member of the IWSS, wrote: 'As suffragists we are to have a single aim until we have the vote – party politics and party concerns are not for us.' Her use of the phrase 'a single aim until we have the vote' is revealing and suggests that suffragists realised the unity amongst them was purely temporary. She seemed to accept that party politics would divide women once the vote had been won. This was an accurate prediction.

Maud Joynt favoured unity with British suffragists in demanding a government measure to bring in suffrage. Mary Lawless of the IWRL took a similar line: 'Let our fight be as uniform as possible with that of our sisters across the water, so that our united demand may be the more effective.' She was critical of the IPP, and proposed 'to fight them uncompromisingly'. She said that the real enemy was caucus government,[1] whether Irish or English, and that should be rooted out.

Representatives of the Conservative and Unionist Women's Franchise Association (Irish Branch) wrote that they would support a move for a private member's bill to introduce suffrage in parliament. Interestingly, they made no mention of home rule. It should be pointed out that the suffrage movement had been relying on private members' bills since the 1860s. Such bills lacked party backing and invariably failed.

On 22 February, Helen Morony, a poor law guardian and a member of the Limerick branch of the MWFL, made her contribution to the *Irish Citizen* debate. She had no faith in a private member's bill. Like her fellow MWFL member, Susanne R. Day, Morony declared that Irishwomen could not adopt the policies of the English suffragists. The home rule issue made everything in Ireland much more complicated than in England; an anti-home-rule stance would severely damage the suffrage cause in Ireland, she wrote.

Mrs Coade of the Newry Suffrage Society was very critical of this type of view. Why, she asked, must women once again subject their demands to those of men? 'If we are to win our emancipation in this generation we must put suffrage and the woman's cause before and above everything.'

Louie Bennett contributed to the debate on behalf of the IWSF, saying that a private member's bill had shown itself to be futile, and so a government measure was the only hope. She concluded that in Ireland there was simply not enough support for an anti-government policy. Representing an opposing view, Lilian Metge, honorary secretary of the Lisburn Suffrage Society, wrote to the paper in favour of anti-government militancy.

---

1   This refers to a process of government driven by the interests of a minority.

These letters demonstrate the main differences among the various groups in Ireland. The militant suffragists like McCoubrey, Metge and the IWSS demanded an anti-government policy like the one that the Women's Social and Political Union in England had already embarked on (see Hill, 2007). Meanwhile, constitutional suffragists like Louie Bennett from the IWRL and contributors from the MWFL believed that home rule should not be opposed, and that a government measure was the only hope of ever achieving the vote. This roughly divided the suffragists into constitutional and militant. However, as I have written elsewhere, such a sharp dichotomy may be misleading and overly simplistic (Ryan, 2006).

In January 1914, the *Irish Citizen*, in reviewing the suffrage activities of the past year, stated that during 1913 there was virtual unanimity among Irish suffragists in demanding a government measure to introduce suffrage. The Irish Women's Reform League led all non-militants in this demand, and their 'government measure' line was quickly adopted by all societies in the Irish Women's Suffrage Federation, which included almost all the suffrage groups in the country (see *Irish Citizen*, 17 May 1913, for details of membership). However, the article went on to say that the IWFL and IWSS continued to carry out anti-government policies, such as, for instance, campaigning against the government candidate at the Derry by-election. The review claimed that 1913 had been an important year for many reasons. First, because public support was growing:

> This year has been marked by a great increase of strength and confidence in the movement in Ireland. All societies are growing in number and increasing in activities … The latent sympathy of the Irish people for the cause of women is coming to the surface in spite of the politicians. (Jan. 1914)

Second, because the Ulster Unionist Council had announced its support for the suffrage cause (though they later reneged – see Hill, 2007). The paper called this 'the most important single development that has taken place in the suffrage movement in Ireland'. This point reflects attempts, on the part of the *Irish Citizen's* editors, to appear as impartial as possible and welcome unionist initiatives. Clearly, this was informed by a desire to maintain unity in the suffragist ranks and avoid sectionalism by keeping unionist suffragists within an integrated movement (Ryan, 2006).

As the following quote indicates, the *Irish Citizen* saw itself as playing a crucial role in promoting unity among all suffragists; the piece concluded with an important statement, saying that in the past year there had been:

steady growth of good feeling, mutual understanding and cordial co-operation on occasion between militant and non-militant sections of the movement in Ireland ... of that essential unity ... the *Irish Citizen* claims to be the symbol and bond. (Jan. 1914)

However, agreement and unity were rather fragile things.

Cumann na mBan and the Irish Citizen

In May 1914, Mary MacSwiney wrote to the paper on the topic of home rule. She said Irish women, unlike British women, were not in a position to put 'suffrage first'. Ireland had the question of national sovereignty to settle and to oppose the government would, in effect, mean to oppose home rule. She accused many Irish suffragists of being political ostriches with their heads in the sand: 'Mr Redmond's one and only business at Westminster is to secure Home Rule. He received no mandate for women's suffrage and thoughtful and fairminded Irishwomen of every political belief recognise that' (23 May 1914).

Home rule, she argued, was the most important issue in Irish politics and suffragists would do well to accept that reality. The suffrage cause, she claimed, was becoming synonymous with unionism and was, therefore, daily losing nationalist supporters. She also expressed her doubts about the sincerity of English suffragists, whom, she felt, would gladly wreck Irish suffrage to further their own cause. She asserted that Irishwomen did not want the vote at the expense of home rule. MacSwiney and many of her ilk believed that once home rule had been achieved in Ireland, then the Irish government would grant votes to women.

MacSwiney was originally a suffragist and a member of the Cork branch of the MWFL (Fallon, 1986). However, she left that group due to their stance on the First World War. As a nationalist, she had no desire to support the British cause during the war. She was outraged by the MWFL decision to engage in fundraising to buy an ambulance in support of the war effort. She wrote to the *Irish Citizen* to express her fury. She condemned the members of the MWFL as 'Britons first, suffragists second and Irish women perhaps a bad third' (21 Nov. 1914).

Cumann na mBan (the Irish women's council) was set up in 1914 as an auxiliary to help the Irish Volunteers. Although women were not admitted to the Volunteers, Cumann na mBan organised along military lines and were part of the armed campaign that would eventually lead to the 1916 Rising (Ward, 1989).

As one of the most outspoken members of Cumann na mBan, MacSwiney kept up a regular correspondence with the *Irish Citizen*. Today this stands as a valuable record of the nationalist-versus-feminist clash. It is made all the more interesting by the fact that those defending nationalism's priority over feminism were women. The tone of these exchanges was not only very critical, but also angry; insults were hurled in both directions. That anger is a mark of the enormous passion and commitment that both sides felt for their cause. However, a short contribution by Rosamund Jacob (July 1914) following the outbreak of the First World War, when John Redmond effectively sidelined Cumann na mBan by setting up the Irish Volunteers' Aid Association, revealed a sense of disillusionment among at least some nationalist suffragists.

On 9 January 1915 the 'Current Comment' section of the paper admitted that the suffrage cause in Ireland had been badly affected by home rule and by the war, which had taken attention away from the suffrage campaign. The article also attacked Cumann na mBan as a group of women who were displaying a 'slave like mentality' by giving their unconditional support to the Volunteers, with no guarantees of future enfranchisement.

The 'Current Comment' piece went on to attack the Sinn Féin convention of 1914, which had ruled the matter of suffrage out of order when Countess Markievicz, Hanna Sheehy Skeffington and Jennie Wyse Power all attempted to raise it for discussion (see Van Voris, 1967: 126). The paper commented favourably upon Edward Carson's willingness to consider suffrage in Ulster.

On 3 April 1915, the editorial continued its bitter criticism of IPP leader John Redmond. It described him as being as much of an anti-suffragist as Prime Minister Asquith. The article accused Redmond of doing everything in his power to quash suffrage at Westminster.

In the next issue of the paper, the editor warned Redmond that the crowd at a recent meeting in Dublin, which had included many members of the Irish Volunteers, had responded very well to suffragists. While in 1912 these very same people had jeered at suffragists, they were now much more sympathetic to the cause of female enfranchisement. The *Irish Citizen* took this as a sign that the Volunteers were losing their loyalty to Redmond. 'Redmond's day is over,' the paper forecast with a certain amount of accuracy, though perhaps a few years premature. The article did not miss the opportunity to criticise the women who continued to offer their work freely to the Volunteer movement – Cumann na mBan. 'On such women is the slavery of their sex built,' said the editor.

The sympathy these Volunteers now displayed towards the suffragists should not, however, be seen as total support for the cause of votes for women. Many Volunteers' growing dissatisfaction with Redmond, plus the fact that home rule was now officially on the statute books though postponed because of the First World War, and their gradual drift towards the notion of an armed uprising, are probably more accurate explanations for their apparent lack of hostility towards the suffragists. In other words, suffragism and home rule were no longer in competition for political expediency. However, it was also reported that the sale of copies of the *Irish Citizen* and the distribution of suffrage leaflets among the Volunteers had increased.

After the 1916 Rising: suffragists rethinking nationalism

In an article in the September 1916 issue of the paper, the change in opinion of the editorial team is very apparent. Those like Hanna Sheehy Skeffington, who had been so sharply opposed to armed violence, were now full of praise and sympathy for the dead:

> The ranks of the suffragists have been sadly depleted by the events of Easter week: the Irish Volunteers and Citizens' Army were suffragists almost to a man, the women prominent in the movement were all convinced and practical exponents of the doctrine of equality of the sexes.

This is high praise indeed for the women who only months previously were being criticised by the *Irish Citizen* editorials for their 'slave-like mentality'. In an interesting piece of research Beth McKillen (1982) claims that nationalist and suffragist women actually grew closer after 1916 and had a significant influence on each other's thinking. Margaret Ward, in her important and influential study of Cumann na mBan (1989), claimed that nationalist women became more aware of gender issues after the Rising. It is necessary to remember that Cumann na mBan women were assigned fairly menial tasks during the Easter Rising (Taillon, 1996; McDiarmid, 2015; McAuliffe & Gillis, 2016). Their main tasks involved stereotypical female roles such as cooking and nursing the wounded, although, of course, some women undertook the more unconventional role of dispatch carrier (Taillon, 1996). It was women from the Irish Citizens' Army such as Dr Kathleen Lynn, Constance Markievicz, Margaret Skinnider and Winifred Carney who took a more active part in the Rising.

One can surmise that their limited participation in the uprising was a source of frustration to some Cumann na mBan members. Perhaps they realised that the Volunteers did not appreciate their true capabilities. In any case, the years after 1916 saw a change in Cumann na mBan culminating in their active and highly significant role in the War of Independence and Civil War (Buckley, 1938; Conlon, 1969; McCoole, 1997; Ryan, 2000; Ryan &

Ward, 2004). During these pivotal years, Markievicz became president of Cumann na mBan, even though she had earlier been quite critical of its functions in support of the Volunteers (*Irish Citizen*, Oct. 1915). Her influence in changing the organisation was highly significant.

In remembering the fallen of 1916, the *Irish Citizen* singled out James Connolly, leader of the Irish Citizens' Army, for special praise: 'He recognised that the cause of women and labour was twin … James Connolly deserves a shrine in the heart of every suffragist' (Sept. 1916). This statement is probably true, as Connolly had been devoted to the cause of feminism and had written of the exploitation of women (Innes, 1993). He had admitted women to the Citizen Army on equal terms with men. He probably influenced the equality guaranteed to women in the 1916 Proclamation of the Irish Republic.

The *Irish Citizen* declared that the Proclamation was of more value than any of those produced as a result of the American or French revolutions, as these had reserved freedom only for (some) men. One could argue that it was this Proclamation and the rights which it guaranteed to women which actually softened suffragists' attitudes toward the 1916 Rising. The document is brief, and yet it encompasses a wide range of issues, including equality between the sexes. If fully implemented, it would have made the Irish republic very advanced in all areas of human rights. However, in hindsight, this document may have made suffragists and nationalist women overly optimistic about the rights they would enjoy in the republic that was to come (see Beaumont, 2007). The *Irish Citizen* demonstrated some of this optimism when it said of Ireland: 'as of old her civilisation was based on feminism'.

The glorious past?

As I have discussed elsewhere (Ryan, 1995), suffragists often appealed to the 'glorious' feminist past of Ireland, when women apparently enjoyed equality with men. This is clearly illustrated by Sydney Gifford, a member of Inghinidhe na hÉireann, when she wrote to the *Irish Citizen* in September 1912 under her pen name – John Brennan. She claimed that Irish women had always played an active part in public life, giving such examples as the Ladies' Land League. But before drawing simplistic conclusions about the naivety of suffragists, more analysis is required.

Is it possible that nationalist suffragists, like Gifford, genuinely believed that all of Ireland's problems would be over as soon as the last British soldier withdrew from Irish soil? That Ireland would simply return to its feminist past? This seems highly unlikely given the suffragists' writings on the many deep structural problems in Irish society, such as the existence of slum dwellings, overcrowding, pay inequality, sexual violence and child abuse. Their writings on work, trade unionism, legal injustices, double moral standards, the workhouse and poverty reflect their concerns for the harsh realities of Irish society – problems that could not be quickly or easily ameliorated.

Some suffragists suspected that many of these social problems would continue even in an independent Ireland (see Louie Bennett, Apr. 1914). It is more likely that suffragists glorified the past in the hope of winning nationalist support for feminism as an ancient Irish tradition. While nationalists looked back into the Celtic past to discover true Irish culture (see Innes, 1993), they often dismissed feminism as a modern British invention. By cleverly reinterpreting or reinventing Irish traditions through a feminist lens, suffragists sought to counter nationalist opposition (Ryan, 1995). Feminism was evoked as an ancient Irish tradition as old and as Irish as Cuchulann. If Irish men turned their back on feminism, they were insulting part of their Irish heritage.

In April 1917, an article appeared in the paper, entitled 'Political Morality', in which the writer expressed hope for a new Ireland under a new administration. The writer asked of the new political movement in Ireland: 'Will it be true to the fine traditions of Ireland's past, when Ireland's men and women were equally honoured and equally free?'

Suffragists looked to the forthcoming Sinn Féin convention for an answer. In November 1917, the *Irish Citizen* carried a full report on the convention, which had been held in the previous month. It praised the organisers for endorsing and embodying in their constitution the complete equality of men and women in Ireland. 'Irishmen by their actions have not merely honoured themselves and their countrywomen but they have added immeasurably to the glory and renown of Ireland's name.'

At the convention, the article reported, Councillor Sean Kelly had 'pointed out that in endorsing this principle Irishmen were only returning to the traditions of Gaelic Ireland and rejecting the teaching of an alien civilisation; and any Irishman who could oppose women's claim for equality would be acting in an un-Irish spirit'.

At the same convention, Eamon de Valera was unanimously elected president of Sinn Féin, and four women were elected to the twenty-four-person executive. The women were all nationalists and only two of them – Countess Markievicz and Dr Lynn – had been active in the suffrage movement. This is a very familiar pattern, which was to continue in Irish politics (Beaumont, 2007). The women who were elected to the Dáil after 1919 were also nationalists, and no suffragist per se was ever elected (they were rarely even put up by national parties). Hanna Sheehy Skeffington ran for election once and was defeated, though she was elected a local councillor (Levenson & Natterstad, 1986). It would thus appear that suffragists' suspicion of the nationalists was well founded. The more progressive leaders were among those executed in 1916, which left the way free for more conservative men like de Valera to come to the fore. He also employed the ideal of the great Gaelic civilisation, but used it not to improve the lot of women but to endorse a reactionary and conservative value system, heavily influenced by the Catholic church (see Ryan, 2002; Beaumont, 2007).

Suffragists were not to be fobbed off with empty promises that the issue of votes for women would be resolved after national independence, and continued to demand the vote. The *Irish Citizen* was especially anxious that Irishwomen would be included in any proposed change to the electoral system in England. This demonstrated their reluctance to throw in their lot with the nationalists. In 1917, the Representation of the People Act came under discussion at Westminster largely with a view to enfranchising (male) soldiers (Pugh, 1992). The suffragists called for women to be included in the amendments to the act. In January 1918, the paper warned that Irish women might be tricked and deliberately excluded from an extension of the franchise: 'Mr Redmond's political power for doing ill is strong even yet although his moral power – the sanction of the people – is almost nil.' The article urged all suffrage societies to take action: 'Let each society in its own way harass the enemy ... either by lady like appeals or more vigorous attacks – each way helps to gain public opinion' (*Irish Citizen*, Jan. 1918).

Anna Haslam, the veteran suffrage campaigner of the IWSLGA, initiated a conference of the various suffrage groups in the country. It was discussed whether or not the groups could work together as a lobby group to press for other reforms concerning women. The societies unanimously agreed not to amalgamate: 'The feeling of the conference being that political differences are at present so strong in Ireland that a closer union in a society or federation would be out of the question' (*Irish Citizen*, Apr. 1918). This statement reveals that the political differences that had always existed under the surface had now come to the fore. Clearly, the campaign for the vote had been a unifying symbol which held together a complex mixture of liberals, socialists, nationalists and unionists (Ryan, 2006).

In the following selection of extracts from the *Irish Citizen*, I have chosen to include a lengthy piece in which the veteran nationalist campaigner Maud Gonne describes her experiences in an English prison. She shared these experiences briefly with Hanna Sheehy Skeffington, although Hanna was quickly released due to her clever use of the hunger-strike tactic (Ward, 1997). Gonne's article is included among the following extracts not only because of its interest as an account of prison life, but also because it foreshadows the role which both Maud and Hanna would later play in the Women Prisoners' Defence League. Following the establishment of the Free State in 1922, this group would absorb much of the energy of women activists as the new government clamped down on all political opponents and the prison population began to soar.

Clearly, the complex relationship between feminist activists and nationalist politicians remained troubled and troublesome following the establishment of the twenty-six-county state (Ryan, 2002; Beaumont, 2007). Feminist voices continued to play a role in demanding rights and tackling inequality throughout the twentieth century (Connolly, 2002).

" Mr. Judge said the movement was one in which there was no room for the ladies. They would want at least two million pounds, and the ladies could form a society, and collect money for that, and put their hearts and souls into it. (Cheers)."

—" Irish Volunteer."

The *Irish Citizen* was sceptical about the role of women within the nationalist movement, as this cartoon of Cumann na mBan illustrates.

Extracts from the *Irish Citizen*

Home Rule and Votes for Women
by F. Sheehy Skeffington MA
13 JULY 1912

The third Home Rule Bill is now before the House of Commons.

It is a different Bill, in many respects, from the previous two. Speaking as a Nationalist, I regard it as a better Bill than either of them. New ideas and new developments in the political situation have made it imperative to depart in many particulars from the model of 1893. For example, the financial clauses are altogether different; they had to be, because since 1893 we have had the Financial Relations Commission, and a quantity of other information on the financial position of Ireland which was not then obtainable.

Again, the principle on which the question of Ireland's representation at Westminster has been considered is quite different in the new Bill from that adopted in 1893; because since then the Federal idea has come to the front, and the framers of the measure have had to take it into consideration. There are many, however, who think that the Bill has not yet been brought sufficiently up to date. They think the finances of the scheme do not adequately represent the information now at our disposal as to the financial situation. There are others who hold that the recent development of Proportional Representation, as an electoral system capable of securing fair representation for all, should be recognised by its adoption in the Bill. On all sides there is a general desire to recognise the passage of time and the emergence of new facts since 1893, and to remould the Bill accordingly.

Now one of the most important changes – with the possible exception of Land Purchase, the most important of all – which has taken place in the condition of Ireland since 1893 is the revolution in Local Government brought about by the Conservatives in 1898. In 1893 Local Government was entirely in the hands of the Grand Juries. The masses of the people had no experience whatever of managing local affairs. Consequently, it was said, they were unfit for Home Rule. Five years after the Bill of 1893, the complete management and control of those local affairs passed into the hands of popularly elected local bodies. These bodies have on the whole, it is universally admitted, performed the duties allotted to them with efficiency and economy. The men and women chosen by the Local Government electorate for these bodies have been, on the whole, capable for the task.

This is admitted, not merely by the Liberals and the Nationalists, but by Mr Balfour and Mr Wyndham. Hence no one can any longer say the Irish have given no proof of capacity for self-government. No one can contend that the electorate which has exercised wisdom in the choice of its local representatives will not display similar wisdom in the choice of its representatives for a Home Rule Parliament.

And, as a matter of fact, it has not been said. The argument that the Irish are incapable of self-government, that there exists no proof of their ability for self-government, has, thanks to the Local Government Act and the Local Government Electorate, disappeared from the Unionist armoury. The success of the Local Government has become the strongest practical argument for Home Rule on English platforms. Mr Redmond, Mr Devlin and other leading Nationalists have repeatedly recognised this and, in fact, they use the argument continually.

This is the new fact which Nationalists who are consistent want to have definitely recognised in the Home Rule Bill.

We claim that those people who have proved their capacity in local affairs, that electorate whose working of the local government system has furnished the strongest argument for Home Rule, should be entrusted with the working of the system of National Self-Government as soon as that system is established. In this respect, as in others, we want the Bill brought up to date. The Bill as it stands ignores the change that has taken place since 1893; its electoral provisions are identical with those of the last Home Rule Bill. Irish women have contributed to build up local government and to make it a success. We claim for them a free entry into the edifice of which they have helped to lay the foundations. To refuse them that entry is inconsistent with the spirit of Nationalism.

What excuse can be given for this exclusion of women? Some excuse could plausibly be made in 1893, when the women's movement was hardly yet articulated in this country; to-day there can be none that will stand a moment's examination.

'We want Home Rule for all Ireland or no Home Rule,' said Mr Dillon lately; and all Nationalists who have a sense of their duty to their fellow countrywomen will echo this declaration. Home Rule for men only would clearly not be Home Rule for all Ireland. The chief excuse urged for the exclusion of women is that 'this is a matter for the Irish Parliament to determine for itself'. Now if the Irish Parliament were left to determine its own franchise from the beginning, there might be some point in this; but it is not so permitted. The franchise for the Irish Parliament is being fixed at Westminster; we should see then that it is fixed justly, and not on the basis of sex-inequality. The Proportional Representation Society, which also seeks to have the electoral system of the Bill brought up to date, in another direction, has argued with much force that the first three years of the new Irish Parliament will be critical years, during which traditions will be formed and vested interests established and constitutional customs developed; consequently it is of the utmost importance that the representative character of that Parliament should be beyond all doubt from the beginning, as it can only be if it includes women.

Moreover, those who argue that the existing franchise ought not to be changed until it is done by the Home Rule Parliament are themselves, with astonishing inconsistency, assisting the Imperial Parliament to make a still more drastic change in the franchise. Manhood suffrage is not being left to the Irish Parliament to decide on; if the Government's Franchise and Registration Bill be carried into law before or simultaneously with the Home Rule Bill, then the Irish Parliament will be elected from the beginning, not on the existing register, but on the new Manhood Suffrage Register. The Irish Party, led by Mr Redmond, are supporting that Manhood Suffrage Bill; and that shows the hollowness of their pretence that 'this must be left to the Irish Parliament'. Their real motive, it is evident, in refusing to allow the Local Government Register to be incorporated in the Home Rule Bill is hostility to the cause of women – a hostility which they are afraid openly to express, but which their actions prove.

This is not the only sign of their hostility. Every reader of the *Irish Citizen* knows how they killed the Conciliation Bill, breaking their pledges at the nod of their leader. This might have been forgiven them – Nationalists at all events could have forgiven it – had they shown a determination to give votes to their own countrywomen in the Home Rule Bill; but they are just as hostile to the women of their own country as to those of England. Hostility to women has even led them to break away from their old tradition with regard to political prisoners, a tradition recalled and endorsed by their leader ever since militancy began in the suffrage movement, and with direct reference to it. The men whose proud boast it has been that they were in favour of the special treatment of political prisoners everywhere and under all circumstances – who supported political treatment for Dr Jameson, though they detested his politics – have now placed on record their votes in favour of the forcible feeding in prison of political offenders when they happen to be women demanding the vote.

These are the reasons why the militant women's movement in Ireland, after long delay and with great reluctance, after infinite patience with the trickery and tergiversation of the Irish Party, has been forced into an attitude of opposition to the Party on the question of votes for women, because that Party has declared war upon women. At the last two elections in South Dublin, militant women suffragists, Nationalist and Unionist alike, worked for the

Nationalist candidate because he was a declared supporter of Woman's Suffrage, while the Unionist candidate was an opponent. One woman, a Unionist, travelled from the West of Ireland to help Alderman Cotton on this ground. The Irish Party and its backers, who try to set up a monopoly in Nationalism, say the woman's movement is hostile to the Nationalist movement. This is untrue. Fortunately the cause of Irish Nationality, the cause linked with the names of Emmet and Tone, of Mitchel and Davitt, is not the sole possession of the gentlemen who break their pledges at the nod of Mr Redmond. There are better Nationalists in this movement than there are in the ranks of the Irish Party.

There is a stronger and purer Nationalism in Mountjoy Prison at this moment than any Mr Redmond's followers can boast.

There was a time when the Irish Party used to go to prison in pursuance of their ideals. Those were the days when the spirit of true Nationalism blazed in their blood, when the Party and its leaders were worthy of respect. To-day that spirit of Nationality is gone from amongst them, and their highest ideal is the transference of the jobs and jobbery of Dublin Castle to the hands of their sectarian societies. It is not to the Irish Party that we look to-day for courage, for sincerity, for self-sacrifice in a great cause. If we seek these things, if we seek to find the essentials of the spirit that made Irish Nationality great and worthy of respect, we must look to Mountjoy Prison, where women, Nationalist and Unionist, are sacrificing their liberty for the liberation of the human spirit and the enfranchisement of the entire Irish Nation.

The True-Born Irishman

by John Brennan

14 SEPTEMBER 1912

If it were possible to define and honour by a public vote which qualities make men good citizens and good patriots, the country would be saved all those troublesome disputes which occur between adherents of different leaders; we would turn the lawyers and police out on grass, the lawyers with their golf sticks, the police with camans, and the true-born Irishman would find himself all of a sudden in a true-born Ireland, thinking clearly and calmly, his mind free from cant phrases and party-cries. But at the present we call by the names of citizen and patriot such widely differing types of men that the words are losing their old glory. There are many of them who claim the names, and who know a great deal about their country, because they see it discussed in English papers, who claim that they have patriotic feelings about a large part of the earth, and are 'citizens of the British Empire', which places on them municipal and patriotic duties in such far off places as Delhi, London, Cape Town and Ontario. They believe that while they are busy looking after the world, we will not be so provincial and narrow-minded as to call on them to fulfil their duty to their own land and their native town. These bosses of dreamt-of places far away dispute the title of citizen and the claims to the name of patriots with those men who are fighting for 'Ireland's freedom', and who define 'freedom' as a limited power given to a limited number of the minority of the population.

As the official leaders of both these classes are entirely foreign to Ireland, and in fact the direct results of English rule in our country, and as the two policies which they represent may be called Ireland's foreign policy, it is unnecessary and useless to look to them for any true expression of Irish thought. They have long since lost touch with Irish ideals and Ireland's mental growth; they represent some of us perhaps for material wants, but of the important changes in Ireland, her spiritual growth and progress, they are as ignorant as the English. Indeed, as often happens to exiles, they have become more English than the English themselves. It is to the native growths of Ireland, whether they be ornaments or abortions, that the women of Ireland must look if they would discover the feelings of Ireland on the subject of woman's freedom. For too long the Irish suffrage societies have devoted all their energy to petitioning and blaming members of the English Parliament who are indifferent and unreachable, because women have no power to make or mar a bill, to overthrow a government, or to win the balance of power between two parties. Whilst Irishwomen were hammering away at the Irish members for years, they made very little impression on those same delegates.

> With pipes in mouths they go their way
> With hands in pockets; they are blest
> With grand digestions, only they
> Are such hard morsels to digest!

They have disagreed with a number of Irishwomen, and even some of our fighting men cannot swallow them at all; but still the franchise leagues have gone on nibbling at them, believing that constant chewing wears a stone. In the meantime, they have had very little time or inclination to work on those voters who can make their opinions felt with the stony members, or to make their own power felt in those places where they can. By swarming into the councils and corporations, and putting their own supporters in power everywhere, possibly women could boss a great deal of the power which is becoming important in urban and rural Ireland, and give expression to public opinions on the subject of the franchise, which they cannot do until they are public opinion.

When Irish women study the history of the English suffrage movement (which they do too often) and read of the savage treatment which those women have received from their own Government, they fear that the Irish members, who have lately shown themselves hostile to the woman's franchise will use the Home Rule Parliament to crush the feminist movement. But when we leave out of the consideration this body of delegates to the English Parliament and study the country behind them, with its social and political organisations, we find in every group, and on every council, that women are not only eligible, but well represented. In the Gaelic civilisation, which was never quite cast down and trampled out, and which the Gaelic League and Sinn Fein organisation are attempting to rebuild, the woman was the equal of the man in all things; she was never the woman of the harem, but the proud and independent comrade of her mate. The Irish were not a barbarous race glossed over with a semblance of civilisation as were the English by the Romans, but they were a cultivated and civilised people, who were subjected and glossed over with a thin veneer of English barbarity. Consequently, under the semblance of civilisation, in the English there is the old brutal savage, who used his club on his wife to convince her of his superiority; traces of it are seen in the Englishman of to-day, who the papers tell us, uses his 'club' as a weapon of defence or offence to his womanhood.

In Ireland, however, there peeps out through the worn particles of English influence the somewhat gaunt bones of that fine old civilisation which was ours. The Irishwoman has not been subjected and clubbed into obedience. She was not driven back with sneers and told to darn stockings when she stood by the men during the siege of Limerick. She was not told to go home and mind her babies when she came to the aid of the men of '98 – and in the days of the Land League no Irishman feared his country-women would be 'soiled by mixing in politics'. Irishwomen have been active through all ages in physical and political strife, very often there have been no stockings for them to darn, many a time there has been no hearth for them to keep, too often there were no babies for them to mind when the invaders or the great starvation had stricken down the children. But all the time they have obeyed the call of Ireland and of human reason to fight for their homes and their motherland, and many of them have lost their lives in defence of their country; it has never been said yet that their age long intrusion into politics 'has soiled and degraded' them and broken up the homes in Ireland. They have been foremost in nation-building, they are the foremost colonists in the small Irish-Ireland settlement in Ireland, they are the staunchest of the Gaelic garrison, and the question of their emancipation rests with those people who have been their neighbours in the colony, their comrades in the garrison, not with the bald-headed back-numbers of Irish nationalism who are rooted in a foreign parliament, and have forgotten the native soil.

Editorial: The Slave Women

2 MAY 1914

A perusal of the full report, in the 'Irish Volunteer', of Miss O'Farrelly's speech at the foundation of the 'Irishwomen's Council' confirms and deepens our first impression of the slavish character of this new project.

'We offer our homage to the men' – 'Our first duty is to give our allegiance and support to the men' – these are the kind of phrases that are scattered through it and give its keynote. We are satisfied that this movement like the movement of Ulster Unionist Women which it is imitating, is a thoroughly reactionary one, and opposed to the best interests of the women's movement in Ireland.

We have in type, and hope to publish in our next issue, an article from an Ulster correspondent, which puts this point of view clearly with regard to the Northern movement. Its arguments may be commended, not only to these Unionist women with whom it is primarily concerned, but also to their Southern Nationalist imitators. We publish this week a letter from a Southern Nationalist, Miss McSwiney [*sic*] – whom we know to be an active suffrage worker, and who is therefore welcome in these columns though her views are totally opposed to that policy of Suffrage First for which the *Irish Citizen* stands – in which a defence of the Women Volunteers is attempted. Miss McSwiney, though a suffragist, puts Party first. Of course she does not call it 'Party'; she attempts, as party camp followers always do, to persuade herself that she is upholding some great principle that is above Party. For her, it is 'Nationalism' that ties her to the chariot wheels of Mr Redmond, just as it is 'Unionism' that ties the Ulster woman to the chariot of Mr Edward Carson, and Liberalism that leads patient thralls of Mr Asquith in the Women's Liberal Federation. Miss McSwiney's argument is sheer sophistry.

There can be no nation without women, and there can be no free nation without free women. By denying freedom to the women of the nation, the

Party led by Mr Redmond have lost the right to call themselves 'Nationalists' in any other than a Party sense; and the Nationalist woman who supports them is false not only to her sex, but to the highest ideals of Nationalism. Miss McSwiney promises us a further contribution on the subject, which we shall be glad to publish and to deal with, in the hope that the full discussion of the subject may lead her, and those who think with her, to a clearer conception of the realities of the political position.

Correspondence

2 MAY 1914

Miss McSwiney, BA writes: I wish to protest in the most emphatic manner against the remarks made in your 'Current Comment' recently about those Irish women who consider that in the present crisis their country's interests must come first. You cannot be ignorant that that attitude is adopted by the vast majority of Nationalist suffragists. Are you so totally devoid of commonsense – not to speak of political acumen – that you cannot discriminate between the attitude of Nationalist women in Ireland and Party women in England? To characterise our point of view as 'slavish' and a display of 'crawl-servility to men' is the very best anti-suffragist campaign you can carry on in this country.

I say our point of view, because, as a Southern woman, I am in hearty agreement with my fellow-countrywomen of the Irishwomen's Council, and totally opposed to the attitudes of the Women Guardians who meet with your approval.

If you continue at the present rate alienating Nationalist opinion from the Suffrage cause, I should advise you to use as a subtitle for your paper – 'Chief Anti-Suffragist Organ in Ireland'.

Correspondence

9 MAY 1914

Miss Mary McSwiney writes: In your 'Comments' on my letter in last week's *Irish Citizen*, you speak of me as being 'tied to the chariot wheel of Mr

Redmond.' I am not a follower of Mr Redmond – nor of Mr O'Brien either – I use the word Nationalist to include all those who believe that self-government for Ireland is the most important question in this country at present, and must be paramount until Home Rule is attained. I do not put Party first; I put Ireland first.

Mr Redmond is offering the Irish people a very poor mouse after such years of labour; but, inadequate as the Home Rule Bill is, any Irishwoman who rejoices in its possible wrecking – because women are not included in it – is sadly in need of that 'clearer conception of the realities of the political position' in Ireland which you so kindly desire for my poor self.

I quite agree with you that there can be no free nation without free women; but the world – women included – has taken some thousands of years to realise that fact. Three years more, in our very exceptional circumstances, will not hurt us.

*

Miss Helena Moloney writes: It is with great regret I see the *Citizen* ranging itself on the side of those who are against women taking part in the armed defence of their country – because they may, incidentally, be a source of strength to Mr Redmond. This is an attitude which, as Miss McSwiney says, will do much to injure Suffrage in Ireland. The Volunteers, men and women, have been called into being to defend the liberties of all Irish citizens. I was not at the meeting at which Miss O'Farrelly made the speech which you quote, but I have no hesitation in saying that you put a wrong interpretation on the words – 'We offer our homage to the men', etc. It is no evidence of a slavish spirit, but an expression of allegiance to anti-English militancy.

Every Nationalist knows this to be true. You do not alter the facts of a case by dubbing other people's principles 'party' and calling your own party 'freedom'. It is possible, and may be desirable, to support the Parliamentary Party without necessarily supporting Mr Redmond's anti-suffrage opinions; and, personally, I have great confidence in the ability of Irish suffragists to deal with Mr Redmond and other antis on the subject of women when we get them away from the protection of the English Parliament. It is also possible for some women, without being what you call 'camp-followers', to imagine the freedom – even the partial freedom – of a nation to be of more importance than the partial freedom of the feminine portion of it. You say, truly, 'there can be no free nation without free women', but neither can there be free women in an enslaved nation, and it seems to me sound citizenship to put the welfare of the whole nation before any section of it.

Of course these views are opposed to the policy of 'Suffrage first' for which you stand, but I do not think the fact of our holding different views justifies your accusing us of being 'reactionary', 'camp-followers', 'patient thralls', and 'false to our sex and the highest ideals of Nationalism'. Such an article is calculated to make the *Irish Citizen*, and what it stands for, unpopular with many Nationalists; and that is a thing, I am sure, most of the women Volunteers would be very sorry to see.

Suffragists and Home Rule: a Plea for Common Sense
by Mary McSwiney, BA
23 MAY 1914

To plead with suffragists for a little common sense and political insight may be looked upon nowadays as a request for a dispatch of coals to Newcastle, and yet it seems to be true that many Irish suffragists are rather losing their heads, and by their present tactics injuring their own cause. This does not apply to Militants only, but to all those whose views are expressed in recent 'leaders' of the *Irish Citizen*. In England, convinced suffragists rightly place Votes for Women above and before all other reforms, and this policy expresses itself in consistent and continual opposition to the Government, while the Government, as such, is opposed to Woman Suffrage. No question of Party – no reform of any kind – social, fiscal, agrarian – can in any way compare with the dominant need in England today – the Woman's Voice – backed by the power of the Vote – in all questions of reform. But in Ireland, even those who place suffrage first must take the special circumstances of the country into consideration if they wish to win adherents to their cause. Ireland is struggling to settle not a Party question, but a National one, and opposition to the Government in the present crisis means opposition to Home Rule.

The fact that many Irish suffragists play the political ostrich and refuse to recognise the essential difference between this and English Party questions does not minimise that difference; it simply blinds their political intelligence and injures the cause they wish to promote.

Let us take England in an analogous position. Suppose her in thrall to Germany, and that after many fruitless struggles she is at length on the road to receive a measure of freedom. Can you imagine England refusing that measure because it only enfranchised half her people, but left her to enfranchise the other half within a few years? Is it thinkable that English women would try to ruin that measure because for a few years they would have to be governed by English men instead of Germans? Can you fancy Christabel Pankhurst herself hesitating, even if she honestly believed that by clinging to Germany she would get the women's vote sooner? Even if such an unpatriotic course were possible to Englishwomen, it would be none the more acceptable to Irishwomen.

It is idle to pooh-pooh this point of view; it is the actual point of view of the majority of the Irish people, and it has to be reckoned with. If, then, suffragists do not wish to alienate the sympathy of the Irish people – women as well as men – they must not hail with delight the prospect of the destruction of the Home Rule Bill.

Many Nationalist women are of the opinion that Mr Redmond made a big tactical blunder in opposing the Conciliation Bill and thus setting the English suffragists so hotly against him. But we must remember that whatever his private opinions, he was helpless here. He could not, even if he had wished, risk the Home Rule Bill by opposing the arch-anti Mr Asquith on his pet prejudice. Mr Redmond's one and only business at Westminster is to secure Home Rule.

He received no mandate for Woman Suffrage, and thoughtful and fairminded Irishwomen of every political belief recognise that.

To maintain that Home Rule is not Home Rule, and should not be accepted unless women are included, is puerile. The point for Irish suffragists to note is this: that no question but the Home Rule one will turn a single vote at an Irish election until Home Rule is finally attained. Therefore it is an absurdity to write that 'In Ireland the opposing parties are not yet fully convinced of the importance of the suffrage movement or the need to make terms with it.' The suggestion made lately that Irish suffragists should help to 'drum Asquith out of Fife' shows so little grasp of the situation in Ireland that one almost asks if we are supposed to be content to be cats-paws for English suffragists. In consequence of such deplorable partisan tactics, the suffrage cause is rapidly becoming synonymous with the Unionist cause and is losing day by day many Nationalist supporters.

Englishwomen want the vote for themselves first and foremost. That is natural, and we applaud and sympathise with their efforts. But in order to hasten their political enfranchisement – even by a year – they would not hesitate to wreck the cause of suffrage in Ireland for a generation or more. The sooner Irishwomen open their eyes to that fact, the sooner they will get back to sane methods. What is good for England is not good for Ireland in suffrage tactics any more than in other matters; and as Irishwomen we are concerned with our own country first.

It is no kindness to the cause of suffrage in Ireland that has brought an English society to carry on an active campaign in this country. We cannot logically complain if Englishwomen damage Irish interests in England in order to further their own; but let them confine their campaign to their own side of the Channel. It is not 'playing the game' to deliberately injure our movement in our own country, in order to advance theirs. The sophistry that answers that in winning the vote for themselves they are winning it for us does not blind us. The women of Ireland want the vote but they do not want it nor would they take it at the expense of Home Rule – even if we have to wait three years! What are three years in the life of a nation? To those suffragists who are truly sincere in their policy of 'suffrage first', I earnestly appeal for wiser methods for the sake of the cause they have at heart. Let them take into account the special conditions of their country – as wise politicians will – and, whatever their private opinions may be, cease to injure that cause by knocking their political heads against the stone-wall of the National Will.

Let us make no mistake. These tactics if persisted in, will not injure Home Rule; they most undoubtedly will injure the suffrage movement, and postpone indefinitely the fulfilment of our hopes.

Editorial: The Slave Women Again

23 MAY 1914

We publish this week another of those wrong-headed appeals by which Miss McSwiney, the spokeswoman of the Slave Women (Nationalist variety) seeks to justify her placing of a party Nationalism above the cause of her sex. We say a party Nationalism; for in seeking to show that her adherence is not to a party, but to the principle of Nationalism, Miss McSwiney begs the very question at issue. It is not Nationalism as such, but Nationalism as perverted by Mr Redmond, that calls for the uncompromising opposition of Irish suffragists. Miss McSwiney's position shows some advance in that taken up by similar partisans a few years ago. Then Mr Asquith was sacrosanct; now Miss McSwiney admits Mr Asquith's sinister role in wrecking women's hopes, but seeks to exculpate Mr Redmond. The Irish leader, she says, 'could not even if he wished' have supported the Conciliation Bill in opposition to Mr Asquith's pet prejudice. Will Miss McSwiney apply herself to this question: Why did Mr Redmond not say so? The excuse she puts forward for him is one he had never dared put forward himself. Had he done so – had he said frankly that his action in deliberately killing the Conciliation Bill was due to the exigencies of the English political situation and had he accompanied that plea by a promise to take up Votes for Women in a Home Rule Parliament – Miss McSwiney's position would be a logical and tenable one. Nationalist suffragists might then, quite reasonably, have regarded the pledge for the future as a fair recompense for the postponement of their hopes – just as Unionist suffragists were satisfied with Sir Edward Carson's pledge to give them votes under his Provisional Government. But Mr Redmond's course was doubly different. He denied in the face of all the evidence, that he had anything to do with the killing of the Conciliation Bill. He stated categorically that he would always oppose Votes for Women, in a Home Rule Parliament as well as at Westminster. It was this double treachery and hostility that made opposition to him, and to the Party which was the weak instrument of his will, imperative on the part of self-respecting Irish women. Those who do not recognise this categorical imperative are Slave Women, whether they realise it or not.

It is this identification, in Mr Redmond's personality, of official Nationalism with the most virulent anti-feminism that renders irrelevant Miss McSwiney's attempted Anglo-German parallel. To make sure a parallel is at all conceivable, we must imagine Mr Asquith as an English 'Nationalist' leader, fighting a German sovereignty. In such a case we hope, and believe, that English women suffragists would have more self-respect than to work for Mr Asquith or facilitate a campaign destined to place them absolutely under his control; they might well think the Kaiser's rule preferable. If they wanted to work for English Nationalism they would form a party of their own for that purpose – a party in which women's right to English citizenship would be explicitly recognised. Here is where the 'Irishwomen's Council' might come in. If that body were to declare definitely in favour of the equal citizenship of women, and were to refuse its assistance to any party or leader failing to recognise that principle, it would justify itself, and might do useful work among those Nationalist women who are not yet prepared to put suffrage first. Until it makes such a declaration it is an organisation of Slave Women.

We do not question Miss McSwiney's personal sincerity in the line she takes up. That a woman suffragist should find it possible to take such a line makes it all the more necessary to write plainly on the subject. What Miss McSwiney lacks is political education. It is not at all surprising that many Irish women, both North and South, should suffer under that disability. We are grateful to Miss McSwiney for having put the view of the Southern section of politically uneducated women so forcibly. We are satisfied that the more the question is discussed, the more clearly will Irish women, Nationalist and Unionist, North and South, perceive that an independent suffragist policy, opposing every body of responsible politicians which is hostile to women's citizenship, is the only one consistent with self-respect.

Editorial: Women and the Irish Volunteers

4 JULY 1914

When Mr Redmond captured the Irish Volunteers a fortnight ago, by securing the addition of 25 of his nominees to the Provisional Committee, we asked Miss McSwiney, Miss Jacob, and other defenders of the Volunteers and their women's auxiliary, 'Cumann na mBan', to explain how they now stood in regard to these organisations. There has been no response. Yet surely the position requires definition.

The Irish Volunteers were started, nominally, as a non-party force, on a broad national basis, for defensive purposes only; and in this spirit many people not usually associated with party politics (notably the Rev. Dudley Fletcher) associated themselves with the new departure. We recognised the existence of a good spirit in many of the rank and file of the Volunteers; but from the first we suspected possibilities of mischief in the handling of the central machinery. Consequently, we asked that the Volunteers who professed to stand for 'the rights and liberties of the Irish people', should definitely state that they included women's rights of equal citizenship among those which they were prepared to maintain, in accordance with the sprint of ancient Irish civilisation.

We pointed out the inconsistency of ignoring women in the objects and the control of the movement, while at the same time inviting women to subscribe money for the equipment of the Volunteers; and we advised Irish women in general not to associate themselves with this movement unless they received definite guarantees that their status as citizens would be formally recognized by the leaders of the movement. When the 'Irishwomen's Council', or 'Cumann na mBan', was formed, with the object of collecting money for the Volunteers, we protested against women allowing themselves to be used for the purpose of helping a men's association over which they had no effective control, and urged that, at the very least, subscriptions should be conditional on a share in the government.

Miss McSwiney, Miss Helena Moloney, and Miss Jacob defended the Volunteers in our columns. Their chief argument – the only one with the slightest cogency – was that the Volunteers were on a 'broad national basis' and that support of them did not by any means imply support of Mr Redmond.

Even then the position they defended was sufficiently slavish with regard to the men actually at the head of the movement; but the position has now materially altered. The Irish Volunteers have become a mere annex of Mr Redmond's Party, a pawn in his political game. What are the suffragists on the 'Irishwomen's Council' going to do?

Are they prepared to continue to assist a movement which has been captured by the leading anti-suffragist politician in Ireland?

Mr Redmond has lost no time in showing his contempt for the slave women. Ignoring the 'Irishwomen's Council' he has formed a new body, the 'Irish Volunteer Aid Association', to do precisely the same auxiliary work which the 'Irishwomen's Council' (farcical misnomer!) set before itself. But the new Association is officered and governed by men; women are to be allowed to join it, to subscribe to it, to work for it; but not one woman is given a place on its Committee.

We cannot pretend to regret this plain demonstration of Mr Redmond's attitude. But, if there are still any free-minded women left in the 'Irishwomen's Council', surely this deliberate insult will arouse them to a sense of the ignominy of their position.

Correspondence

11 JULY 1914

Miss R. Jacob writes: As my name is mentioned, along with those of Miss Moloney and Miss McSwiney, in your last week's leading article, 'Women and the Irish Volunteers', I am quite ready to admit that 'the position has materially altered' since Mr Redmond has obtained control of the Volunteers, and I deplore extremely the silent acquiescence of the executive of Cumann na mBan in the present altered state of affairs.

The Future of Irishwomen

Speech delivered by Countess Marcievicz [sic]
at IWFL Meeting, October 12th

23 OCTOBER 1915

By a law passed at the Council of Drumceat, 590, the women of Ireland were exempted from military service. Over 100 years after, the law had to be renewed as it had become inoperative! Ancient Ireland bred warrior women, and women played a heroic part in those days. To-day we are in danger of being civilised by men out of existence. What distinguished Ireland chiefly of old was the number of fighting women who held their own against the world, who owed no allegiance to any man, who were super-women – the Maeves, the Machas, the warrior-queens. Beside the Penelope type of women, like Emer, who sat at home and span, we have these; beside our Helen, Deirdre, we had also the great fighting women:

> Alas! for the deeds of the dead forgotten and out of mind,
> Lavarcam, the Wise and Fand and the Faery-woman Feithleen;
> Alas, for the sword of Fleeas, red flaming along the wind,
> And Skiah from the Isle of Mists, the dark and terrible Queen.
> Their souls were fierce with freedom, they loved and they called no man
>   lord,
> Freely the winds of Eirinn could tangle their loose-flowing hair;
> Here in the sunny grianan the days are weary and long,
> Weary are we of the sunshine and the cry of the wind and the rain.[2]

That spirit is now only alive in the suffragettes. Throughout later history, though Irishwomen have suffered and worked, they have as a rule taken no prominent part; there are no great leaders. Dervorgilla was a creature of sex simply. Granuaile, true, went back to the older type and was a fighting queen, but not much is known of her. Countess Marcievicz here touched on many of the women of '98, and pointed out how little is known of them. She went on to say that of all these we get glimpses, from male chroniclers, but their roles seem to have been passive. They followed and helped the men, they did not initiate enterprises of their own. The same is true even of brave Anne Devlin, true of weak Sarah Curran, who drifted to madness after Emmet's death, and married one of his bitter foes.

---

2 This is from the poem 'Lament of the Daughters of Ireland' by Eva Gore-Booth, Markievicz's sister.

The Ladies' Land League, founded by Anna Parnell, promised better things. When the men leaders were all imprisoned it ran the movement, and started to do the militant things that the men only threatened and talked of, but when the men came out, they proceeded to discard the women – as usual – and disbanded the Ladies' Land League. That was the last of women in national movements down to our time. Today the women attached to national movements are there chiefly to collect funds for the men to spend. These Ladies' Auxiliaries demoralise women, set them up in separate camps, and deprive them of all initiative and independence. Women are left to rely on sex charm, or intrigue and backstairs influence.

Tommy Moore, the popular poet of his day, and also, many days later, has set Ireland a very low idea of woman to worship. To him woman is merely sex, and an excuse for a drink. Not a companion or a friend, but a beautiful houri holding dominion by her careful manipulation of her sex and her good looks. In particular does the young lady annoy one, who started to walk around Ireland with all her jewels on, a golden wand in her hand, and a sly appeal to 'man' from out the corner of her down-cast eyes. She is very like the lap dog which, when it meets a larger animal, rolls over on its back, turns up its toes, and looks pathetic. The better ideal for women who, whether they like it or not, are living in a work-a-day world, would be – If you want to walk around Ireland or any other country, dress suitably in short skirt and strong boots, leave you jewels and gold wands in the bank, and buy a revolver. Don't trust to your 'feminine charm' and your capacity for getting on the soft side of men, but take up your responsibilities and be prepared to go your own way depending for safety on your own courage, your own truth, and your own common sense, and not on the problematic chivalry of the men you may meet on the way. The two brilliant classes of women who follow this higher ideal are Suffragettes and the Trades Union or Labour women. In them lies the hope of the future. But for them women are everywhere today in a position of inferiority. And the Churches, both Catholic and Protestant, are to blame for this, for both foster the tradition of segregation of the sexes.

A consciousness of their own dignity and worth should be encouraged in women. They should be urged to get away from wrong ideals and false standards of womanhood, to escape from their domestic ruts, their feminine pens. It would be well to aim at bringing out, as it were, the masculine side of women's souls, as well as the feminine side of men's souls. War is helping to do this by shaking women out of old grooves and forcing responsibilities on them. We have got to get rid of the last vestige of the Harem before woman is free as our dream of the future would have her.

Editorial: Suffrage Casualties

SEPTEMBER 1916

The ranks of suffragists have been sadly depleted by the events of Easter Week: the Irish Volunteers and Citizen Army were suffragists almost to a man, and the women prominent in the movement were all convinced and practical exponents of the doctrine of equality of the sexes and, like Chaucer's Parson, what they preached they always practised in themselves. When the true history of those days comes to be written, that of the women deserves a special chapter. Many are now learning the bitter truth that it is often easier to die than to live for a cherished cause. A great living poet has paid tribute to them; we hope his words will soon be 'released' for publication. Of the dead leaders James Connolly stands foremost as a friend of suffrage, and of many a progressive cause an unfailing and courageous champion. In perilous days when obloquy was our portion from orthodox Unionist and Nationalist, Redmondite and Carsonite alike, James Connolly stood by us: never a jibe at womanhood fell from his lips – with the wisdom of true statesmanship, that ought to have something of the seer, he recognised that the cause of Woman and Labour was twin, and this gospel he preached unfailingly to his followers. James Connolly deserves a shrine in the heart of every suffragist.

Pearse in his philosophic pamphlet 'From a Hermitage' also gave eloquent testimony to the feminist faith that was in him. Thomas MacDonagh, the 'gentle poet of the sword', as Robert Lynd calls him, was ever ready to support our cause and voice our claims. From Joseph Plunkett, the youngest, to Thomas Clarke, the oldest of the signatories to the Proclamation, all were friends to our movement. The Proclamation gave equality of citizenship to women and men alike on the human basis, and might well be taken as a model by more imposing commonwealths and empires which prate of the Rights of Man so glibly, while ignoring the Rights of the Mothers of Man. What if it were all the dream of visionaries? Irishwomen were not excluded from the Paradise! Liberty-loving France and free America in establishing their Republics included in their dream of freedom only the male; like the Mohommedan's, their paradise was strictly masculine. Ireland, left to her true self, takes a larger view: as of old her civilisation was based on feminism, giving under the Brehon Laws equal rights to men and women, so in modern days the two Provisional Governments – in aught else so unalike – that were planned by Irishmen, recognised women. Carson's Provisional Government and Connolly's Provisional Government extended citizenship to Irishwomen and gave them a place on the Executive. Ireland should never permit other leaders to fall below this high standard.

Other outstanding personalities deserve well of suffragists. Madame Marcievicz will be remembered to readers of the *Irish Citizen* for her striking historical articles on 'The Women of '98'; Partridge, T.C.; R. O'Carroll, T.C.; Gerald Crofts, Mallin, John McBride, William O'Brien, Philip Sargent, Helena Moloney, Sean Connolly, Henry Dixon, Ald. T. Kelly, William Sears, Sean T. O'Kelly, Sean Milroy, Miss Nellie Gifford, Miss Kearney, and many others now in prison, deported, or released after a long detention, are among our supporters – in fact, any attempt to name them all would exhaust our space. Others well known to suffragists are Dr Kathleen Lynn, who mercifully helped the wounded and the dying, Ernest Kavanagh, the gentle pacifist, shot in the streets, who contributed our suffrage cartoons; Crawford Neil, the charming poet, killed by a stray bullet of a looter, renowned for his songs at our social gatherings. Whatever the opinions of Irish suffragists may be on the rising (and our readings include every possible divergence of view) all must realise that in these men and women we have lost (some, happily, only temporarily) friends and champions difficult, if not impossible, to replace. It is the tragic lesson of militarism, in whatever guise – it sweeps away the bravest and the best.

F.S.S.

A Dedicatory Poem
by James H. Cousins

When with dark wrongs we waged our strife,
I found you pure, past praise or frown,
But, in the blinding light of life,
Saw not your hovering martyr crown;
Nor dreamt that when in April showers,
New life's green banners were unfurled –
You, in the clash of deadly powers,
Should fall and falling, shake the world.

Oh! now forgive these eyes that far
Held me from measure of your heights,
And saw not, in your war with war;

You of your end had inward sight,
And heard round your vicarious head
God's thunder to the Nation's call:
Life is not nourished on the dead:
Who take the sword by sword shall fall.

Forgive my love that saw no need
For such loud end in face of spring
For you, who were a selfless reed
Where freedom's breath ceased not to sing.

Oh! honour, honour – dogs your feet,
Who, with a moment's breath to live,
Let not death's bitter spoil life's sweet,
But stood as One who said: 'Forgive,
Father! they know not what they do.'

Ere, the reluctant rifles cried
(Nay to new life saluted!) You
On their blind error smiled, and died.

Yea, and upon our shattering grief
You smile, in knowledge deeper grown,
Saying: 'You count my life a leaf
By some dark wind to darkness blown.

It is not so.' And there you leave
The fact, and to new business press –
A soul one-purposeful to weave
Love's garment for a world's distress.

Surely, in that exalted place
Where lauding seraphs round you press,
Some wistfulness will cross your face
Echoed from our heart-loneliness;
And through Heav'n's harpings you will find
A hallowness in praise of Him;
Our strife in darkness call to mind,
And slip between the Cherubim
Crying: 'I want no starry crown;

I want no harp save one that thrills –
Marching the hosts of Reason down
To war with darkness 'twixt the hills'
And somehow – though we know not how,
Or may not know the well-known face –
Someone will glimpse your placid brow,
And feel you strongly in your place –
You whom no power or pride e'er awed;
Whose hand would heal where sharp it fell,
Smite Error on the Throne of God
And smile truth though found in Hell.

My Experiences in Prison
by Maud Gonne MacBride
JUNE–JULY 1919

Read at the I.W.F.L.

While so many of our best citizens are locked up by England in her prisons it is well for us to consider the question of prison conditions, and realise the wickedness of the whole system, which results in the majority of cases in breaking down the health of the prisoners; it is well for us to remember what so many who are working for Irish liberty are enduring, so that individually and collectively we use every means in our power to obtain their release. Under the Irish Republic actually proclaimed, and which I hope we shall soon see in effective operation, we shall have to consider the question of prisons generally, and make up our minds what we want them to be like, or if we want them to exist at all. I should like to see them done away with altogether; they are useless, expensive and immoral. If we except the political, of whom I believe there were several hundreds last year (and they would disappear automatically with English rule) the prison population in Ireland is very small, so that most of the prisons could be closed and the others run as hospitals for medical and curative treatment rather than as places of punishment. Certainly inveterate drunkards, for instance, who render their homes intolerable, break the furniture, beat their children must be restrained in some way, and kept from spoiling the lives of those around them. Certainly, the community must be protected from hideous crimes happily rare in Ireland, but increasing since military service and the war sent so many men mad, familiarising them with every sort of horror and crime and violence – but in all these cases medical and spiritual care of the criminal, and not punishment, is needed.

Few people would be criminals if they were happy. Most criminals have something wrong with their nervous system either from the over strain due to bad social conditions or perhaps to heredity, it is the priest or the doctor and not the jailer, who should cure them.

That the actual prison system does not cure them or act as a deterrent is proved from the way the prison population return again and again to jail. Once a criminal always a criminal is the result of the English system. In Holloway the star class, i.e. the first offenders, was, as far as I could see, comparatively small, and generally composed of very young girls. Most of the prisoners had been in many times; during the six months I was there I used to see the same faces returning after short intervals of freedom. One old woman I was told was in after her 45th conviction! From the English prison system one may learn all that should be avoided in a decent community, for this reason I will describe Holloway.

Outside it looks a charming place, picturesquely built, I think on the model of Chester Castle; it has turrets and battlements overgrown with Virginia creeper and bright flower beds each side of the entrance, which makes it look quite reassuring to the general public who pass by, and who I dare-say think with smug English complacency, 'How well we treat even our criminals, what a noble people we are.'

Inside it is very different. I believe there is lodging for some 3,000 prisoners, and it seems always crowded. There are four stories of cells in most of the wings which ray out starfish fashion from a central building between them, are narrow, black, asphalted yards where in dreary rings the prisoners take their exercise; no sun penetrates in some of these, the surrounding buildings are too high; no flowers or creepers here, only black coal or coke dumps. I was told by the wardress that there was a large exercise ground with grass in the middle in another part of the prison, but I never saw it. Mrs Clarke, Countess Markievicz, and myself exercised in a small asphalted yard with a coke dump on one side as high as the second storey, when the wind blew the fine dust from it used to hurt our eyes, and in conjunction with the ill-ventilated cells was, I think, the cause of the lung trouble I developed. This yard was surrounded on three sides by prison buildings, and on the fourth side by the laundry and disinfection furnaces.

After we were transferred to hospital we used to exercise in the hospital yard on an asphalt path surrounding a grass patch and a geranium bed. On the grass the bandages used in this hospital used to be dried, and sometimes mattresses aired after disinfection. There was a hedge of Michaelmas Daisies, there was also a never-ending procession of poor syphilitic women going into the hospital surgery for treatment. The stream never ceased all day long, for Holloway prison is at the same time a vast lock hospital. One often heard distressing cries and groans from the surgery, and the smell of disinfectants was sickening. On our way to chapel we used to pass through sunless gloomy yards, and see the unfortunate women pacing in single file about five feet apart in hopeless rings which never met, a wardress seated in the centre or at the end to see they did not talk or leave the ranks. The women in the centre must get giddy walking round and round the circle was so small. The rings where they walked were marked on the asphalt.

The cells where we were at first confined in the wing were on the fourth story, they measured about seven feet by thirteen feet. They were lighted by a tiny barred window at the top too high to see out of except by standing on a chair. These windows could not open, only one pane of the glass could slip aside leaving about half a foot where the fresh air could penetrate. It was impossible to clean the glass on the outside, so the little light they admitted was veiled by dust. Of course, we always kept this half foot open, but it was too high up to air the cells. There were various gratings which, I suppose, were meant to stimulate ventilation, but no air penetrated through them, though, no doubt, they satisfied visiting justices and health commissioners, and allowed them the comfortable consciousness that England is a wonderful country and understands sanitation and fresh air. The cells, really aired when the doors were opened for cleaning, opened into the hall or well round which the four tiers of cells ran, and on each tier there were four open lavatories, the smell from which was beyond description. English lavatories, it appears, are always open, they have half doors, over which and under which one can see from outside. And when, as was the case during the six weeks of my stay in the wing, workmen were employed in the galleries there is very serious cause and ground for complaint from the point of view of ordinary decency, a fact which I pointed out on more than one occasion to the authorities, as an example of the English sense of delicacy.

The air in the cells was so bad that no growing flower could survive more than three days without its leaves withering and turning yellow. Our friends often sent us plants, but not even the hardiest geranium would survive till we discovered that by leaving them in the exercise yard alternate nights we were able to prolong their lives, and we generally descended to the exercise ground each carrying her pot of flowers.

The ordinary prisoners were shockingly underfed, the girls who cleaned our cells (for we refused to do any prison work) told me they were starving, and it became our principle amusement passing food to them or to any of the prisoners who passed near us. We politicals were almost at once put on hospital diet and could get food sent in which the ordinary prisoners could not, and every Sunday in chapel one saw the faces of the poor girls getting whiter, thinner, and more pinched as the starvation and bad air told on them. The newcomers could be picked out easily by their complexions; they had not yet got the prison pallor. In prison all acts of kindness are forbidden, they are the greatest crime of which either a prisoner or a wardress can be guilty. A word of sympathy is a crime, a prisoner who would help another weaker than herself is liable to punishment. A wardress who wishes for advancement must report often, i.e., get the unfortunate girls under her charge into punishment, or her fellow wardresses fined. Secret reports are encouraged. The consequence is an abject state of suspicion and fear on all sides. The prison officials fear one another, the wardresses fear the officials and suspect each other, the prisoners fear everyone and also suspect each other, for talebearing is encouraged and rewarded. Even the chaplains are afraid. I saw one young wardress get into trouble through my fault. She had been over a gang of prisoners who were carrying the coal from the dump in the exercise yard of the wing, and had seen me taming and feeding the pigeons, who seem to be particularly jail birds for they are in all prisons. After we were in the hospital this same wardress with her gang of prisoners brought coal one day to the hospital dump. I nodded to her, and she said: 'The pigeons have followed you here, they have quite deserted the other exercise yard.' For that remark I believe the poor girl was fined. I saw her afterwards, but she did not dare to raise her head or even to glance in my direction.

That is the English prison system. There are schools for the illiterate, there are lady visitors who patronise the prisoners, there are visiting Justices, but what good can they accomplish against an immoral system based on meanness and tyranny, a system calculated to destroy the souls and bodies of the victims? They can only make futile though praiseworthy efforts. Few, if any, of them understand the first word of the problem they are up against. I doubt if even the chaplains understand, though they feel there is something wrong. To understand one must have seen it from the prisoners' view point.

All the espionage and reporting does not prevent the contagion of vice. One of the girls who cleaned my cell said: 'This is a wicked place. Whatever I didn't know before I know now'; and another said: 'I have learned a lot here, and I mean to use it when I get out.' And it was not good she meant.

Some of the old jail-birds take pleasure in instructing the young in the ways of vice. Rendez-vouz are arranged for the jail gate, receipts for abortion are freely passed along, forbidden intercourse makes it daily necessary. I have described the English prison system to show what should be avoided. If prisons must exist: − 1st, Let them be small; huge institutions can never be humane. The individual gets lost, and the only hope of reform is through the individual; 2nd, Put away the idea of punishment. Men have no right to judge or apportion punishment. That right belongs only to God. The magistrates who condemn are probably far more criminal than the poor victims they judge. If certain individuals have to be restrained for the sake of the community, an effort should be made to cure them.

Prisons should be thoroughly sanitary; prisoners should be well fed, for with lower vitality and shattered nerves prisoners when they return to the world have no chance. I would like to see prisons conducted as much on home lines as possible, the matron or governor to be simply the head of the household. Work there should be; gardens and farms should be attached so as to make them as far as possible self-supporting. Each prison should grow its own vegetables, bake its own bread, rear its own fowl, but the work should not be punitive, it should be useful; recreation should be provided and intercourse allowed, though I think, probably the presence of some safe person who would turn the conversation into harmless channels would be necessary. Countess Markievicz told me that when she was a convict at Aylesbury the filthy conversation of her fellow-convicts was at first very painful to her, but that very soon she was able by her influence to change it.

All law not based on Christ's law of love is a very dangerous thing, more dangerous than the crimes it is supposed to prevent. It is often the cause of crime and protects the rich against the poor, the strong against the weak; as understood by the English it is organised tyranny. The English prisons are the outposts of Hell.

Shifting feminism from the periphery to the centre

The significance of the Irish suffragists can be understood on a number of levels. At a rather simple level one could argue they are important because they helped to ensure that Irish women won the vote. However, as this book has attempted to demonstrate, they are also important for a wider range of reasons.

Through their actions, speeches and writings, suffragists help us to challenge the 'truism that prior to the 1960s, Irish women were passive victims of Catholicism' (Connolly, 2002: 59). On the contrary, as this book has shown, Irish feminists showed ingenuity, courage and determination to resist oppression in both the public and private spheres. In particular, the *Irish Citizen* newspaper documents a feminist critique of early twentieth-century Irish society, a counter-narrative that has rarely been seen or heard elsewhere. Through this medium, feminist campaigners tackled numerous forms of inequality and oppression – 'ventilating evil', as Meg Connery so eloquently described it. They discussed problems that are still part of Irish society in the early twentieth-first century. In addition, as many of the articles cited in this book reveal, they presented sophisticated feminist analyses drawing on a range of arguments and philosophical insights inspired by diverse writers and theorists, developing theses that in some cases seem radical even by today's standards.

Therefore, I believe that the *Irish Citizen* represents a crucial part of the history of Irish feminism. In a country that has been dominated by records of men's deeds and men's words, Irish suffragists illustrate that Irish women were not just active agents in our history but that they offered a different understanding of that history. Their writings on class, trade unionism, morality, sexual abuse, the law and nationalism challenge a monolithic view of Irish society. They gave voice to a multiplicity of opinions and life experiences. The fact that, until recent decades, they have been absent from recorded history has led to a narrow understanding of the discourses in Ireland prior to partition and independence.

According to Eavan Boland, women have often appeared in Irish writings as myths and symbols, as passive and decorative – 'raised to emblematic status' (1989: 12). She says:

The more I thought about it, the more uneasy I became. The wrath and grief of Irish history seemed to me – as it did to many – one of our true possessions. Women were part of that wrath, had endured that grief. Once the idea of a nation influences the perception of a woman then that woman is suddenly and inevitably simplified. She can no longer have complex feelings and aspirations. She becomes the passive projection of a national idea. (1989: 12–13)

Writing about the traditional representations of Irish women, Gerardine Meaney says: 'Sexual identity and national identity are mutually dependent. The images of suffering Mother Ireland and the self-sacrificing Irish mother are difficult to separate. Both serve to obliterate the reality of women's lives' (1991: 3). Nonetheless, Meaney expresses wariness about falling into a revisionist trap. She has argued that some revisionists have used feminism as a way to attack or dismiss nationalism. On a similar theme, Linda Connolly offers a different approach, arguing that feminism challenges the 'grand-narratives' of Irish social history, presenting new perspectives which help us to go beyond the narrow dichotomy of nationalism versus revisionism (Connolly, 2002: 5–6). Hence, while nationalist and revisionist historians challenge each other's interpretations of Irish history (Fennell, 1989), the suffragists provide a contemporary feminist analysis of Irish society. This is a slant that has been considerably under-utilised by historians and political analysts (see Ryan & Ward, 2004; Pašeta, 2013).

On the international level, the history of feminism cannot be understood without a recognition of the interconnections and interactions between colonialism, nationalism and feminism (Delap et al., 2006). Delap, Ryan and Zackodnik argue that attention to feminists' work within national discourses 'begins to shift feminisms from political periphery to centre, to recast women from passive symbols of nation to active participants in the articulation of national identity' (2006: 242). This book, by re-assessing feminists' engagement not just with Irish nationalism but with various political, economic and social challenges, has sought to contribute to that shifting of feminism from periphery to centre. In so doing, I argue that the *Irish Citizen* is an invaluable resource.

As Delap et al. have argued, 'while autobiographies, biographies and specialist collections are usually only associated with a small minority of feminist campaigners, periodicals have tended to be a much more accessible medium of expression for a greater diversity of activists' (2006: 241). Thus, 'feminist print culture in its diversity' offers insights into 'great complexity' and so furthers our historical understanding (Delap et al., 2006: 242).

Through the pages of the *Irish Citizen* we learn that suffragists were women (and in some cases men) of many different ideas and backgrounds, religious, social and political. Yet they shared a common faith in suffrage and the difference that it could bring to the lives of women – rich and poor. However, they were not naive that the vote would solve all problems. They argued for a wider campaign of social reform to tackle inequality and oppression at all levels of society.

As demonstrated by that plucky and defiant little paper, Irish feminists did 'interrogate nationalism'. During those years of the home rule movement, the Easter Rising of 1916 and the election victory of Sinn Féin in 1918, no Irish suffragist could ignore nationalism. However, in engaging with nationalism Irish suffragists raised fundamental questions of loyalty, duty, priority, militarism, citizenship and access to power.

Nonetheless, I am wary of presenting suffragists simply through a feminism-versus-nationalism lens. While acknowledging the importance of the anti-colonial context, I have deliberately sought to widen the discussion to include pacifism, internationalism, socialism, moral reformism and egalitarianism, to illustrate not only the broad agenda of feminism but also to shift the narrative to topics that have been less studied in the Irish context.

As illustrated by the *Irish Citizen*, the suffrage movement was involved in lively debates and discussions about women's nature, women's roles in public life, housework, sexual abuse, morality and so on. They were attempting to create new models of behaviour for women by breaking down traditional stereotypes. They were questioning the taken-for-granted world and exploring new possibilities.

This book has, of necessity, been selective. Obviously, there were many articles and writers who have not been included here for reasons of space. For example, the *Irish Citizen* devoted considerable space to discussing the arts, especially theatre (see Reynolds, 2007), but unfortunately that was beyond the scope of this book.

Of course, one may wonder how representative were those suffragists who actually wrote in the *Irish Citizen*. Perhaps they were simply a minority of outspoken feminists? This might be true. However, it is important to remember that almost every single suffrage group in the country – from the MWFL to the IWSLGA, the IWRL to the IWSS – had regular contributions printed in the paper. Numerically such groups accounted for the vast majority of Irish suffragists, so in that respect, they must have reflected the views of their members.

Still, there is undoubtedly a repetition of certain names among the list of regular contributors, including Duggan, Bennett, Connery, MacSwiney,

Cousins and Sheehy Skeffington. Clearly, there was a small core of writers who regularly expressed their views in the paper. These writers developed their arguments and feminist beliefs through the pages of the *Irish Citizen*. They became involved in ongoing debates with other contributors. In addition, it is significant that they did not all come from one suffrage group, and they did not advocate merely one approach to feminism.

The *Irish Citizen* is important precisely because it does represent a relatively small and minority voice – the voice of Irish feminism. This highlights an alternative voice that challenged the dominant views of the church, the state and the law – and, in so doing, it offers us a very different understanding of Irish society in the early years of the twentieth century.

Ireland in the twenty-first century, of course, is very different to the Ireland of one hundred years ago. The lives of women have improved immensely in several important ways. Nonetheless, many of the issues tackled by our feminist foremothers remain pertinent to feminists today: equal pay, sexual abuse, domestic violence, war and pacifism, and so on.

We need to hear the voices of our foremothers and learn from their experiences. In this way perhaps each generation of feminists can stop reinventing the wheel. We can conclude where we began by quoting Margaret Cousins, whose words capture the essence of the *Irish Citizen*: 'It is the visible demonstration of our continuity and purpose and of our capability in action … it is the voice of the woman crying in the wilderness …' (*Irish Citizen*, Jan. 1917).

Bibliography

Banerjee, Sikata, *Muscular nationalism: gender, violence, and empire in India and Ireland, 1914–2004* (New York, 2012).

Banks, Olive, *Faces of feminism: a study of feminism as a social movement* (London, 1986).

Beaumont, Caitriona, 'After the vote: women, citizenship and the campaign for gender equality in the Irish Free State (1922–1943)' in Louise Ryan and Margaret Ward (eds), *Irish women and the vote: becoming citizens* (Dublin, 2007), pp 231–50.

Bland, Lucy, 'Heterosexuality, feminism and *The Freewoman* journal in early twentieth-century England', *Women's History Review*, 4:1 (1995), pp 5–23.

Boland, Eavan, *A kind of scar: the woman poet in a national tradition* (Dublin, 1989).

Bolt, Christine, *The women's movements in the United States and Britain from the 1790s to the 1920s* (London, 2014).

Bryson, Valerie, *Feminist political theory: an introduction* (London, 1992).

Buckley, Margaret, *The jangle of the keys* (Dublin, 1938).

Burton, Antoinette, 'Colonial encounters in late-Victorian England', *Feminist Review* 49 (1995), pp 29–49.

Candy, Catherine, 'Relating feminisms, nationalisms and imperialisms: Ireland, India and Margaret Cousins's sexual politics', *Women's History Review*, 3:4 (1994), pp 581–94.

—, 'Untouchability, vegetarianism and the suffragist ideology of Margaret Cousins' in Louise Ryan and Margaret Ward (eds), *Irish women and the vote: becoming citizens* (Dublin, 2007), pp 154–70.

Clancy, Mary, 'Women of the West; campaigning for the vote in early twentieth-century Galway' in Louise Ryan and Margaret Ward (eds), *Irish women and the vote: becoming citizens* (Dublin, 2007), pp 45–59.

Clear, Caitriona, *Women of the house: women's household work in Ireland, 1926–1961: discourses, experiences, memories* (Dublin, 2000).

Conlon, Lil, *Cumann na mBan and the women of Ireland* (Kilkenny, 1969).

Connolly, Linda, *The Irish women's movement: from revolution to devolution* (Amsterdam, 2002).

Connolly, Linda and Niamh Hourigan (eds), *Social movements and Ireland* (Manchester, 2006).

Corish, Patrick J., *Radicals, rebels and establishments* (Belfast, 1985).

Coulter, Carol, *Hidden tradition: feminism, women and nationalism in Ireland* (Cork, 1993).

Cousins, James and Margaret, *We two together* (Madras, 1950).

Cronin, Anthony, *An Irish eye: viewpoints* (Kerry, 1985).

Crossman, Virginia, *The poor law in Ireland, 1838–1948* (Dundalk, 2006).

Cullen, Mary, 'How radical was Irish feminism?' in Patrick J. Corish, *Radicals, rebels and establishments* (Belfast, 1985).

—, 'Feminism, citizenship and suffrage: a long dialogue' in Louise Ryan and Margaret Ward (eds), *Irish women and the vote: becoming citizens* (Dublin, 2007), pp 1–20.

Cullen, Mary and Maria Luddy, *Women, power and consciousness in nineteenth-century Ireland* (Dublin, 1995).

—, *Female activists: Irish women and change, 1900–1960* (Dublin, 2001).

Cullen Owens, Rosemary, 'Votes for Ladies', *Saothar*, 8 (1983), pp 32–47.

—, *Smashing times: a history of the Irish women's suffrage movement, 1889–1922* (Dublin, 1984).

—, Rosemary, *Louie Bennett* (Cork, 2001).

Day, Susanne R., *The amazing philanthropists* (London, 1916).

Delap, Lucy, Louise Ryan and Teresa Zackodnik, 'Self-determination, race, and empire: feminist nationalists in Britain, Ireland and the United States, 1830s to World War One', *Women's Studies International Forum*, 29:3 (2006), pp 241–54.

EC (European Commission Representation in Ireland), 'The EU and Irish women', 2017, https://ec.europa.eu/ireland/node/684_en.

Edwards, Gemma, 'Infectious innovations? The diffusion of tactical innovation in social movement networks, the case of suffragette militancy', *Social Movement Studies*, 13:1 (2014), pp 48–69.

Fallon, Charlotte, *Soul of fire: a biography of Mary MacSwiney* (Cork, 1986).

Fennell, Desmond, *The revision of Irish nationalism* (Dublin, 1989).

Ferriter, Diarmaid, *The transformation of Ireland, 1900–2000* (Dublin, 2010).

Fox, R.M., *Rebel Irish women* (Dublin, 1935).

Gray, Breda and Louise Ryan, 'Politics of Irish identity and the interconnections between feminism, nationhood, and colonialism' in Ruth Roach Pierson (ed.), *Nation, empire, colony: historicizing gender and race* (Bloomington, 1998), pp 121–38.

Hall, Lesley, 'Hauling down the double standard: feminism, social purity and sexual science in late nineteenth-century Britain', *Gender & History*, 16:1 (2004), pp 36–56.

Haque, Md. Rezaul, 'Educating women, (not) serving the nation: the interface of feminism and nationalism in the works of Rokeya Sakhawat Hossain', *An International Journal of Asian Literatures, Cultures and Englishes*, 7:2 (2013), pp 95–113.

Hazelkorn, Ellen, 'The social and political views of Louie Bennett', *Saothar*, 13 (1988), pp 32–44.

Hearne, Dana, 'The *Irish Citizen*, 1914–1916: nationalism, feminism and militarism', *Canadian Journal of Irish Studies*, 18:1 (1992), pp 1–14.

Hill, Myrtle, 'Ulster: debates, demands and divisions: the battle for and against the vote' in Louise Ryan and Margaret Ward (eds), *Irish women and the vote: becoming citizens* (Dublin, 2007), pp 209–30.

Holton, Sandra Stanley, 'The suffragist and the "average woman"', *Women's History Review*, 1:1 (1992), pp 9–24.

Innes, C.L., *Woman and nation in Irish literature and society, 1880–1935* (London, 1993).

—, 'Virgin territories and motherlands: colonial and nationalist representations of Africa and Ireland', *Feminist Review*, 47 (1994), pp 1–14.

IWSLGA (Irish Women's Suffrage and Local Government Association), *Annual Reports, 1896–1918* (Dublin, 1919).

Jayawardena, Kumari, *Feminism and nationalism in the Third World* (London, 1986).

Jones, Mary, *These obstreperous lassies: a history of the Irish Women Workers' Union* (Dublin, 1988).

Katrak, K.H., 'Indian nationalism, Gandhian 'satyagraha' and representations of female sexuality' in Andrew Parker, Mary Russo, Doris Sommer and Patricia Yaeger (eds), *Nationalisms and sexualities* (New York, 1992).

Kent, Susan K., *Sex and suffrage in Britain, 1860–1914* (Princeton, NJ, 2014).

Kleinrichert, Denise, 'Labour and suffrage: spinning threads in Belfast' in Louise Ryan and Margaret Ward (eds), *Irish women and the vote: becoming citizens* (Dublin, 2007), pp 189–208.

Levenson, Leah and Jerry Natterstad, *Hanna Sheehy Skeffington: Irish feminist* (New York, 1986).

Lewis, Gifford, *Somerville and Ross: the world of the Irish R.M.* (London, 1987).

Liddle, Joanna and Rama Joshi, *Daughters of independence: gender, caste and class in India* (London, 1986).

Luddy, Maria, 'Introduction: an overview of the suffrage movement', Louise Ryan and Margaret Ward (eds), *Irish women and the vote: becoming citizens* (Dublin, 2007), pp 1–20.

Luddy, Maria and Cliona Murphy, *Women surviving: studies in Irish women's history in the 19th and 20th centuries* (Dublin, 1990).

MacPherson, D.A.J., *Women and the Irish nation: gender, culture and Irish identity, 1890–1914* (London, 2012).

Maguire, Moira and Seamus Ó Cinnéide, '"A good beating never hurt anyone": the punishment and abuse of children in twentieth-century Ireland', *Journal of Social History*, 38:3 (2005), pp 635–52.

Matthews, Ann, *Renegades: Irish republican women, 1900–1922* (Cork, 2010).

McAuliffe, Mary and Liz Gillis, *Richmond Barracks 1916: 'We were there' – 77 women of the Easter Rising* (Dublin, 2016).

McClintock, Anne, 'Family feuds: gender, nationalism and the family', *Feminist Review*, 44 (1993), pp 61–80.

McCoole, Sinéad, *Guns and chiffon: women revolutionaries and Kilmainham Gaol, 1916–1923* (Dublin, 1997).

McDiarmid, Lucy, *At home in the revolution: what women said and did in 1916* (Dublin, 2015).

McKillen, Beth, 'Irish feminism and nationalist separatism', *Éire-Ireland* (Winter 1982), pp 52–67.

Meaney, Gerardine, *Sex and nation: women in Irish culture and politics* (Dublin, 1991).

Murphy, Cliona, *The women's suffrage movement and Irish society in the early twentieth century* (New York, 1989).

Murphy, Cliona, 'The tune of the Stars and Stripes: the American influence on the Irish suffrage movement' in Maria Luddy and Cliona Murphy, *Women surviving* (Dublin, 1990).

—, 'Suffragists and nationalism in early twentieth-century Ireland', *History of European Ideas*, 16:4–6 (1993), pp 1009–15.

—, '"Great gas" and "Irish bull": humour and the fight for Irish women's suffrage' in Louise Ryan and Margaret Ward (eds), *Irish women and the vote: becoming citizens* (Dublin, 2007), pp 90–113.

Murphy, William, 'Suffragettes and the transformation of political imprisonment in Ireland, 1912–1914' in Louise Ryan and Margaret Ward (eds), *Irish women and the vote: becoming citizens* (Dublin, 2007), pp 114–35.

O'Neill, Marie, *From Parnell to de Valera: a biography of Jenny Wyse Power* (Dublin, 1991).

Offen, Karen, 'Defining feminism: a comparative historical approach' in Gisela Bock and Susan James, *Beyond equality and difference* (London, 1992).

Parker, Andrew, Mary Russo, Doris Sommer and Patricia Yaeger (eds), *Nationalisms and sexualities* (New York, 1992).

Pašeta, Senia, *Irish nationalist women, 1900–1918* (Cambridge, 2013).

Pugh, Martin, *Women and the women's movement in Britain, 1914–1959* (London, 1992).

Quinlan, Carmel, 'Onward hand in hand: the nineteenth-century Irish campaign for votes for women' in Louise Ryan and Margaret Ward (eds), *Irish women and the vote: becoming citizens* (Dublin, 2007), pp 21–44.

Reynolds, Paige, 'Staging Suffrage: the events of the 1913 Dublin Suffrage Week' in Louise Ryan and Margaret Ward (eds), *Irish women and the vote: becoming citizens* (Dublin, 2007), pp 60–74.

Roper, Esther, *The prison letters of Countess Markievicz* (London, 1987).

Ryan, Louise, 'The *Irish Citizen* newspaper, 1912–1920: a document study', *Saothar*, 17 (1992), pp 105–11.

—, 'Women without votes: the political strategies of the Irish suffrage movement', *Irish Political Studies*, 9 (1994), pp 119–39.

—, 'Traditions and double moral standards: the Irish suffragists critique of nationalism', *Women's History Review*, 4:4 (1995), pp 487–503.

—, 'A question of loyalty: war, nation and feminism', *Women's Studies International Forum*, 20:1 (1997), pp 21–32.

—, 'Negotiating modernity and tradition: newspaper debates on the "modern girl" in the Irish Free State', *Journal of Gender Studies*, 7:2 (1998), pp 181–97.

—, '"Drunken Tans": representations of sex and violence in the Anglo-Irish War (1919–21)', *Feminist Review*, 66:1 (2000), pp 73–94.

—, *Gender, identity and the Irish press, 1922–37: embodying the nation* (New York, 2002).

—, 'An analysis of the Irish suffrage movement using new social-movement theory' in Linda Connolly and Niamh Hourigan (eds), *Social movements and Ireland* (Manchester, 2006), pp 40–57.

—, 'Publicising the private: suffragists' critique of sexual abuse and domestic violence' in Louise Ryan and Margaret Ward (eds), *Irish women and the vote: becoming citizens* (Dublin, 2007), pp 75–89.

Ryan, Louise and Margaret Ward (eds), *Irish women and nationalism: soldiers, new women, and wicked hags* (Dublin, 2004).

—, *Irish women and the vote: becoming citizens* (Dublin, 2007).

Sharkey, Sabina, *Ireland and the iconography of rape: colonisation, constraint and gender* (London, 1994).

Sheehy Skeffington, Hanna, 'Reminiscences' in Rosemary Cullen Owens, *Votes for women: the Irish women's struggle for the vote* (Dublin, 1975).

Somerville, Edith and Martin Ross, *Irish memories* (London, 1917).

Steele, Karen, *Women, press, and politics during the Irish revival* (Syracuse, NY, 2007).

Steiner-Scott, Liz, '"To bounce a boot off her now and then …": domestic violence in post-Famine Ireland' in Maryann Valiulis and Mary O'Dowd (eds), *Women and Irish history* (Dublin, 1997), pp 125–43.

Swanton, Daisy, *Emerging from the shadow: the lives of Sarah Anne Lawrenson and Lucy Olive Kingston: based on personal diaries, 1883–1969* (Dublin, 1994).

Taillon, Ruth, *When history was made: the women of 1916* (Belfast, 1996).

Thapar-Björkert, Suruchi and Louise Ryan, 'Mother India/Mother Ireland: comparative gendered dialogues of colonialism and nationalism in the early 20th century', *Women's Studies International Forum*, 25:3 (2002), pp 301–13.

Urquhart, Diane, *Women in Ulster politics, 1890–1940: a history not yet told* (Dublin, 2000).

Valiulis, Maryann (ed.), *Gender and power in Irish history* (Dublin, 2009).

Van Voris, Jacqueline, *Constance de Markievicz: in the cause of Ireland* (New York, 1967).

Vellacott, Jo, 'A place for pacifism and transnationalism in feminist theory', *Women's History Review*, 2:1 (1993), pp 23–56.

Watkins, Sarah-Beth, *Ireland's suffragettes* (Dublin, 2014).

Ward, Margaret, 'Suffrage first', *Feminist Review*, 10 (1982), pp 21–36.

—, *Unmanageable revolutionaries: women and Irish nationalism* (London, 1989).

—, *Maud Gonne: Ireland's Joan of Arc* (London, 1990).

—, *Hanna Sheehy Skeffington: a life* (Dublin, 1997).

—, '"Rolling up the map of suffrage": Irish suffrage and the First World War' in Louise Ryan and Margaret Ward (eds), *Irish women and the vote: becoming citizens* (Dublin, 2007), pp 136–53.

—, *Hanna Sheehy Skeffington: suffragette and Sinn Féiner: her memoirs and political writings* (Dublin, 2017).

West, Lois, 'Feminist nationalist social movements', *Women's Studies International Forum*, 15:5–6 (1992), pp 563–579.

Women's Aid, 'Domestic Violence Matters during #GE2016' (2016), https://www.womensaid.ie/about/campaigns/election2016, accessed 20 Dec. 2017.

Yuval-Davis, Nira, *Gender and nation* (London, 1997).

Index

Page references in **bold** refer to illustrations.